D1034761

The American Immigration Collection

The Negro Immigrant:

His Background, Characteristics and Social Adjustment, 1899-1937

IRA DE A. REID

Arno Press and The New York Times

NEW YORK 1969

*

Library of Congress Catalog Card No. 69-18771

*

Reprinted from a copy in the collection of
Harvard College Library

*

Manufactured in the United States of America

STUDIES IN HISTORY, ECONOMICS AND PUBLIC LAW

Edited by the

FACULTY OF POLITICAL SCIENCE
OF COLUMBIA UNIVERSITY

NUMBER 449

THE NEGRO IMMIGRANT

BY

IRA DE AUGUSTINE REID

THE NEGRO IMMIGRANT

His Background, Characteristics and Social Adjustment, 1899-1937

BY

IRA DE A. REID, Ph.D.

PROFESSOR OF SOCIOLOGY IN ATLANTA UNIVERSITY

NEW YORK
COLUMBIA UNIVERSITY PRESS
LONDON: P. S. KING & SON, LTD.
1939

PRINTED IN THE UNITED STATES OF AMERICA

To

W. J. R.

AND

G. S. R.

". . . . not to laugh at the actions of men, nor yet to deplore or detest them, but simply to understand them."

—Spinoza

PREFACE

THE effects of the migration of 100,000 foreign-born Negroes to the United States are scarcely known, and before they can be understood an outline of the existing frontiers of knowledge on the subject should be available. The first task of the researcher became, therefore, that of discovering what is known about Negro immigrants and Negro foreign-born peoples. Upon this information was to be developed a coherent body of knowledge on the subject which might be used as the basis for continuous accretions. This was conceived as the scope of this study.

Some ten years ago when the author first became interested in this subject he was somewhat disconcerted by the magnitude of the task on the one hand, and by the paucity of specific documentary materials, on the other. This absence of basic materials necessitated resolving the problem and the methods of research into specific divisions—(1) the human materials, (2) general documentary materials, and (3) the specific observations of the author.

Human materials deal with data related to the direct investigation of the Negro foreign-born population through the author's personal contact with members of the group. Because it was impossible to undertake a thorough scientific analysis of the physical, mental, cultural and economic aspects of the individuals concerned, it became necessary for the author to rely heavily upon his objective and subjective observations as a participant observer.

Objective observation covered an investigation of foreign-born individuals and their social roles when they were not aware of this observation. It necessitated talking with them, asking questions, observing them at work, at play, and on the job. It meant becoming familiar with the patterns of their behavior in the land of their birth as well as in their new clime. The author's familiarity with the social environment of New York and his experience in social investigation did not make this process an arduous one. Despite the possession of these tools the process was a slow one, and would not have produced the materials obtained had they not been supplemented by the cooperative services of many foreign-born persons who understood our professional interest.

The *subjective approach* to the problem consisted in finding out from the individuals and the groups concerned the nature of their physical and mental individual and corporate lives. In this respect we were faced with the problem of finding adequate and accurate measurement of what people think and of what they do. Two devices were employed—the first *social intercourse,* and the second *life histories.* Through social intercourse we were able to move freely in and out of groups, as a participant observer, learning the points of view, observing the shaded differences of class role, and obtaining the spontaneous reactions to adjustment situations. In the course of time the notebook technique of recording these materials became necessary only for the identification of specific situations.

Additional subjective data were secured through the use of life histories and the written reactions of foreign-born persons to specific situations. The life histories, obtained by means of a prize contest and limited only by the specification that individuals limit their statements to five thousand words, indicated what has been so frequently related by sociologists and social psychologists—that the general value of these documents is relative to other materials collected, to the situation being considered. Thomas and Znaniecki maintain "it is clear that for the characterization of single social data—attitudes and values—personal life records give us the most exact approach. . . . A social institution can be fully understood only if we do not limit ourselves to the abstract study of its formal organization, but analyze the way in which it appears in the personal experience of various members of the group and follow the influence which it has upon their lives".[1] With the materials

1 Thomas, W. I. and Znaniecki, F., *The Polish Peasant in Europe and America,* Chicago, University of Chicago Press, 1920, Vol. II, p. 1833.

used in this study it was noted in many instances that the written analysis of one's responses and attitudes was comparable with the observed behavior; in others that the autobiographical material on this subject was written in terms of what seemed feasible, advisable and correct. The true sense of introspection was not always evident in these documents, but the emotional responses to the situations were. Yet, no materials could more adequately reflect the numerous conflicts of the social adjustment of Negro immigrants. All in all, the combined objective and subjective observations provided a body of data on various cultural or civilizational aspects of the adjustment, on social movement, and on physical adjustment that permitted the determination of the study's focus.

Documentary materials were necessary to obtain a valid statistical frame of reference for our study, on the one hand, and to give credence to our observation of the human materials, on the other. The chief sources of the statistical information were the publications of the Bureau of Immigration of the Department of Labor, the Immigration Commission Reports of 1911, and the reports on Migration of the International Labor Office at Geneva, Switzerland. Other matters of international import were cleared through the various consular offices in the United States, and through publications and reports of the immigration services of the various nations, particularly England and France.

All statistical data covering the migration of Negro peoples between other countries and the United States are subject to a few limiting interpretations. The use of the "race" concept is only now being regarded as important for the accurate presentation of immigration statistics. This is being occasioned in part by the high mobility of colored peoples in the Caribbean area, and in part by the restrictive immigration legislation of countries in that region. Between 1908 and 1932 immigrant and emigrant statistics of the United States were very fully reported by race and nationality. Since that time, because of governmental budgetary limitations, these specialized statistics by race have not been available. The immigration statistics of all countries supplying our foreign-born population are reported by nationalities rather than by races.

Because the race-nationality concept does not receive uniform international treatment, it has been reasonable to suppose that a large number of Negroes entering the United States from the British West Indies are not recorded as Negroes, but as West Indians. They, therefore, do not appear as "Africans, black" in the immigration statistics. Furthermore, because the stereotype "Negro" does not include the connotation "immigrant", it is reasonable to conclude that many persons of color are able to enter the United States illegally, and without fear of successful apprehension. Both of these facts seem to account for, in part at least, the discrepancies between the number of Negro foreign-born reported by the various censuses, and the statistics of the Bureau of Immigration.

It is, therefore, generally true that statistical data on the Negro foreign-born and immigrant populations are scattered, diverse, and, from the viewpoint of validity, almost non-existent. The qualitative rather than the quantitative character of the problem is partially responsible for this lack of adequate statistical data.

No primary source material was found that would give information on such social characteristics of the foreign-born population as intermarriage and institutional forms. Furthermore, the only published data on relationships between native and foreign-born Negroes tended to be that focused upon improving the relations rather than upon interactions of the cultures. Meanwhile, practically nothing has been written about the cultural characteristics of the Negro immigrant. Newspapers, magazines, tracts and pamphlets published by foreign-born persons, and reports of various societies, clubs, and other organizations provided much useful information. The most elaborate body of published information was found in those Negro newspapers reporting foreign news of interest to colored peoples. These were the *New York Amsterdam News,* the

Pittsburgh (Pa.) *Courier,* the *Chicago* (Ill.) *Defender* and the *Boston* (Mass.) *Chronicle.* The tracts of the Universal Negro Improvement Association and its organ *The Negro World* gave many valuable leads in analyzing the foreign-born problems of the nineteen twenties.

A geographic focusing of the material was necessary from two points of view—first, the geographic distribution by place of origin of immigrants arriving from the Caribbean, and, second the geographic distribution of immigrants by place of concentration in urban centers of the United States. The first problem demanded an exhaustive analysis of published materials on the cultural traits of the indigenous peoples of the various islands. Checking these findings with native-born and foreign-born Negroes who had lived in these islands or who had recently visited them gave the material as reasonable an amount of authenticity as could have been secured without extensive travel. The second problem was that of definitely locating immigrant colonies in the United States. Large groups of foreign-born Negroes are to be found in New York, Massachusetts and Florida only. Ninety per cent of the immigrant and foreign-born Negro populations are located in these areas. Furthermore, approximately sixty-five per cent of both these groups are located in New York City. It was in this last area that most of the materials herein presented were developed.

ACKNOWLEDGMENTS

To scholars in the field of population problems the author's numerous obligations will be abundantly evident. Yet, full and complete acknowledgment for the many fruitful contacts and aids that friends, acquaintances and advisors rendered the researcher, is in no way possible. It is most pertinent, however, that a few of the more pronounced and sustained ones be herein mentioned. I am tremendously indebted to Professor Robert M. MacIver for guiding me into this field; to Professor Robert E. Chaddock for timely criticism and guidance in this phase of population problems, and for pains-taking readings and criticisms of the manuscript; to Professor Frank A. Ross, Chairman of the Department of Sociology at Syracuse University, for his personal interest and encouragement.

Dr. Donald Young of the University of Pennsylvania and the Social Science Research Council, and Dr. Maurice R. Davie, Chairman of the Department of Sociology of Yale University, read the preliminary manuscript and offered valuable suggestions for revision. To Miss Ruby M. Bryant of the National Urban League I am indebted for the steady flow of materials and contacts she made possible. From the late A. A. Schomburg, former curator of the 135th Street Branch of the New York Public Library, I acknowledge valuable historical orientation for much of the background data.

A grant from the Julius Rosenwald Fund made possible the collection of life histories. To the J. B. Lippincott Company, the Associated Publishers, and the Clarence Williams Music Publishing Company I am indebted for permission to quote from their copyrighted works.

Above all I am indebted to friends and acquaintances who have endured the persistency and frequency of my queries and my presence while I sought to observe and learn the ways of the cultures some dared call strange.

IRA DE A. REID

ATLANTA, OCTOBER 25, 1938.

CONTENTS

CHAPTER VI

The Adjustment of the Negro Immigrant (*Continued*)

CHAPTER VII

The Adjustment of the Negro Immigrant (*Continued*)

CHAPTER VIII

The Negro Immigrant's Life Story

CHAPTER IX

CONCLUSION

LIST OF TABLES

CHAPTER I

INTRODUCTION

IMMIGRATION is the entrance into an alien country of persons intending to take part in the life of that country and intending to make it their more or less permanent residence.

Negro immigration as a modern aspect of the phenomenon has received only passing attention in the myriad works on the immigration policies and problems of the United States. A sentence here and a paragraph there—frequently to the effect that this immigration is not extensive—represent the sum total of references in immigration literature. When, however, it is realized that the present foreign-born Negro population numbers approximately 100,000 persons, and is larger than the number of foreign-born Japanese, or Chinese—in fact, is larger than all other groups of foreign-born colored peoples in the United States combined—Malayans, Samoans, Filipinos, Hawaiians, Turks, Hindus, and Koreans—the subject does become significant. (Table 1) *All tables referred to in the text are to be found in Appendix A.*

Sociologists have always regarded the subject of immigration as their special province. However, it has been only since the World War that they have given it any especial attention. Earlier studies in the field have, as a rule, contained much history, economics, and crude statistics, and very little sociology. A most trenchant criticism of these approaches maintains that—" As a result of the mixed academic history of the field, adequate attention has been paid neither to fact nor analytical methodology in nationality comparisons and contrasts, with the consequence that even today white immigrants from all countries are distinguished for purposes of economic study only in gross statistical groupings based on political boundaries ".[1] As a field for research, therefore, immigration

[1] Young, Donald, *Research Memorandum on Minority Peoples in the Depression*, prepared under the direction of the Committee on Studies in Social Aspects of the Depression, New York, Social Science Research Council Bulletin 31, 1937, p. 85.

offers a unique opportunity. And, when the racial factor in immigration is considered the possibilities for further study appear extremely fruitful.

Carr-Saunders has given a basic lead to this problem in saying " The black peoples have suffered heavy relative losses, for they once formed about a fifth of the population of the world and now form about a fifteenth. It is impossible to say whether they have gained or lost absolutely; they have apparently decreased in Africa, but against this has to be set the fact that about a third of all black peoples are now outside Africa ".[2]

The United States is one of the few nations that analyzes its international migration on the basis of race. " Africans, black " is the cover-all term employed by the Bureau of Immigration and Naturalization to cloak with racial identification all persons of Negro extraction admitted to or departing from the United States. It is a conjure-word that metamorphoses persons who, prior to embarking for the United States, may have been known as " coloured ", " mulatto ", or " black ", or, who, had not been grouped by race or color.

Negro immigration to the United States is a phenomenon of the western world. Despite the name " Africans, black ", very few of the Negro immigrants are either Africans or black. They come largely from the Caribbean area, and represent a polygot collection of racial mixtures, and cultural adaptations. This study, therefore, endeavors to pass under the marque of immigration statistics and see what is significant in the fact that between 1899 and 1937 approximately 150,000 Negro aliens were legally admitted to the United States. How does a group theoretically regarded as biologically unassimilable in the United States' melting pot accomodate? What type of assimilation does take place? What significant effects does its presence have upon the national and racial, social and economic structure?

2 Carr-Saunders, A. M., *World Population: Its Past Growth and Present Trends*, London, Oxford Press, 1936, p. 44.

The Negro group in the United States is not a distinct ethnic group which has maintained its original racial characteristics and social customs. Contacts with other racial and cultural groups have resulted in an increasing blend of diverse bloods and modification of customs. The background for such a study as this is furnished by one of the most universal American stereotypes "all Negroes". As has often been remarked, no sentence beginning with those words is true. However, if there is a clear and concise understanding of the socially valid subgroups that go to make up "the Negro" then the statement may acquire significance. Negroes of the United States, even as white persons, must, for social research purposes, be divided on the basis of their biological mixtures and cultural heritages. Accurate research results may be expected only as the phenomena under discussion take these specifics into consideration. Within this stereotype are small aggregates of Negroes with culturally diverse customs, traditions, institutions and ideas of homeland. These cultural traits are not only modified to permit conformity within the place accorded Negroes in the United States, but they in turn modify the culture of the native Negro. This new infiltration keeps in a fluid state the intra-racial adjustment of the native Negro population.

Conflict situations between the foreign-born Negro groups and the native ones, between two Negro immigrant groups, and between different generations of the same immigrant group make us aware of definite phases of social process. Negro immigrants being largely from the Americas do not possess many of the outward manifestations of the stranger that are common to European immigrants. This standardization of external characteristics makes for less immediate social visibility. (For further elaboration of this point see pp. 113-114.) However, alien standards do provide a sharp and distinctive cleavage between the two groups. Being a minority within a minority, Negro immigrants disturb intra-group relations because of their partial accommodation. In times of social stress, or if the foreign Negro group is highly visible, or, when it is in competition with native Negroes this lower role is most operative. As competition and visibility disappear, the role of *immigrant* or " monkey chaser " or " Spic " or " Garveyite ", tends to lose its broad identity and disappear.[3]

The Negro immigrant presents a field for the analysis of the intra-racial aspect of the processes of acculturation—of accommodation and assimilation. While it is generally accepted that individuals reared in one culture and migrating to another can never be completely absorbed in the new culture, it is noticeable that the old culture fades more and more as time goes on, and that there is always a residue of habits, ideas, points of view and ways of doing things which is never completely changed. Meanwhile the foreign Negro group develops special cultural norms resulting from the fact that it lives and works under special circumstances; that it is compelled to contrive patterns of defensive behavior because of its role, and also because of the inescapable confusion that results from its compulsory adoption of new and majority modes of behavior. Accompanying these changes are the less inventive devices of the Negro majority and of the white group, which render new schemes of relationships and action less than satisfactory. Techniques to maintain status, to restrict and suppress—even oppress—the immigrant deviate not one whit from those employed by other groups. Their major significance is in the changes they evoke in the pattern of social role known as Negro.

It is in this respect that the adjustment of Negro immigrants differs from that of white immigrants. The Negro immigrant undergoes a reorganization of status involving adjustment to an intra-racial situation and to an inter-racial one. Leaving communities where he was part of the numerical majority, he moves into one where he is parcel of the numerical and social minority. This change presents two distinct types of social prob-

3 A " monkey-chaser " is the United States Negro's name-calling device for all West Indian Negroes. " Garveyite " has a similar meaning. " Spic " refers to Spanish-speaking Negroes, particularly Puerto Ricans and Cubans.

lems which are intimately related—one involving the outer or material aspects of adjusting in the new environment, such as earning a living, making a home and looking and acting as do the native-born, and the other having to do with the less tangible differences found in cultural patterns and standards of thought and action. The former are the more easily discernible differentials; the latter are the more subtle, but of equal importance. Once the former have been determined the latter may be more easily deduced. Thus, the Negro immigrant finds his usual ways of conduct inadequate to the new environment. He discovers the native Negro's attitude of amused superiority, and, while thrilling to the incentive of the new locale, he frequently remains bewildered and self-conscious for some time. The Negro immigrant becomes a *déraciné*—a man without roots—who has lost something of a former self which provided the " push " for his migration and has not yet acquired a new and stabilized self. He becomes aware of his almost automatic exclusion from numerous areas of social activity because of a system of group relationships called " race ". He realizes that culture differentials within this area of " race " tend to resolve themselves into class lines and to make the immigrant group a formally recognized " out-group ".

Within recent years there has been an increasing tendency to treat problems arising within the area of race adjustment as phases of class and caste phenomena. *Class* is identified as a loose form of social grouping to which opinion attaches some degree of status with reference to other groups called classes, the members of which share some implied common interest. In its more rigid form a group membership with status implications in which social rank may be lost but not gained, is called *caste.* Within this framework the Negro group in the United States is regarded as a caste. Thus, Warner in his approach to racial aspects of social organization in the Deep South describes caste as a " theoretical arrangement of the people of the given group in an order in which the privileges, duties, obligations, opportunities, etc. are unequally distributed between the groups which are considered to be higher and lower. There are social sanctions which tend to maintain this unequal distribution. Such a definition also describes class. A caste organization, however, can be further identified as one where marriage between two or more groups is not sanctioned and where there is no opportunity for members of the lower groups to rise into the upper groups or for the members of the upper to fall into the lower ones. In class, on the other hand, there is a certain proportion of inter-class marriage between lower and higher groups, and there are, in the very nature of the class organization, mechanisms established by which people move up and down the vertical extension of the society ".[4]

In a further development of this thesis Dollard maintains that caste in the United States is pinned not to cultural features, but to biological ones—color, hair form, and the like, providing a categorical badge which transcends in importance any social value the individual might have.[5] Inferior caste tends to create a degree of social isolation for the individuals so grouped, and to limit their personal development by removing from their reach the higher social gains of the community. Thus, in the United States there develops the white-caste and the Negro-caste—the former proud of its achievement and stressing its superiority in the realm of social organization; the latter developing an emotional set to the situation and realizing its relative social immobility beyond the caste barriers.

In the United States Negroes, Orientals, and Jews who can rise out of their original group membership only by hiding hereditary physical features or their origins, or by other unusual circumstances, are caste groups. Within each one of these groups there tend to arise status differences or class lines. By this token, Negroes are not " just Negroes " to each other.

4 Warner, W. Lloyd, *American Caste and Class*, American Journal of Sociology, 42: 234-237, No. 2, Sept. 1936.

5 Dollard, John, *Caste and Class in a Southern Town*, New Haven, Yale University Press, 1937.

Cutting across their social relationships are myriad status lines that make for important distinctions within the group.[6]

The most widely known features of such sub-class and sub-caste distinctions and social stratifications within the Negro group are those based on skin color in which higher status has been acquired within the group through the biological accident of the individual's physical resemblance to the white group. Between the days of the Civil War and the World War this sub-caste distinction was based largely upon family membership and relationship. Within the last twenty years a rather unique development has indicated that this color-caste feature is no longer a unit based on family membership but one based on the individual. Intermarriage of members of different sub-castes did not necessarily uncaste the member holding superior status. Beyond this distinction there is no outstanding sub-caste feature in the Negro group.

There are among Negroes, however, numerous class lines corresponding in structure and function to those social stratifications which characterize the majority white group. The laboring classes, the "capitalists", professional people, "middle classes", the "individualists" or self-made individuals, typify this stratification. Not least among these is the stratification based on nativity and ancestry. It is in the class stratification resulting from place of birth that the role of Negro immigrant operates.

While it may be assumed that there is a strong cohesive bond operating within the Negro group, the evidence of stratification frequently belies its existence. Struggles between sub-groups appear to have an intensity equal to, and a time sequence that closely parallels, the struggle between the majority and minority groups in relation to economic opportunity and successful competition for a stated objective.[7] The role of the

6 For a more complete statement of this thesis see Young, Donald, *op. cit.*, pp. 17-30.

7 See the views of Professor Robert M. MacIver, on inter-class competition. MacIver, Robert M., *Society: a Text-book of Sociology*, New York, Farrar and Rhinehart, 1937, pp. 173-183.

Negro immigrant then becomes significant in determining what may and may not be subsumed about the Negro group's adjustment in the United States. Young's statement to the effect that immigrant Negroes disappear among native Negroes and create no special issue of race relations states the problem too simply.[8] The Negro immigrant's advent introduced new problems of social status and social process that throw light on many aspects of the inter-racial pattern. A fundamental tenet of this thesis is that those problems are not problems about a natural fact called race; they are social problems—problems of social life, of economics, and of the political state. The "race" concept is simply a framework within which these factors function. Variations in the manifestations of race prejudice against Negroes as a whole in the North and in the South substantiate the presence of this social basis.[9]

In view of these facts, therefore, we shall aim to present the significant aspects of Negro immigration; to analyze the impact of the United States culture upon the immigrant Negro groups and the effect of their cultures upon the native Negro population; and, finally, to present an inductive analysis of the problems and conflicts arising from this inter-cultural and intra-racial differentiation.

8 Young, Donald, *American Minority Peoples,* New York, Harper and Brothers, 1932, p. 41.

9 See Barzun, Jacques, *Race: A Study in Modern Superstition,* Harcourt, Brace and Co., 1937, pp. 270-299.

CHAPTER II

THE NEGRO IMMIGRANT

The Problem—Number and Sources of Negro Immigrants

A. IMMIGRATION AND THE LAW

There are three fundamental principles involved in any nation's immigration policy—the policy of *exclusion,* which may be applied to any peoples so as to stop all immigration absolutely; the policy of *free immigration* which would allow anybody from anywhere to enter; and, the policy of *regulation* through which a country seeks to control the movement of peoples into its borders. Operating under the aegis of *regulation* is the quasi-selective policy of *restriction* through which the numbers and types of immigrants admitted are revised to meet current opinion and conditions. At various times in its history the United States has enacted immigration laws emphasizing each of these policies.

Operative against Asiatic peoples has been the government's policy of excluding all such people who intend to live and work here, and who might compete with native workers. This law has been applied solely to the darker-skinned races. And while the " low standard of living " of the excluded peoples has been voiced as the determining factor, the exclusion policy seems to have been based largely upon the thesis that the biological assimilation of darker races is well-nigh impossible. Davie states: " Experience shows that the yellow, brown, and black races are unassimilable, at any rate by us, and the United States would only be inviting trouble and adding to her already large and serious race problems by admitting members of such races. This exclusion is indispensable to the welfare of the United States ".[1]

1 Davie, Maurice R., *World Immigration,* New York, MacMillan, 1936, p. 368.

When the 1924 revision of the immigration act was under consideration Davie wrote: " There is need at the present time of excluding other dark skinned races, a need which will undoubtedly increase unless some action is taken. From 1899 to 1922 there were admitted to this country over one hundred and fifteen thousand African Blacks, and during the same period more than 25,000 West Indians other than Cubans. One would think that our Negro problem was already large enough without adding to it that way. The recently enacted 3 per cent restriction law, to be sure, applies to Africa and allows a yearly quota of only one hundred and twenty-two, so that now there is less danger from that source. But it would seem since we have applied the principle of exclusion to such people as the Chinese and Japanese that we should go the whole way and exclude the black-immigrant aliens. The barred zone should be extended to Africa and also to the West Indies, especially to Jamaica and the Bahamas, to stop the coming of blacks from these quarters ".[2]

The first inclusive immigration law in the United States was passed in 1882. Prior to that time immigration was practically free. The law of 1882 prohibited the entry of convicts, lunatics, idiots and persons likely to become public charges. Laws passed since that time (1885, 1888, 1891, 1903, 1907, 1917, 1921 and 1924) have become increasingly severe and restrictive. With the coming of the World War it became evident that the " melting pot " theory of immigrant adjustment was not effective. There were fourteen million persons of foreign birth in the United States, nearly five million of whom could neither read and write, nor speak the English language, and over half of whose male population of voting age were not citizens. Foreign-born colonies were arising and being perpetuated; alien residents were retaining their foreign citizenship. The Act of 1917 established an Asiatic barred zone, excluding inhabitants of India, and islands surrounding Asia, territory not already

2 Davie, Maurice R., *A Constructive Immigration Policy*, New Haven, Yale University Press, 1923, p. 7.

covered by the Chinese exclusion laws of 1880, and 1882. It also established a literary test which excluded all aliens over 16 years of age, physically able to read, who cannot read English or some other language or dialect.

The immigration act of 1924 provided that no alien ineligible to citizenship shall be admitted to the United States. This act excluded Chinese, Japanese, East Indians and other peoples not whites or Negroes of African descent. It set up thereby a quota rule that was considered a permanent solution of the problem of immigration restriction. In 1921 a quota act provided that "the number of aliens of any nationality who may be admitted under the immigration laws to the United States in any fiscal year shall be limited to three per cent of the number of foreign-born persons of such nationality resident in the United States, census of 1910". The law exempted from the quota aliens who had been residents for at least one year previous to admission in Canada, Newfoundland, Cuba, Mexico, the countries of Central or South America or adjacent islands. The 1924 act shifted the basis for the quotas from 3 per cent of the 1910 foreign-born population to 2 per cent of the 1890 population. Persons entering the country were divided into three classes: non-immigrants, non-quota immigrants, and quota immigrants. Non-immigrants were government officials, aliens visiting the United States for business or pleasure—persons in transit to another country, and bona fide seamen.

Non-quota immigrants included (1) an immigrant who was the unmarried child or the wife of a citizen; (2) an immigrant who had been previously admitted to the U. S.; (3) an immigrant who was born in Canada, Newfoundland, Mexico, Cuba, Haiti, Dominican Republic, Canal Zone, or an independent country of Central or South America and his wife and unmarried children under 18 years of age; (4) an immigrant who has been a minister or a professor for two years preceding application for admission; (5) students; (6) women who had lost their citizenship through marriage to aliens. All other persons were quota immigrants.

The principles established by the act of 1921 and extended by the act of 1924 thus marked an entire change in immigration policy. Since that time the volume of immigration has not been considered too large. The quota method was used to limit the number of immigrants entering the country, and, though not specifically mentioned, the ideas of racial preference and eugenic differences were implied therein. The effect of this restrictive policy has been to flexibly regulate the flow of immigration to the United States. Thus in September, 1930, by Presidential order, consular officers were advised not to issue immigration visas to applicants who were likely to become public charges, and who did not have sufficient resources to maintain themselves for an indefinite period without employment. As a result of these restrictions the number of immigrants admitted dropped from 241,700 in 1930 to 50,244 in 1937 and the number of quota immigrants from 141,000 in the earlier year to fewer than 15,000 in 1937.

But while the laws have diverted European emigration to other countries, it has stimulated movement into the United States from non-quota countries. Two-thirds of all the immigrants now entering the United States are from non-quota countries. The situation has been described as one where " we have locked the front door but left the side door open ". The sharp curtailment of European immigration is in marked contrast to the rather unlimited flow of immigrants from North and South America. It is through the side door of the Americas that the bulk of the Negro immigrants have come.

Immigration from the dependencies of the United States has markedly increased since 1917. Although residents of our island possessions are citizens of the United States, their move to the mainland presents some diverse racial and cultural problems. The statistics available do not differentiate between white Americans and native members of colored races in this movement. What amount of it may be attributed to the movement of unskilled Negro and other colored labor, supposedly large, is really a matter of conjecture. But let us examine this movement of the Negro immigrant from the point of view of the culture group which he leaves. Does his movement involve problems that are not so prominent in the larger patterns of the emigrant-immigrant process?

B. THE PROBLEM OF NEGRO IMMIGRATION

The Negro immigrant to the United States is faced with grave problems of social adjustment. Not only is he an alien by law and fact, but he suffers a complete change in status by emerging from a group setting where he was the racial majority into one where he becomes part of a racial minority. He brings a cultural heritage that is vastly different from that of the American Negro. In the majority of cases he speaks English, sometimes French or Spanish, less frequently Portuguese. His mode of living, his relationship with government, his idea of "liberty", even his traditions, are vastly different. Briefly, then, the immigrant who becomes Negro upon arrival brings to the United States Negro population a different set of mores, with a different life experience. The problem he faces is distinctly one of cultural adjustment.

Furthermore, this immigrant usually comes from a rural, or rural-urban background where life is less complex than in the new areas of settlement. Though he has been advised as to working conditions, and the possibilities for employment, he is not versed in the ways of job-seeking. He is not particularly disturbed about living conditions since the older immigrants have let it be known that there are "colored sections". He is a stranger, even as is the immigrant from our insular possessions. Being a stranger he is ignorant of the law, the modes of life and the prejudices he is about to face. As a result, he becomes the unwitting victim of a direct and indirect type of exploitation. But what is there in the background of the Negro immigrant, particularly the Caribbean immigrant, that makes this cultural adjustment necessary?

The chief factor in immigration is the transfer of the individual from one social group to another. In the case of many non-colored immigrants, this acculturation involves a change in nationality status, a new language, and the necessary personal adjustments involved in settling in a new land. The Negro immigrant finds that he must adjust in a three-fold way—from the point of view of *nationality, mores,* and the *social role played by his racial group.* He experiences a complete change in his environment. And it is this environment which he has left behind, that constitutes his background.

These factors in the environment have been classified by Fairchild as physical and human. In them anything which tends to provide " coherence, unity, character and self-consciousness to the human group " combines to form the group environment.[3] From the physical point of view, we find the Negro immigrant coming from a semi-tropical area, where the significant factors of climate, temperature, rain fall, winds, elevation, topography, earthquakes, all have had their importance in determining the thoughts and movements of the population.

The human environment, on the other hand, is more complex and more important. It is the most significant part of the background and consists of the characteristics of the human group within which the individual has lived up to the time of his migration, and to which he is necessarily adapted. The geographical environment constitutes an environment for the group and for the individual members; the human environment is an inner environment as well as an outer environment and consists of the social heritage and the community, both of which provide a setting for the individual.[4] The immigrant's problem of adjustment would be more simple if only the physical or geographical environment were involved. The real problem, however, inheres in the group differences which are part of the

3 Fairchild, Henry Pratt, *Immigrant Backgrounds,* Wiley and Sons, New York, 1927, pp. 1-6.

4 MacIver, Robert M., *Society, Its Structure and Changes,* Long and Smith, New York, 1931, p. 343.

respective backgrounds. The chief factors in this human environment are race and culture.

It is very easy to over-weight the importance of race as a factor in social affairs, though its influence cannot be ignored. Though it is a biological characteristic by which individuals in one group are more closely related to each other by blood than they are to members of another race, it also has a social significance. This is particularly true in any areas of pronounced social and economic problems. The mere factor of racial color has influenced the social processes of the area in which the problems are located. In the Caribbean area where there are more than 7,000,000 colored persons, including mixtures of Negro stocks, and where they form approximately 70 per cent of the total population, there is not only an increasing fusion or mixture of the racial stocks, but there is also a tendency for the races to voluntarily remain apart and socially isolated. Thus, there is a distinct role for blacks, for mixed peoples, and for whites in these areas. There is no lumping of race problems as in the United States, nor is there any clearly defined line between what is possible for colored folk and what is not possible as is true in this country. The concept of race in the Negro immigrant's background, therefore, is an important index to his adjustment, for it indicates not only how he felt and how he acted in his home environment, but it also indicates what he was prior to the migration.

This racial background indicates how the Negro immigrant feels and reacts to other Negroes and to the white population. The disgust that a Negro immigrant experiences when he sees a white American doing unskilled labor may be a profound shock to his preconceived notions of the role of the white person in society. The realization that a Negro of "good birth" and performing a " gentlemanly " role as a professional person, may be forced to suffer the same social indignities as those experienced by the Negro laborer may be an initial shock that is soon rationalized into reactions as to why any Negro should suffer such treatment. The sympathy for the " we-group " is at first in terms of the racial situation as it has been experienced in the old culture, and of antipathy for the " they-group ". Nothing could be more misleading in analyzing the racial backgrounds of Negro immigrants, than to assume that they are all Negroes, in the American sense of the word.

In the United States all persons with Negro blood, no matter what amount, are classified as Negroes. In the West Indies those persons having admixtures of white and Negro blood are recognized as colored, and form a separate, though not so rigidly defined, caste. Their social position is distinctly superior to that of the black population. Within this color maze, there is a diversified system of castes in which prestige and stratification are determined not only by the amount of " white " blood possessed, but also by the social and economic position attained. European customs have combined with racial mixtures to produce a more flexible physical and social type than is found in the United States. The colored population constitutes a real middle caste, just as the blacks constitute a lower caste. This does not mean that the darker populations are openly excluded from the larger activities of the area, rather, that they are the poorest group, the most rural, and that only the exceptional individual is able to overcome the obstacles to success. In the West Indies, it is largely the colored person who fills the responsible positions that lie between higher administrative control and menial labor. Why? Weatherly states:

The whites deny any intention of excluding blacks as such from responsible positions, and claim that, with rare exceptions, it is only the colored who have sufficient mentality for them. Some observers believe that the reason lies in the prestige of lighter color, since in trade it is a business asset, while in administration it carries greater dignity and authority. Sir Sydney Olivier, who has had some experience in West Indian administration, holds that, whatever the fact as to capacity, mixed bloods in a tropical environment make a useful buffer between white and black by easing the shock between two types otherwise alien for successful cooperation.

What appears to be certain is that the existence of a colored group at least tends to fracture race solidarity among those who have African blood.[5]

When Marcus Garvey was attempting to initiate his program for an industrial school in Jamaica, one to be patterned after the Tuskegee Institute idea in the United States, he bemoaned the fact that he received more cooperation from the white population of the island than from the colored.

From the French and British possessions in the Caribbean have come thousands of colored persons, to whom the concept " race " has never been important. To them the badge of culture or nationality has been the outstanding symbol. The confusion of culture and race becomes increasingly significant upon migration. Their social heritage represents and includes the devices that have been utilized by Negro groups in other sections to solve their life problems. Racial amalgamation is regarded as a definite " way out ". By and large their social devices are based upon procedures for establishing contacts and relationships with other groups. As a result race and culture become closely intertwined.

The ways in which the Negro immigrant groups have worked out this matter of relationships with other groups are important values. They represent an accumulated life experience. They are supported by custom, usage, tradition—and, in the homeland, even by merit. These ways are tenacious and tend to survive in both the pure and hybrid forms in certain relationships abroad. These differences in settings afforded by the homeland and the new environment may be reconciled if they are based upon reason, but if they are purely matters of convention or usage they are rather irreconcilable. Disgust arises, remains and conquers. Some of the most important of these cultural factors in the background of the Negro immigrant that are of importance in analyzing the American adjustment are:

5 Weatherly, U. G., *The West Indies as a Sociological Laboratory*, *American Journal of Sociology*, Vol. XXIX, No. 3, November, 1923, p. 300.

Religion—a background of ritualistic religion evidenced through affiliation with the Catholic and Episcopal faiths;

Politics — a profound interest in self-government among the British and the practice and philosophy of *liberté, égalité* and *fraternité* among the French. Yet, political stagnation;

Economic System—areas that are still productive, greatly populated but exploited;

Moral and Social Usages—essentially European and bourgeois;

Social Institutions—patterned upon an imitation of European experiences and forms.

These factors include not only those influences that Boas has classed as the " strong African background in the West Indies, the importance of which diminishes with increasing distance from the South ", but also the significant factors of family institutions, leisure, food habits, education, and superstitions.[6]

While none of these factors is a matter of race, all of them are so closely identified with the racial group that they give the appearance of having racial character. These factors are the products of group life in the homeland—are acquired and become deeply etched in the individual and the group. On the whole, the Negro immigrant is much more aware of them than he is of his physical manifestations of race. These factors in his background become infused with the sentiments of " loyalty, devotion, patriotism, justice, truth and rightness. To depart from any of its canons involves not only the pain of the unfamiliar, but also the guilty sense of treachery ".[7]

This close association of language, religion, moral standards, customs, and racial identity effects a sense of nationalism that is not typical of the American Negro. The Negro immigrant brings to the racial American scene a national character that has been impressed upon him by the area in which he previously lived. Substituting the American Negro character therefore becomes assimilation, a process not too easily nor very readily

6 Boas, Franz, Introduction to Hurston, Zora Neale, *Mules and Men*, Philadelphia, J. B. Lippincott, 1935, p. 3.

7 Fairchild, *op. cit.*, p. 11.

achieved. He must become " denationalized " and renationalized at the same time. Doing so involves recognition of a lower status than was held in the homeland, not as a national, but as a member of a rigidly defined color-caste—the Negro. Let us look at the make-up of a singular group of people who undergo a strange metamorphosis between the time when they leave their homeland either without racial identification, or as *colored* persons, or *blacks,* who upon arrival become to the immigration authorities *African Blacks,* and, who, if they identify themselves with the colored citizenry of the United States, become *Negroes.*

C. NUMBER AND SOURCES OF NEGRO IMMIGRANTS

Number

The first Negro immigration was a forced one. Slavery was its vehicle. Estimates on the number of Negro slaves imported into the United States prior to 1810 have varied from 300,000 to 400,000. A " Mr. Carey " cited in *A Century of Population Growth* [8] estimates that up to 1808 a total of 333,000 slaves had been imported as follows:

Prior to 1715	30,000
1715 – 1750	90,000
1751 – 1760	35,000
1761 – 1770	74,000
1771 – 1790	34,000
1791 – 1808	70,000
Total	333,000

The Federal Census of 1790 estimated that the survivors and descendants of the African slaves imported into the colonies numbered 757,208. This census represents the first analysis ever made of the size of the Negro population of foreign stock in this country. The foreign-born colored population " exclusive of Chinese, Japanese and civilized Indians " numbered 4,067

8 Bureau of the Census, U. S. Dept. of Commerce, *A Century of Population Growth,* 1909, p. 36.

in 1850. By 1870 it had increased to 9,494. The census report of 1880 listed 14,017. No other computation was made until 1900 when the total foreign-born Negro stock numbered 54,737. Between 1900 and 1930 this population increased to 181,981, or by 232 per cent, forming slightly more than 1.5 per cent of the total Negro population. (Table II)

The reports of the Bureau of Immigration give another aspect of the picture. Between 1899 and 1937 a total of 143,797 Negro immigrants were admitted to the United States. Between 1908, the first year for which statistics on emigrants departing were available, and 1937, the total number of Negro emigrant aliens departing was 36,937. For every 100 Negro immigrant aliens arriving during this period, 29 left the country.

Between 1908 and 1924 the number of Negro aliens admitted exceeded those departing. In 1925 the departing aliens exceeded those admitted by 303. There followed another period of five years when admissions exceeded departures. Then came the depression. Since 1932 the movement of Negro immigrants has been away from this country, reaching its all-time peak in 1933, when the admissions totaled 84 and the departures 1,058. For white immigrants, who had maintained a constant excess of admissions over departures since 1908, the all-time peak was reached in 1932, one year earlier than that of the Negro immigrant. The number of Negro aliens admitted in 1937 was larger than in any year since 1931. Negro aliens departing, however, out-numbered those entering the United States. Between two-thirds and three-fourths of the Negro aliens leaving the country between 1923 and 1932 had resided in the country less than ten years. (Table III)

The foreign-born Negro population of the United States in 1930 numbered 98,620 and formed 0.9 per cent of the total Negro population. The total foreign stock, which includes 83,361 native-born persons of mixed or foreign parentage, numbered in the same year 181,981. If one includes the 17,625 Negroes born in the outlying areas of Cuba, Puerto Rico and the Virgin Islands, who are alien by culture though not by law, the total Negro foreign population in 1930 numbered 199,606.

Ever since 1900, the foreign Negro population has increased at a more rapid rate than the foreign-born white and the native-born Negro populations. While the rate of growth for most of these groups declined during this thirty-year period, the foreign-born Negro groups continued to show a more vital rate of growth than either of the other groups. Between 1900 and 1930 the native Negro population increased 33.9 per cent, the native white 68.4 per cent, the foreign-born white 30.6 per cent, and the foreign Negro population (all stocks) 232 per cent.

The relative recency of this immigration is indicated by the fact that only 7.7 per cent of the present immigrant survivors arrived in 1900 or earlier, as compared with 32.7 per cent of the foreign-born white population and 6.3 per cent of the Mexican immigrant population. As among all migrating groups, the immigration of males preceded that of females. The percentage of all arrivals coming in during 1929 and 1930 (approximately 7 per cent) is similar for whites and Negroes of both sexes. (Table IV)

Sources

At the time of the census of 1870, there were 9,494 foreign-born Negroes in the United States. Reflecting the interrelation of population movement and economic practices attending the decline of slavery in the western world is the fact that 2,645, or 28 per cent, of them were from Canada, 1,982, or 21 per cent were from Africa, and 16 per cent were from the West Indies and other Atlantic islands. The remainder were from Portugal, Spain and Mexico. Since 1870, there has been a broad change in the sources of Negro immigration. No longer does Africa supply the bulk of Negro immigrants. Today, they come from the various islands of the Atlantic, particularly the British West Indies, from Canada and from the Cape Verde Islands. In 1930, 86 per cent of the Negro immigrants residing in the United States, as compared with 12 per cent of all foreign-born persons, were born in some American country. Furthermore, 73 per cent of all Negro immigrants residing in the United States in 1930 were born in the West Indies, and 82 per cent in the combined areas of the West Indies, South America and Central America. The bulk of them have come from the British West Indies, falling under the quota of Great Britain. A comparison of the birthplaces and places of last permanent residence of immigrant aliens admitted between 1923 and 1932 reveals little variation over the years, Negro immigrants, in the main, migrating directly to the United States. (Table V)

CHAPTER III

THE BACKGROUNDS OF NEGRO IMMIGRATION

THE West Indies, principal source of Negro immigration, is composed of an almost innumerable number of islands, ranging in size from Cuba with an area of 44,164 square miles, to islets scarcely bigger than a sandbar. These islands may be divided into three groups: The Greater Antilles, composed of Cuba, Jamaica, Haiti, Puerto Rico and their satellite islands; the Lesser Antilles, of which Guadaloupe, Dominica, Martinique, St. Lucia, Barbados, Tobago, and Trinidad are the principal islands; and, the Bahamas. With the exception of Cuba, Haiti and the Dominican Republic (which shares the island of Haiti with the republic of that name) all of these islands belong to Great Britain, France, or the Netherlands. While there are noteworthy differences among them there are certain marked similarities in their histories and economic development.

The population of these islands varies greatly. In Cuba there is a substantial proportion of whites, although the majority of the inhabitants have some Negro blood. In Haiti the population is practically entirely colored, while in the neighboring republic of Dominica most of the population is of Indian mixture. In Jamaica the mass of the population is Negro or mulatto, with a small dominating white class. In Puerto Rico the population is largely white with some Negro and a very little Indian blood. In most of the other islands the mass of the population is Negro or mulatto with a ruling white class. The large proportion of Negro blood found in the population is due to the extensive importation of Negro slaves during the colonial period. (Table VI)

A. QUOTA IMMIGRATION

Almost the entire body of Negro immigration to the United States comes from the Crown Colonies and the Dependencies of Great Britain and France, located in the West Indies.

(Table VII) Both of these countries undertook colonization to secure economic advantages for the nation or for selected individuals. England, because of her military power, and because of her then unparalleled success in industry and commerce, had an advantage in the material development of her possessions. Her methods did not permit a facile adjustment of culture to the indigenous colored population. France, on the other hand, was less industrial and apparently more congenial in handling the native temperament. Johnston reports that " intelligent travellers in Africa and America during the last half of the eighteenth century recorded opinions of their own and answers to their questions from Negroes which went to show that in the opinion of Negroes themselves the slave-holding nations stood thus in order of merit as regards kind treatment of slaves: the Portuguese first; then the Spaniards, the Danes, the French, the English and Dutch ".[1]

Other factors contributed to the background of the Negro immigrant. The West Indies were mainly black settlements. When the West Indian Negroes were granted their freedom in the British possessions they found their lives proscribed in other ways. The ruling classes provided a four-year apprenticeship system, that while enabling the newly-freed serfs to develop tools for economic freedom also kept them under a form of indentured labor. Nevertheless this new freedom did provide them with cultural contacts that had not been possible under slavery. During these days of development no new problems of race and conflicting cultures were introduced because of the immigration of new peoples. The West Indian Negro was without racial competition. He developed the area and acquired that sense of " belongingness " which is so much a part of the spirit of nationalism. Later he acquired the intra-racial conflicts that divided the mulatto from the black.

The Negro immigrant comes from an area in which he does not have complete political control, despite the fact that he is

1 Johnston, Sir Harry H., *The Negro in the New World*, New York, Macmillan Co., 1910, p. 47.

the majority population. The mother countries have devised ways and means whereby a certain amount of political freedom is possible, but never complete autonomy. In the Crown Colonies of Great Britain there are Governors assisted by Legislative and Executive Councils composed of officers of the state and representatives of the commercial and industrial and agricultural interests. In a few colonies as, Jamaica, Trinidad, and Barbados, there are a few elected members of the Legislative Council, largely representative of the middle-class colored population. While the members of the legislative assemblies are elected by popular vote, the laws upon which they pass are introduced either by the Executive Councils appointed by the Crown, or by Assemblymen chosen by the Governor. The French colonies likewise are administered by Governors assisted by Councils. These islands, however, are represented by Senators and Deputies in the French Chamber. Martinique and Guadeloupe are Departments of the Republic of France with full citizenship and full representation in the French Parliament. Haiti is an independent republic.

Though Barbados is known as " Little England " and Trinidad as the " New York of the Antilles ", the West Indian islands are primarily agricultural, relying upon England, France and the United States for their manufactured goods. Even today handicraft is the accepted mode of production, and the work of the individual artisan—the tailor, seamstress, wheelwright, blacksmith, boatbuilder and carpenter—is of utmost importance. The development of small farms, approximately one hundred years ago, paralleled the expansion of the sugar plantation system for which coolie labor was then being introduced. Upon the breakdown of the sugar market during and following the World War, the plantation system was reorganized and lands have been concentrated in the hands of native planters with large holdings, absentee landlords and foreign corporations. At one time the single-crop system, the so-called " money crop " method of agriculture, was so pronounced that the islands were called " the sugar islands ". Diversified production was completely unknown. When efforts were made to introduce such crops as limes and cocoa they usually gained a monopoly for the time being. So thoroughly had the idea of a money-crop pervaded the area that for a considerable time these islands did not produce any considerable share of their food products. As a result the system became disastrous to both planter and laborer, since neither could control the price and marketing factors. Yet, climate and soil have combined to render these islands potentially economically independent. To-day the land problem constitutes one of the gravest menaces to the future welfare of the West Indies.

The Negro immigrant—French or English—comes from a background of active superstitious practices. Though the practices of obeah and voodoo are legally prohibited, the beliefs still prevail in the peasant mind. Obeah is used to influence the activities of the white man, for it is " one function that the white can neither work nor understand ". Through many changes it now survives largely by identifying itself as science and by practicing on a lurking superstition that education has as yet been unable to eradicate. Today it is regarded by students of the problem as a common form of witchcraft, not infrequently associated with devil worship. But " duppies " and " jumbies ", even " celts ", are stern realities in many an island, intellectually doubted, perhaps, but instinctively accepted.

Education in the islands has a very different flavor from that provided for Negroes in the United States. The mission schools there were provided for alien groups—the Chinese and East Indians, in order that they might overcome the language handicap. In Barbados they exist for the poor whites. As soon as the deficiencies are removed these people may enter the elementary schools of the islands. In the British West Indies racial schools exist only for the removal of language handicaps. In the United States they provide for four-fifths of all Negro higher education. British West Indians send their children to England and Scotland for their higher education; the French

West Indians send theirs to France. In recent years more have been securing their higher education in the United States.

Class barriers are extremely important, and class distinctions are more closely observed in both the British and French communities of the West Indies, than in the United States. The black and colored populations of Barbados, for example, look down upon the poor whites of the island, known as " Red Legs " or " Scotland Johnnies ". Likewise do the colored populations of the Virgin Islands look down upon the " Cha-Chas " of St. Thomas, St. Kitts and the neighboring islands. Meanwhile, " white " looks over his nose at " colored ", and " colored " does the same to " black ".

The history of many of these islands is one long story of upheavals brought about by internal revolutions or by radical shifts in governmental control. Early in the nineteenth century the colored population of Haiti drove what was then the greatest overseas expedition ever assembled by France forever from the island. This fact is an integrated part of the French colonial's background. Haiti became the first Latin-American country in the new world to achieve its independence. The Jamaicans rose against the British and the Spanish time and time again, and secured for themselves a greater measure of independence. Coming from the slave clearing house for the United States, the Caribbean Negro has developed into a spirited, aggressive culture-type, whose program and principle of accommodation has been singularly different from that of the American Negro. Meanwhile, migrations, economic revolutions and agricultural crises have played an important role in determining the characteristics of the people and the character of the change evolved.

The population from these areas is a product of free and indentured immigration. Spanish, English, French, Dutch, Danes and Portuguese have contributed the European elements; while Africans, Chinese and East Indians represent the non-European types. The white population has not increased perceptibly, even when augmented by new colonists from the mother countries. Meanwhile the vagaries of the sugar industry led to the introduction of coolie laborers from India, and to the migration of Negroes to the Canal Zone, Central America, South America, Cuba and the United States.

One of the most singular phases of the West Indian's background, however, is that involving the emancipation of the free colored population in the British possessions. The long struggle for civil and political equality after the abolition was one in which the natives fought side by side with their former owners. Mathieson reports that the slave in the British colony had no right of redemption, that "one cannot read the Spanish regulations without seeing that their main object was to promote the moral and social welfare of the slave, and they were designed only incidentally and as a matter of course to secure him from ill-treatment. In our colonies only the second of these purposes was attempted, and we shall find that its accomplishment was rendered hopeless by the entire neglect of the first."[2]

Freedom for the slaves came only after bitter parliamentary struggles. The first phase of this emancipation included the diplomatic endeavors from 1807 to 1823 to make the anti-slave trade laws effective and the effort to obtain a universal abolition of the slave trade. The second was the abolition of laws that prevented the free Negroes of the British possessions from being actually free.

Even in the early days of the nineteenth century the free Negroes in the British colonies were divided into two groups, the free colored—the mulattoes—and the free blacks. Law and custom had ordained differences between them. They were neither slave nor free, and had no status in their middle position. Meanwhile there was a development in property holdings and in "respectable living". Many free persons in Kingston, Jamaica, were referred to as persons of great wealth. It was said that seventy persons among them had an aggregate wealth

2 Mathieson, William Law, *British Slavery and Its Abolition 1823-1838*, London, Longmans, Green & Co., 1926, p. 40.

of approximately one million pounds as early as 1825. Their occupations were becoming increasingly diversified. Yet the laws made drastic distinctions between them and the white population.

Restrictions were placed upon real property, so that a donor could bequeath real property to the extent of only two thousand pounds. Prior to 1813 it was unlawful for free Negroes to navigate vessels or to receive clearance papers at the port of Jamaica. Even burial grounds provided separate resting places for mortal remains. In an election held in Montserrat in the same year, the votes of non-white persons were thrown out after they had been permitted to vote and had elected their candidate. Colored votes were not recognized in an election held in Antigua in 1820. Upon this action an appeal was made to England.

Then Grenada, Dominica, Jamaica and Montserrat appealed to the Colonial Office. They even organized to secure their rights. In Barbados the colored population armed itself in defensive protection against the physical onslaughts of white inhabitants. When in 1827 a petition was presented to Parliament on behalf of the free colored persons of Jamaica, asking that they be granted the rights of British citizens, the white West Indian representatives maintained that the colored population was not sufficiently advanced in wealth and culture to be immediately worthy of such a privilege. Yet the agitation continued, and beginning in 1829 the several islands began easing the regulations that had proscribed the free colored and free black populations. In this respect England was asked only to follow the pattern already established by France, Holland, Sweden and Denmark, who had already completely emancipated their Caribbean colonials.

But for long periods divisions had been existing between the free colored and the free black populations. This cleavage resulted from the attitude of the white population on the color question. The free colored people were more acceptable to the whites, and were granted a higher social standing than the blacks. This separation on the basis of color had registered itself in public affairs, private associations and social diversions. The struggle for the liberation of the free colored and the free black populations, therefore, drew the two groups together and by the late twenties of the nineteenth century had broken down some of the tradition of caste which had been attributed to color.[3]

Yet, the color complex survives in some forms. It has become an issue in the present effort for West Indian self-government. In criticizing the colonial policy of Great Britain, one observer noted that

> it has been the policy of the Government for some years past to appoint a few Negroes to those positions. They have usually been Negroes of fair, and not of dark skin. And that type of man, whether on the Council or in the other departments of government, is often a more dangerous opponent of the masses of the people than the Europeans themselves.[4]

Regarding the Trinidad Legislature the author maintains:

> The majority of them hate even more than white men any talk about colour. For if they stand up against colour discrimination they will be noted by the Government as leaders of the people, and then goodbye to some of their dearest hopes; while for some it will mean facing in public the very obvious but nevertheless dreadful fact that they are not white men.[5]

These immigrants come from areas that essentially are isolated from each other and from larger cultural areas. It has only been since the World War that any appreciable traffic has taken place between the islands and the North American mainland. Trinidad and Barbados have long had abundant outside

3 For a more extensive treatment of this subject see Wesley, Charles H., "The Emancipation of the Free Colored Population of the British Empire," *The Journal of Negro History*, Vol. XIX, 1934, pp. 137-170.

4 James, C. L. R., "The Case for West Indian Self-Government," *Day to Day Pamphlets*, No. 16, The Hogarth Press, London, 1933, p. 21.

5 *Ibid.*, p. 29.

contacts, but some of the smaller islands are as isolated today as they were twenty years ago. As a consequence a " high degree of particularism characterizes the whole group, and this has hitherto rendered futile all attempts at federation or even co-operation in common concerns. Much the same spirit of detachment and localism that permeates remote rural communities elsewhere is found in the oceanic islands ".[6] Thus there is developed an insular personality that is not in keeping with the cosmopolitanism of the new world into which the Negro immigrant enters. Furthermore, there are created problems of adjustment that are in no way settled when the immigrant reaches these shores, but which add to the confusion of resettlement.

The French islands provide an entirely different background. In Martinique and Guadeloupe a small percentage of the population is black, the majority being the colored. In Martinique, especially, there is greater freedom of race. During the days of slavery the French attempted, unsuccessfully, to keep the white stock pure by making stringent laws against the freeing of black women for the purpose of marriage, but the present highly varied colored population is evidence of their ineffectiveness. The fact was that the French colonial in those days was more free and humane in his relations with dark women than the other European races.[7] In Martinique, it was customary for the white man to give land or houses to his colored mistress, to admit the relationship. The French colonial is not a black, or a white, but a Frenchman. Between the European stock and the colored and black persons there is no conflict. But " if ever there is a race conflict in the French islands it will come about because of competition for control between the pure black, the plantation hands, who are less advanced, and the mixed breed who are socially conscious and ambitious—not between the white and the black." [8]

6 Weatherly, U. G., *op. cit.*, p. 294.

7 Herrick, Robert, " The Race Problem in the Caribbean, II: The French Way," *The Nation*, Vol. 118, June 18, 1924, pp. 669-670.

8 *Ibid.*, p. 670.

Two agencies have entered the French colonies to make a distinct colored civilization, the Catholic Church and the public schools. The French colonies are predominantly Catholic. In the schools the colonials are taught to read and write intelligible French, aside from the *patois* they use in daily life. Here also there is a poise not noted elsewhere in the Carribbean. Weatherly remarks, " However much the Barbadian may flaunt his ultra-English character, it is still a somewhat extraneous thing of which he is never quite sure. The French islanders have the assured manner of those who do not need to be self-assertive ".[9]

The Caribbean is a vast melting pot. According to Beals,[10] " Islands and mainland swarm with races of every hue, living in every epoch of society, from that of the primitive African jungle to the effete degeneracy of Havana creole aristocracy. Habitats originally thousands of miles apart have been lifted and set down side by side in the countries to the southeast. The Caribbean is a vast ethnological laboratory, Spanish and Portuguese meet French, Dutch, English and Americans. Jews fled there from the Spanish Inquisition. Full-blooded Negroes practice the fearful obeah. East Indian coolies and Hindus tread new tropics. Chinese have flowed in by tens of thousands. The descendants of native Indians who greeted Columbus still lounge under the native palms. Most intense and most vital are Negroes who swarm out of over-populated Haiti, Jamaica and Trinidad until it seems that Africa will rule racially if not politically and economically ".

Lord Olivier, who spent twenty-five years in the British colonies, points out what he believes to be the essential factors in the background of the colored West Indian as follows:

1. The absence of a " colour bar ". This does not mean that there is no color prejudice, but that there is in the minds of the " domiciled " white people nothing answering or

9 Herrick, Robert, *op. cit.*, p. 669.

10 Beals, Carleton, " The Black Belt of the Caribbean ", *The Fortnightly Review*, Vol. 130, No. 777, September, 1931, pp. 356-368.

akin to the hostility and contempt toward black or coloured people which is boasted by many white folk in the Southern States of America and is even more prevalent now in South Africa; or that there is not, conversely, a latent jealousy of and hostility towards the "buckra" in the mind of the black and coloured. Such prejudices do not appear on the surface, and so much as there is is unquestionably diminishing".[11]

2. Such color prejudice as does exist among the whites is stronger against the colored than against the blacks. "This is because the coloured intermediate class . . . encroach upon or threaten to undermine the social and economic ascendancy of the white, traditionally the dominant aristocracy of these communities".[12]
3. There is a healthy balance of social relations between the different racial groups in these islands.
4. Emancipation took place thirty years earlier in the West Indies, and under more favorable conditions than in the United States. "No overwhelming class of new citizens suddenly endowed with democratic power and unqualified and unprepared for its responsible and efficient exercise was created".[13]
5. The people are possessed of "natural good manners and civility of disposition . . . very far . . . superior to the members of the corresponding class in England, America, or North Germany . . . yet they possess enough fundamental independence to resent an uncivil or overbearing address". This, the author maintains, is due to the attitude that has been taken toward them in the Caribbean. Mecklin, however, found the basis for a different background in the benevolent paternalism of the English. He maintains:

11 Olivier, Lord, *White Capital and Coloured Labor*, revised edition, Hogarth Press, London, 1929, p. 63.

12 *Ibid.*, p. 66.

13 *Ibid.*, p. 76.

There are a number of reasons why race antagonisms have always beeen at a minimum, reasons which vitiate entirely the parallel Professor Royce and others have drawn between the Negro in the South and in Jamaica, and upon which he bases his kindly though somewhat condescending advice to his " Southern brethren." Jamaica is far more a black man's country than the South has ever been; there are over 700,000 Negroes upon the island and something over 15,000 whites, but these whites dominate in the governing and employing class and as merchants or planters lead or direct the industrial life of the island.

" There never was a time ", states Dr. Mecklin, " since the English set foot upon the island when they had not been complete and undisputed masters of its destiny, barring perhaps the episode of the Gordon riots of 1865 which only convinced them of the folly of trying to do otherwise." In Jamaica where the whites constitute the apex, the coloured, the middle class and the masses of Negroes make up the broad base, the " orderly, law-abiding and contented character of the Jamaican Negro, which Professor Royce found so charming, is the outcome of the benevolent paternalism of the English regime, the fundamental idea of which is the complete subordination of the Negro to the will of the white. The Negro has never known any other condition ".[14]

It is not to be concluded that all is lovely and gracious in the West Indies for either the colored or the black man. If it were so there would be no large amount of emigration. Economic depression, and what appears to be a large amount of interracial prejudices, are everywhere manifest. This unrest was the soil in which Marcus Garvey planted his program of racial nationalism. The natives are well aware of the methods of British imperialism, popularly described as the " divide-and-rule " method, yet they are far from satisfied with the results it has netted. And when grave political problems are involved

14 Mecklin, John M., " The Philosophy of the Color Line ", *American Journal of Sociology*, Vol. XIX, November, 1913, pp. 343 ff.

the color question is bound to enter. It is necessary to quote at length the passionate argument of one advocate for self-government in the West Indies:

> It has to be admitted that the West Indian Negro is ungracious enough to be far from perfect. He lives in the tropics, and he has the particular vices of all who live there, not excluding people of European blood. In one respect, indeed, the Negro of the tropics has an overwhelming superiority to all other races—the magnificent vitality with which he overcomes the enervating influences of the climate. But otherwise the West Indian people are an easy-going people. Their life is not such as to breed in them the thrift, the care, and the almost equine docility to system and regulation which is characteristic of the industrialised European. If their comparative youth as a people saves them from the cramping effects of tradition, it is a useful handicap to be rid of in the swiftly-changing world of today. Yet they lack the valuable basis of education which is not so much taught or studied as breathed in from birth in countries where people have for generation after generation lived settled and orderly lives. Quicker in intellect and spirit than the English, they pay for it by being less continent, less stable, less dependable. And this particular aspect of their character is intensified by certain social prejudices peculiar to the West Indies, and which have never been given their full value by those observers from abroad who have devoted themselves to the problems of West Indian society and politics.
>
> The Negroid population of the West Indies is composed of a large percentage of actually black people, and about fifteen or twenty per cent of people who are a varying combination of white and black. From the days of slavery these have always claimed superiority to the ordinary black, and a substantial majority of them still do so (though resenting as bitterly as the black, assumptions of white superiority). With emancipation in 1834 the blacks themselves established a middle class. But between the brown-skinned middle class and the black there is a continual rivalry, distrust and ill-feeling, which skillfully played upon by the European people poisons the life of the community. Where so many crosses and colours meet and mingle, the shades are naturally difficult to determine and the resulting confusion is immense.

There are the nearly-white hanging on tooth and nail to the fringes of white society, and these, as is easy to understand, hate contact with the darker skin far more than some of the broader-minded whites. Then there are the browns, the intermediates, who cannot by any stretch of the imagination pass as white, but who will not go one inch toward mixing with people darker than themselves. And so, on and on, and on. Associations are formed of brown people who will not admit into their number those too much darker than themselves, and there have been heated arguments in committees as to whether such and such a person's skin was fair enough to have him or her admitted, without lowering the tone of the institution. Clubs have been known to accept the daughter and mother, who were fair, but to refuse the father, who was black. A dark-skinned brother in a fair-skinned family is sometimes the subject of jeers and insults and open intimation that his presence is not required at the family social functions. Fair-skinned girls who marry dark men are often ostracised by their families and given up as lost. There have been cases of women who have been content to live with black men but would not marry them. Should the darker man, however, have money or position of some kind, he may aspire, and it is not too much to say that in a West Indian colony the surest sign of a man's having arrived is the fact that he keeps company with people lighter in complexion than himself. Remember, finally, that the people most affected by this are people of the middle class who, lacking the hard contact with realities of the masses and unable to attain to the freedom of a leisure class, are, more than all types of people given to trivial diversions and subdivisions of social rank and precedence.

Here lies, perhaps, the gravest drawback of the coloured population. They find it difficult to combine, for it is the class that should, in the natural course of things, supply the leaders that is so rent and torn by these colour distinctions.[15]

Many and vociferous will be the denials to such an estimate both at home and abroad, but keen observers attest the truthfulness of such assertions. W. E. B. DuBois [16] recently states,

15 James, C. L. R., *op. cit.*, pp. 7-9.

16 DuBois, W. E. B., "Inter-racial Implications of the Ethiopian Crisis", *Foreign Affairs*, Vol. 14, No. 1, October, 1935, pp. 82-93.

for example, that " The mulattoes of the British West Indies, and the richer and more intelligent blacks, have been so incorporated with the ruling British that together they hold the mass of black workers in a vise. The number of voters and landholders is limited. The means of livelihood depend entirely upon the employers and the wage is low. Masses of the workers migrate here and there. They built the Panama Canal. They work in Cuban cane fields. They come to the United States. The unrest in these islands is kept down only by starvation and severe social repression ". In Barbados, with a population of 180,000, only 18 per cent of the male adult population enjoy the right to vote, and, the legislature has steadily opposed franchise reform, compulsory education, luxury tax, death duties, workmen's compensation act, and the introduction of any bills which have had as their end the amelioration of the terrible economic and social conditions of the struggling mass of people.

The colored Portuguese immigrant comes from a background that is largely Roman Catholic in religion, agricultural in employment and poverty-stricken in its conditions of living. Here no distinctions are made between persons on the basis of color. Masses of the population are tenant farmers employed on large estates. Wages are low and women are found along with men working in the fields, quarries and at the docks. Fisheries give extensive employment to the male population. The typical Portuguese peasant is described by Lewis [17] as "characterized by a quiet determination, industry, brave endurance of hardship, and a persistent longing for better things. He is devout, though religion and recreation frequently go hand in hand as illustrated in the *romarias,* a combination of religious pilgrimage and country fair popular throughout the country. He is superstitious, and often depends on magic and charms in case of illness. Courteous hospitality, good temper,

17 Lewis, Read, in Fairchild's *Immigrant Backgrounds,* pp. 257-258. See also Davie, Maurice R., *World Immigration,* Macmillan, New York, 1936, pp. 177-178.

quiet thoughtfulness and a certain wistful melancholy are equally notable. Amid living conditions which are generally difficult and often squalid, the Portuguese peasantry exhibit an artistic sense manifest in their love of music, their improvisation of poetry, and their native costumes and handicrafts". Because of insufficient economic opportunities on the mainland and in the island possessions of the Azores and Cape Verde, Portuguese have migrated at a much higher rate than their Spanish neighbors. White Portuguese, for the most part, have gone to Brazil and Hawaii. In the latter country, where they were introduced as contract laborers on the sugar plantations, they have since become small farmers, the backbone of the Hawaiian coffee industry.

Throughout the Atlantic Islands the basic concepts of life and institutions and race have a certain similarity. The lack of economic development, the overpopulation, the influences of European culture have made an indelible mark upon the natives. The universal urge in these islands has been to discard the old and put on the new as rapidly as circumstances would allow—but the masses of the population continue to live a marginal and lagging existence.

Thus the Negro immigrant is at a disadvantage after a brief experience on the American racial front. He becomes sensitive to criticism, self-conscious and uncertain of himself and his values. He is conscious of opposition and of the persistent attempts to belittle his presence here. Yet, being ambitious and possessed of a desire to succeed, he tackles the problem and leaves as mute evidence a transfer of culture values that has made the Negro immigrant less foreign, and the American Negro less provincial in his approach to racial and economic problems.

B. NON-QUOTA IMMIGRATION

Before presenting the composite of migration problems introduced by the non-quota areas and the United States' outlying possessions in the Caribbean, it will be well to introduce briefly some of the problems in the Caribbean picture that necessitate the mobility of its peoples. The economic urge is a powerful motive in this movement, and has exercised both a push and a pull on the Negro populations. Emigration has been one way out of numerous difficulties. In recent years, however, the South American republics have set up new political regulations that have restricted the movement of these island populations to so great an extent that they were regarded as having racial significance. Some examples of these restrictions may be noted.

During 1923 Honduras entertained an amendment to its immigration law to bar Negroes from the Republic. The reason for the resolution was the alleged menace created along the Atlantic Coast by the importation of Negroes by banana-shipping companies to compete with native labor. It was stated that numerous clashes, resulting in many casualties among Negroes and natives grew out of earlier immigrations. El Salvador, the coffee-minded neighboring country approved a similar regulation for the restriction of Negro immigration during the same year.

Kepner in his analysis of the banana industry reports that after the completion of the Panama Canal drifters from all corners of the globe turned up in Central America to try their luck in the banana regions.[18] " At the completion of the canal, a large number of laborers were turned loose in Central America. The thrusting of such labor upon the various countries of the mainland led to serious trouble along racial lines." After mentioning the " Babel of tongues " arising from the heterogeneous mixture of colored railway construction men from the United States, blacks from the West Indies and British Honduras, French Negroes from Martinique and Guadeloupe, and Chinese merchants, he adds:

If all these people could abide in harmony there would, of course, be no problem. The Negro from the United States has

18 Kepner, Dr. Charles D., *Social Aspects of the Banana Industry*, New York, Columbia University Press, 1936, pp. 118-120.

no use for the British subjects. The Jamaican has no regard for the black from Belize or Barbados, and still less for the French-speaking Negroes, and the blacks from the United States.

After calling attention to the respect given to white officials by Negroes from the United States and by natives of Costa Rica, Kepner points out that Mexicans and Colombians have caused numerous disturbances but the big problem is the Jamaican Negro—falsely proud of being a British subject.

Beals describes the background for the present immigration restriction policies of the Central and South American countries. He states, "In the old days several of the Caribbean islands, . . . were the seat of the slave distribution to the United States and Spanish America." The modern versions of those "blackbirder" ships still go out from Jamaica and Haiti with cheap contract labor to work on plantations throughout the Caribbean area. In many ways Panama, with a black population larger than the white, has usurped this role. The Isthmus is a sort of labor mart, or at least center, from where the African current radiates north along the Central American coast, south into Venezuela and Colombia.

Hordes of Jamaican, Barbados, Haitian and French colonial Negroes were brought into Panama by the French canal company, still more were brought in by the United States to dig the great ditch, and this vast horde of aliens was then dumped over the border to present the New Republic of Panama with its peculiar set of problems. Even so the bulk of the Canal Zone population still has British citizenship—black laborers and servants from Jamaica. The blacks are the silver employees; whites are the gold employees . . .

The United States is responsible for the sanitation of Panama and Colon, but nothing is quite so horrible as the conglomeration of black folk in a huge fire-trap, two and three story wooden tenements, covering whole blocks. One passes through large sections of both cities where Belzian, Jamaican, Haitian and other Negroes congregate in colonies according to nationality, any number of families occupying a single room, places with no more than one or two toilets for the whole building, without running water, without electricity or gas, so that the hazard of fire is increased by the use of kerosene lamps, candles and oil and gasoline stoves; where disease stalks and black bodies grow limp and juicy with the preventable scourge of elephantiasis. No more tragic contrast is presented between these people, dumped originally on Panama by the Zone authorities, and the great civilized symbol represented by the remarkable operation of the Canal itself.[19]

Immigration restriction has taken on a new significance in southern America. The Republic of Panama has a highly restrictive immigration policy. A quota of only five persons yearly was allowed Chinese, Syrians, Turks and Negroes under its 1928 immigration law. Japanese and Hindus formerly excluded were at this time admitted. The exclusion of Negroes is limited to persons of the American races whose mother tongue is other than Spanish. This avoids any discrimination against the citizens of other Latin-American countries. Panama, however, needs immigrant labor for the development of the Republic. This need previously has been filled by West Indian Negroes, who are now excluded. According to Work [20] this need is now being met in other ways. The United Fruit Company, for example, is reported as " importing laborers from Nicaragua and San Salvador for the development of the banana plantations on Panama's Pacific Coast ".

As early as 1910 Venezuela had approved a constitutional change which would exclude colored immigrants. It did not become a law, however. In the law of June 26, 1918 the following persons would not be accepted as immigrants: . . . " Persons who are not of European races nor islanders of the yellow race of the Northern Hemisphere. . . ." Since 1918 the laws of Venezuela have more nearly approximated the restrictive legislative actions of the more northern American

19 Beals, Carleton, *America South*, Philadelphia, J. B. Lippincott, 1937, p. 158.

20 Work, Monroe N., editor, *The Negro Year Book*, 1931-32, Tuskegee (Ala.) Press, pp. 354-357.

countries. In 1929 the immigration of foreign-born Negroes was prohibited by law. If the family of a Negro resident is not residing in the country those members are not permitted entrance. Foreign Negroes in the country " will in the future only be permitted to travel from place to place under strict police supervision and only when carrying several documents such as passport, vaccination and identity certificate and police permit, the failure to produce any one of which will render them liable to immediate deportation ".[21] This is one of the most drastic alien-control regulations in the Western Hemisphere.

The Venezuelan law had been under consideration for some time. It is based upon the experience the country has had since the big oil fields were opened near Maracaibo. During the past decade thousands of Negro laborers, artisans, chauffeurs and domestics, lured by high wages and shorter hours, swarmed into Maracaibo from Curacao, Trinidad, Barbados and other nearby West Indian islands, until they numbered nearly ten thousand. The reasons therefor were, of course, obvious. A Negro cook earning five dollars a month in Trinidad could easily earn from thirty to thirty-five dollars in Maracaibo. Negro clerks paid from thirty to forty dollars in Trinidad could earn from one hundred dollars upwards in the new country. The Venezuelan government took the view that every West Indian Negro working in the oil fields was robbing a Venezuelan of a job, despite the fact that nearly every Venezuelan in the vicinity was employed by the oil industry in some capacity.

There was, however, one thesis in the government's objection to the foreign Negro worker that is frequently voiced against the least assimilated foreign groups in the United States population. Whereas the native Venezuelan worker spends all his earnings in the country, the foreign Negro spends no more than the bare necessities of life demand and remits a substantial

21 *Ibid.*, p. 355.

sum home to his native land every month. Previously, foreign oil concerns receiving concessions to operate in Venezuela were obliged to have at least eighty per cent Venezuelans in their employ. Contending that this obligation was not being observed, the government urged the passage of stricter regulations, of which the foregoing is a part.

Cuba, the "Pearl of the Antilles", has likewise developed restrictive procedures regulating the immigration of Negroes. The realization that its colored immigration was larger than the white, and the fact that the sugar crisis of 1921 led to many new demands for new economic resources, served as the basis for its immigration regulation. The probability, and the hope of many Cubans, that the mulattoes and Negroes will be completely absorbed, thus making the Cuban nation a homogeneous race, is fast vanishing. The cause of this is found in the condition of the sugar industry. "Seeking to reduce the cost of production, the sugar companies decided upon the experiment of importing blacks from Haiti, where the Negroes speak a French dialect, and from Jamaica, where they speak English."[22] The influx of the Haitians and Jamaicans into Cuba increased greatly. From 709 Jamaicans and 253 Haitians who arrived in Cuba in 1912, the number rose to 27,088 Jamaicans and 33,971 Haitians in 1920, an influx of 63,000 foreign-born Negroes into a population of less than three millions. In 1921, the year of the sugar crisis, the number decreased. The importation was later resumed, however, and in 1921 we find that the number of Negroes from Haiti and Jamaica arriving in Cuba approximated 26,000. Since 1921 the number of Jamaicans has steadily declined, probably partly because of the warnings of the British government about conditions in Cuba. In 1927 the number of Haitians who arrived in Cuba was 14,312 and of Jamaicans only 2,348. These, together with a few hundred other Negroes from the Antilles, totalled 17,000 Negro immigrants. The introduction of so large a volume of

22 Holler, Arnold, "Black Ivory and White Gold in Cuba", *The Nation*, Vol. 128, January 9, 1929, pp. 55-56.

Negro labor led to the restrictions now in vogue. Negro labor may now be imported only under specific regulations provided for by so called " emergencies ".

In Costa Rica the same " emergencies " clause is operative. Under its regulations Negro workers under contract may be imported from Guatemala for a period not to exceed two years, after which time they are to be deported.

Canada, once the haven of British West Indian Negro emigrants, has recently declared itself as preferring settlers " of a readily assimilable type, already identified by race or language with one or the other of the two great races now inhabiting the country and prepared for the duties of democratic Canadian citizenship." The Acting Deputy Minister of Immigration and Colonization is quoted as stating " Canada seeks certain classes of immigrants, and in the search limits the efforts to those classes needed in Canada and those races most readily assimilable. So far as the Negro is concerned we have never encouraged his settlement in Canada regardless of his occupation, although we have admitted and still admit a few colored folk who are able to comply with existing immigration regulations ".[23] The Annual Report of the Department of Immigration and Colonization for 1929 shows that in that year the total Negro immigration numbered 376 of whom 280 came from the United States and 96 from other countries. Negro immigration from the British Crown Colonies of the Caribbean to Canada is definitely not encouraged.[24]

C. INSULAR DEPENDENCIES OF THE UNITED STATES

Amid this area of racial and economic confusion are located three major insular dependencies of the United States—the Panama Canal Zone, the Virgin Islands and Puerto Rico. Each of these presents problems of emigration and immigration that

23 *The Canada Year Book*, 1932, p. 149.

24 Greaves, Ida C., *The Negro in Canada*, McGill University Economic Studies, No. 16, 1929, p. 47.

have had a resounding effect upon and profound implications for the presence of a foreign-born colored population in the continental United States.

The Panama Canal Zone

The Panama Canal Zone, which was acquired by the United States by perpetual lease in 1903, had, in 1930 a Negro population of 20,385, slightly more than one-half the total population of the Zone. Of the total population, 15,101, or 38.3 per cent were foreign-born Negroes, the vast majority of whom came from Central America, South America and the various West Indies Islands.

The varied differences between native-born and foreign-born Negroes,[25] particularly the demographic differences, are nowhere more evident than in the Canal Zone. Here 19.3 per cent of the foreign-born population is unable to speak English; the illiteracy rate (based upon an ability to read and write in English) for the foreign-born Negro is six times higher than that of the native-born; the age distribution is more skewed than that of the population in any continental American community; and less than one per cent of the population is naturalized. Negro immigration to the Canal Zone is not a recent phenomenon. It reaches back to 1880 when the French Canal Company initiated the building of the Panama waterway. The bulk of immigrants arrived prior to the World War. Yet these immigrants are an older element and appear to be a more stable, and a less mobile group than the native-born Negro population, ninety-five per cent of which is less than twenty years of age. More than half of the foreign-born Negro males and females are married as compared with less than twenty per cent of the native-born Negroes of each sex.

Various West Indian islands have supplied the main labor sources of the Canal Zone since 1880. Negroes were preferred to the Chinese and the East Indians by the French, who had an

25 "Foreign-born", of course, refers to being born outside of the United States and its possessions.

unsatisfactory experience with these workers while building the Panama Railroad earlier in the century. The opportunity for West Indian Negroes to work in a money economy for a short while and then to return home after a few years as peasant proprietors was an alluring one. The failure of the French Company when just about one-tenth of its project was completed forced many of these immigrants to remain in Panama.

When the United States reopened the canal project in 1903 West Indian immigration was again encouraged. The United States government detailed labor recruiters to the larger islands, particularly Jamaica and Barbados, and secured some twenty thousand Negro workers. In addition, workers who wanted to enter the Zone independently found every facility at their convenience. Between 1905 and 1913 some thirty-five thousand West Indians went to work on the canal construction. This number was maintained throughout the life of the project, being balanced by the almost equal flow of emigrants and immigrants.

For the first time the race problem, as it is known and understood in the United States, was introduced on a large scale into the Caribbean. Since designation of workers by color was offensive to the Republic of Panama and Colombia, and since the West Indians were unaccustomed to such differentiations, the local representatives of the United States' interests devised a Silver and Gold standard of stratification. There were the Silver Employees who were colored, and the Gold Employees who were white. The difference, theoretically, was based upon the wage scale, the Silver Employees receiving a wage that ranged from twenty to seventy-five dollars a month, and the Gold Employees from seventy-five dollars upward. Every detail of the canal work was subject to this classification, post office windows, commissary store counters, labor trains, mess kitchens, and railroad stations. The classification obtained for the colored citizenry of Panama as well as for the foreign-born Negroes, all of whom were Silver employees.

Labor problems arose in the Zone when the Canal was opened in 1914. The steady growth of the Isthmian population had been at a more rapid rate than the growth of activities following the completion of the locks. The situation was further aggravated by the coming of a large number of Americans who discovered that the wages paid were in some instances higher than those paid in the United States for similar types of work. The real wages were much higher. Many of the American whites supplanted Negroes holding clerical and supervisory positions. This situation resulted in many Negroes returning to their homelands. The majority of those remaining were either permanently employed or found employment on various operating projects. Yet, they, too, faced grave obstacles. As reported by one observer in 1920 they amounted to this [26]:

> . . . black men who sit at desks beside white men and do the same work. What do they receive? The white man from $100 to $125 every month, the West Indian $75 or less. Very often a West Indian doing clerical work with a long and good record is discharged to make room for some white ne'er-do-well. When he complains to authorities he is often told: " Well, we'll give you a job as foreman over a gang in the shops. No matter what class of work you're doing you can't make any more than seventy-five dollars per month ". That's industrial democracy, is it not?
>
> It may be asked: " Why don't the West Indians organize themselves into labor unions? " They do organize, but there are few reasons for these labor unions not being able to accomplish much.
>
> A spirit of hatred has been kindled among the islanders and the spark has been fanned and sheltered by the wretched system of suggestion borrowed from Great Britain. The white Britisher tells the Jamaican that because some Caucasian blood flows through his veins he is better than the Trinidadian. The Barbadian has been taught that because he is more nearly of pure Negro blood he is better than the mixed people of Jamaica. . . . Thus they go, ever fighting, ever hating each other. The Barbadian hates the

26 Patterson, Harvey T., "American Democracy in the Canal Zone", *The Crisis*, New York, Vol. 20, No. 2, June, 1920, pp. 83-85.

Jamaican, the Trinidadian hates the Barbadian and the Jamaican hates them all. So by desperately creating discord among the men, the government keeps them from organizing unions for the betterment of conditions.

A few years earlier than the above complaint, the Metal Trades Council, a Gold Employees labor union, had demanded that Negro workers be excluded from all positions above those of messengers and janitors. The movement gained momentum when in 1920 labor leaders came from the United States and urged the Negro workers to unite. A strike was called, was unsuccessful, and the Negro strikers were forced to leave the Zone. They found temporary shelter in Colon and Panama, cities of the Republic. Later many of them returned to the Zone to seek other employment. The incident, however, provided the Metal Trades Council with a weapon for eliminating aliens which it is using until this day. The Canal Zone Government, however, in maintaining what is regarded to be a reasonable policy of fair treatment for the Silver Employees refused to yield to the Council's demands. But along came the 1929 depression, which seriously crippled Canal Zone operations.

The Negro workers were the first ones affected by the necessary reductions in personnel. The white unions, backed by the native Panamanians and with the backing of the American Federation of Labor, began a fresh campaign against the foreign-born and all other Negro workers. Again they requested that Negroes be eliminated from all grades above janitors and messengers. The native Panamanians, realizing that their labor market was glutted, urged that Negro workers be expelled and deported from the Republic. The activity reached a new high in anti-alien agitation when in February, 1937, a United States Senate Congressional Committee held hearings on the Metal Trades Council's request that the West Indian Negroes be ousted from the Zone. One of the arguments offered by the Council was to the effect that the West Indians could easily commit sabotage in case the United States warred against

Great Britain. In reply the West Indies Employees, Association, representing the Negro workers, complained that the Negro West Indians could not become citizens until after long residence, maintaining that the motive in pressing the passage of such a bill was to permit the offspring of white Americans in the Canal Zone, who were constrained to go outside of the Isthmus to seek employment, a chance at the soft and high paid positions. Politically and socially the Negro workers of the Canal Zone are *déraciné*. They are completely excluded from political activities, and take no part in political movements. They are neither citizens of the Republic of Panama, nor of the United States. Their political status can only be appreciated when it is recalled that many of them have been in the service of this government in the Zone for more than a quarter of a century. Their long absence from the West Indies has made them alien to its traditions and life. Yet the Congress of the United States has made no provision for their naturalization, nor is there any political machinery in the Zone for such a purpose. For the second and third generations now maturing in the areas the situation is even more precarious. They are the new men without a country. Being born in the Zone in no way gives them precedence over their foreign-born parents, and they are without valid claim to British citizenship.

Social legislation as established in the Zone is available only to the Gold Employees. The provisions of the Dennison Retirement Act, covering federal workers in the Zone are not extended to the Silver Employees. Such few benefits as the Negro workers have received, and these are so minor as to be regarded as merely trivial, have come about through the activities of the Silver Employees' Association, recognized by the government as the official spokesman for the entire Silver personnel.

Education for the children of white employees in the Zone encompasses elementary, high school and junior college training. Negroes have only provisions for elementary education. Negro students who wish to acquire more formal education must go to Jamaica or some other country. The schools in Panama and Colon are said not to encourage the attendance of West Indian children.

Here is reflected one of the most complex problems of immigration in the Western World. The Negro immigrant is not only without rights, but he is without the devices for acquiring any. His grave concern is that his deportation will follow the prolonged depression. Meanwhile the whole series of events is said to have produced one marked change in the character of the immigrant—" it has reduced him to docility. He is never the same individual as observed in his island home ".[27]

An interesting corollary of this situation has been the development of the West Indian Communities' Development League by the British West Indian Negroes in New York. The League proposes the following: [28]

1. To use every legitimate means available to unite West Indians at home and abroad for the purpose of embarking upon a colonization and settlement scheme in the Colony of British Guiana;
2. To urge upon the British Government the necessity of undertaking the construction of roads, railroads, hydro-electric plants, and other primary projects, so as to attract labour into the Colony to exploit its natural resources;
3. To request the British and Colonial Governments that a sum sufficient to undertake the colonization and settlement of British West Indians in the Colony of British Guiana, under such conditions as are necessary to establish the colony with adequate means of support, be provided;
4. That a mission of competent West Indians be sent from the United States to British Guiana for the purpose of making a

27 Sutherland, Louis G., " Panama Gold ", *Opportunity, Journal of Negro Life*, Vol. XII, No. 11, November, 1934, pp. 336-339. This article and the aforementioned one by Patterson present interesting historical data on the complex patterns of racial immigration.

28 Malliet, A. M. Wendell, " On West Indian Colonization in British Guiana ", *Education*, a Journal of Reputation, Vol. I, No. 4, July-August, 1935, p. 3.

study on the spot of the whole question of the settlement of West Indians in the Colony;

5. To call for the registration of all able-bodied West Indian men and women in the United States, Cuba, Panama, and other Central American countries, and the British West Indies, in order to determine the number of persons willing to migrate, if and when an adequate scheme of colonization receives the approval and financial support of the British and Colonial Governments.

The Virgin Islands

The Virgin Islands have been possessions of the United States since they were acquired from Denmark in 1917. The major islands of St. Thomas, St. John and St. Croix, with some fifty smaller ones which comprise the Virgin Islands, lie at the eastern edge of the Caribbean Sea in a line between Europe and the Panama Canal. In 1930 the Virgin Islands had a total population of 22,000, of whom less than 2,000 were white.

The Virgin Islands represent the most recent insular addition to the United States. Shortly after their purchase the islands were cast into economic confusion through the passage of the Volstead Act which ruined the St. Croix rum trade and greatly depressed the native bay rum industry. Within recent years the sorrowful economic outlook of the islands has cleared in many ways. Inducements are now offered to tourist trade, and the new policy of homesteading, aided and abetted by an increasingly able and interested governmental personnel, has had tremendous value. So great has been the improvement in the islands that already the Congress has been petitioned for home rule of the area. Even now, however, the poverty of the islands is that of a socially and physically stranded population.

Unreliable rainfall, high evaporation and the distance from sizable markets handicap the agricultural program. Industry is very largely in the handicraft stage and unable to compete with the matching markets of more industrialized Caribbean islands.

The population is divided into four groups—white, Negro, mixed and other. In 1930 the total population was 22,012 of which 17,243 (78.3%) was Negro and 2,719 (12.4%) was mixed. Foreign-born Negroes formed 18.8% of the total Negro population in 1930. In the same year only 8.3% of the mixed (Negro and white) population was foreign-born. The major source of both immigrant groups is the West Indies, with a smaller number migrating from Central and South America. In the last few years a number of Puerto Ricans have migrated from their islands and settled here. These persons are employed largely in business, though a few of them are engaged in agriculture. The white population includes a small number of government employees from the United States, a few Danes, and approximately 700 French who live on St. Thomas.

In spite of the long period of Danish possession the islands are said to show little influence of Danish culture. English, spoken with a slight Scotch burr and intonations similar to those of the more southern islands is the native language.

Immigration to and from the Virgin Islands dates back to the American slave trade when they were the center of the American slave industry. When the traffic was ended in 1848 the islands began a normal marginal existence to which only a few migrants were attracted. Most of the foreign-born present in the islands before 1930 came prior to 1900. Fewer than two hundred migrants who had gone there between 1925 and 1930 were present at the time of the 1930 Census. Yet, heavy has been the relative emigration to the continental United States, particularly of the male population. Because of this male emigration, the female population exceeds that of the males by about 16 per cent.[29]

29 *The Economic Problems of the Women of the Virgin Islands of the United States*, Ethel L. Best, U. S. Department of Labor, Women's Bureau Bulletin, No. 142, 1936, p. 3. See also pp. 5-7.

Puerto Rico

The population of Puerto Rico is largely white and Andalusian. The term " colored " with reference to its population covers all black or mulatto peoples. In 1930 the 397,151 colored persons formed 25.7 per cent of the total population. Of this number 409 were foreign-born colored, the majority of whom had migrated from other West Indian islands prior to 1920. Puerto Rico being only slightly less poor than the Virgin Islands is not an immigrant-receiving domain.

Color, as such, has relatively little significance for the Puerto Rican at home. However, because it does present complications when the colored Puerto Rican comes to the United States, it is interesting to observe that in 1930 approximately forty-five per cent of this colored population that was ten years of age or over was illiterate, and that more than three-fourths of the population was unable to speak English. According to a survey made by the Brookings Institution in 1930[30] " Race lines are not as strictly drawn in Porto Rico as in the Windward Islands. Colored men and women are found in all walks of life, numerous in the teaching profession, and colored pupils attend on terms of equality public schools and higher educational institutions. Yet the changing race attitudes of the emigrants are illustrated by an advertisement inserted in an island newspaper by a Puerto Rican automobile mechanic residing in an upstate city of New York, for a wife who among other qualifications must be either white or mulatto ".

Up to the present the other islands of the Caribbean have not opened their labor market to the unskilled Puerto Rican laborer who is in urgent need of employment. Davie's observation that this group of immigrants " has hardly been noticed by the general community and has only placed a strain on a few neighborhoods and social agencies ", is indicative of the concentration of the problem on the continent.[31]

30 Clark, Victor S., director, *Porto Rico and Its Problems*; A survey by the Brookings Institution, Washington, D. C., 1930; see pp. 8 and 519.

31 For the most recent treatment of this migration see: Chenault, Lawrence

The movement of the Negro population either as immigrants or emigrants in the other dependencies and territories of the United States, the Philippines, Alaska, Guam, Samoa and Hawaii, numbering less than 200 is too slight to warrant detailed consideration.

Thus there may be noted a great deal of churning among the colored populations of the Caribbean area. The same forces that impel and propel colonization and restriction in the neighboring countries of the area have induced emigration to the United States. In brief, these may be summarized as—population pressure, economic motives, adventure, and political and social ambitions.[32] Their movement to "the States" may be regarded as contemporaneous with fundamental changes in the lives of the people in the area. Their migration is a product of forces a long time in the making—forces which reshape the careers of colored peoples in the Caribbean as well as in the United States. How do they adjust in "the States"? Are there any broad new patterns into which they must fit, or which they must fashion? What are the problems faced in effecting the geographical and cultural changes?

R., *The Puerto Rican Migrant in New York City*, New York, Columbia University Press, 1938.

32 Davie, Maurice R., *op. cit.*, p. 558.

CHAPTER IV

COMPOSITION AND CHARACTERISTICS OF THE NEGRO IMMIGRANT AND FOREIGN-BORN POPULATIONS

No understanding of the problems faced in immigrant adjustment would be possible without an analysis of certain facts on the composition and characteristics of the Negro immigrant population. In this study one is compelled to employ the immigration statistics to a great degree, for despite their limitations, they furnish the only clue to certain demographic characteristics of the Negro immigrant. The major analyses of the census returns are concerned chiefly with the foreign-born white population, since the foreign-born Negro group forms such a small numerical unit. Data on age, sex and geographical distribution, literacy, occupational and financial status upon arrival, indicate to some extent certain well defined characteristics which distinguish the immigrant from the native population.

One of the most distinctive characteristics of the data on the Negro foreign-born as reported by the federal census is that the year of immigration is not known for 11.7 per cent of the total population, for 13.8 per cent of the Negro males and 9.3 per cent of the females.[1] This percentage is unusually high, since the year of immigration is unknown for only 4 per cent of the total foreign-born population.

Within recent years (since 1923) the majority of these Negro immigrants have come to the United States " on their own hook ", that is, by paying their own passage fares. Years in which a large number of women and children entered, the

[1] Between 1899 and 1932 a total of 115,222 Negro aliens was admitted to the United States. Debarred from entering were 5,679; 3,522 for physical, mental and moral reasons. Deportees numbered 760. The rate of Negroes debarred and deported during this period was 5.61 per 100 immigrant aliens admitted.

passage was usually paid by a relative. The proportion of Negro immigrants whose passage was paid by individuals or organizations other than themselves or relatives has not exceeded 5 per cent of the total.

Great variations are noticed in the amount of money brought by immigrant aliens. An analysis of the figures for the years 1923 and 1932 reveals that in each year a larger proportion of the Negro immigrants than of the total brings $50 or more, but that the average amount of money shown by the Negro immigrant is less. Thus, in 1923, 48.2 per cent of the Negro immigrants brought more than $50 and showed an average amount of $53.38. Only 46.9 per cent of the total immigrant alien group brought $50 or more, but the average amount shown upon arrival was $94.11. In 1932, the last year for which these statistics are available, 77.9 per cent of the Negro immigrants brought in $50 or more, as compared with 70.9 per cent of the total group. The average amount of money shown in that year by the Negro immigrants was $108.88, by all immigrants $171.63.

Between 1921 and 1932, approximately 5,000 Negro immigrants were debarred from entering the United States. The operation of the quota law was the chief reason for their being denied admission. During this period there were 2,163 applicants for admission who did not have the necessary visas. Prior to 1924, persons likely to become public charges, and persons with loathsome, dangerous and contagious diseases formed the majority of those denied admission. The consequences of the 1924 act, however, are noted in the decline in the number and percentage of such persons applying for admission to the country. Negro immigrants formed 2.6 per cent of all aliens debarred from entering the United States between 1908 and 1937. At no time during that period did they form more than 1.7 per cent of all aliens admitted.

The deportation of Negro aliens, however, has been at a much lower rate than the debarments. Since 1923, Negroes have formed 1.6 per cent of the aliens deported after landing.

The chief causes for deportation have been: (1) charges of criminality and immorality, and (2) becoming public charges from causes existing prior to entry. Deportations to the West Indies, South America and Canada were the heaviest, though they did not exceed the proportions of immigrants received from these countries.

Age

The bulk of Negro immigration has always been in the work-age populations, indicated in the earlier immigration returns by the age groupings 14-44. In 1899, the earliest year for which returns by race were available, 71 per cent of the Negro immigrants admitted were between these ages. The older population —those over 45 years of age—formed 18 per cent of the total. This type of age distribution was typical of Negro immigration until the turn of the century. From 1903 until the World War, the population between 14 and 44 years of age assumed greater proportions, forming from 80 to 86 per cent of the total immigrants. When compared with other racial immigrant groups of the period, the Negro immigrant population in 1910 reflected composition characteristics similar to those of the Italian, Irish and Polish populations, the variation between the older and the newer immigrant groups being interpreted in part at least, by the differential mortalities of the survivors. (Table VIII)

Children under 14 years of age have formed from 12 to 23 per cent of the total immigrants admitted to the United States. At no time prior to 1924 did the number of children among Negro immigrants admitted form more than 11 per cent of the total. Since 1924, the percentage of persons under 16 years of age admitted has steadily mounted, forming from 15 to 29 per cent of all Negro immigrants admitted annually between 1926 and 1932. This proportion may be expected to continue to decline as the male workers arriving within more recent years tend to provide for the establishment of family units.

The age distribution of the Negro immigrant population tends to vary from that of the total immigrant group in other respects. Using the data of 1930, the last year of great immigration, both total and Negro, we find that a larger percentage of the total than of the Negro males is between 22 and 45 years of age, but that the opposite is true for the female population. Furthermore, the proportion of the Negro population in the younger age group (under 16) is higher than that of the same group in the total population. Only 7 per cent of the Negro immigrants admitted were 45 years of age or over, as compared with 9.9 per cent of the total group. An excess of females in the older populations is typical of both groups. Statistics on age distributions indicate that since 1899 an increase in the proportion of young persons admitted is accompanied by an increase in the number of older persons. It appears to indicate an increase in family units among this group. (Table IX)

Since immigration is largely a movement of adult peoples any comparison of the ages of the Negro immigrant population with that of the native-born group is certain to show marked unbalances. Using the 1930 immigrant admissions for comparison, it may be noted that the percentage of persons under 16 years of age is nearly twice as high in the total population as in the immigrant group. Yet, 48.9 per cent of all the immigrants admitted were between 22 and 44 years of age, as compared with 35.7 per cent in the total Negro population. (Tables IX & X)

Statistics on the age distribution of Negro emigrant aliens departing from the country since 1926 indicate this group is composed of an increasingly large proportion of the older groups, and a diminishing proportion of the younger population, the rate of movement for each age group by sex being quite similar. In 1926, 9.9 per cent of the emigrant aliens departing were under 16 years of age, a proportion that steadily decreased until 1932 when that group formed only 3.2 per cent of the total emigrants. In the earlier year, emigrant aliens 45 years of age and over formed 14.6 per cent of those departing.

This proportion increased annually until 1932, when they formed 23.1 per cent of all departing aliens. The largest proportion of emigrant aliens is in the age groups 30-37.

Sex

The permanency of Negro immigration to the United States within recent years is well indicated by the ratio of the number of males and females. Statistics indicate that it is chiefly the males who emigrate. While the proportion of males is particularly high among some groups—the Portuguese and Haitians, for example—it has usually ranged from 51 to 59 per cent of the total Negro emigrants. An excess of female immigrants has been particularly noticeable since 1924, when the total volume of Negro immigration has been small. This follows the observation made by Davie [2] on the sex factor in world immigration. During the period 1917-1934, the era of greatest Negro immigration, males showed a higher proportion. It appears, however, that families were sent for as quickly as possible. The relatively short distances between the homeland and the United States, and the relative cheapness of travel made it possible for the Negro immigrant from the Caribbean to bring together his family unit much more quickly than could the European immigrant.

There is one other factor, however, that must be taken into consideration when analyzing inter-American immigration—that of clandestine arrival. The ease with which males can cross the borders, leave their occupations as seamen, and arrive surreptitiously by various devices, is much greater than among females. While statistical verification is not possible, there is every reason to believe that this factor accounts, in part at least, for the relatively unequal sex proportions indicated by the statistics of arrivals. It is evident, also, in the census statistics on the year of immigrant arrival, and is supported by the naturalization data. For, in 1920, the Negro female foreign-born

2 Davie, Maurice R., *op. cit.*, p. 223.

had a higher naturalization rate than the Negro male—a phenomenon not experienced in any other racial group. The relative preponderance of females immigrating since 1920 has, of course, reduced this inequality. Further weight is given to this observation by the fact that of 2,590 male Negro immigrants brought from the Caribbean by the Federal Government in 1919 to work as construction laborers in Charleston, South Carolina, 227 deserted and were not located.[3]

As is true of other racial and nationality immigration, males have predominated among the Negro immigrants returning to their homeland. Between 1908 and 1927, the proportion of males in the total returning ranged from 51 to 59 per cent of the total departing. Since 1929, however, Negro females have tended to return to their homelands at a more rapid rate than the males. During the four years 1929-1932 Negro females formed respectively 57, 64, 60 and 53 per cent of the total Negro emigrants.

In 1930 the sex ratio of the Negro population of the United States was 91.3 males per 100 females. Among the foreign-born Negro population the ratio was 143.3 males to each 100 females. This is a fact of tremendous social significance. The Negro foreign-born sex ratio is higher than that of races from northern and western Europe, and much lower than that of immigrants from southern and eastern Europe. A comparison of sex ratios (males per 100 females) of foreign-born Negroes, who are largely from the central and southern areas of the Americas indicates that the sex ratio of the Negro immigrant, (13.3 males per 100 females) is exceeded only by the ratio of foreign-born whites from Cuba, among whom there are 145.3 males per 100 females.

MARITAL STATUS

The increase in the proportion of female immigrants following the restriction of immigration affects the statistics on the marital status of the Negro immigrant. Being younger than

3 *Report of the Commissioner of Immigration*, 1919, p. 253.

other immigrant populations, it has a higher percentage of persons in the marriageable age group, 15 years of age and over. Such statistical data on maiital status as cover the Negro population must be obtained from the immigration reports as they are not provided by the census. (Table X)

Available data on the marital status of Negro immigrants permit the following conclusions:

1. That single persons predominate in the Negro immigrant population 16 years of age and over admitted to the United States.
2. That a higher proportion of single Negro men than of single Negro women emigrate to the United States.
3. That the factors of age and sex are important indices to the adjustment problems hereinafter mentioned.

Occupations upon Arrival

Upon arrival the Negro immigrant faces an occupational pattern that is distinctly different from that experienced in his homeland. It is, therefore, significant to observe the occupational classifications into which these workers fit upon arrival. Negro immigration is primarily a movement of future male industrial workers and female domestics. Since 1925, farmers and agricultural workers have never formed more than 4 per cent of the total employable Negro immigrant alien population. Laborers and servants, on the other hand, have formed from one-third to two-fifths of the incoming group. (Table XI)

Distinctly out of proportion to the prevalence of such classes in the occupational schemes of the native-born Negro are the high proportions of workers who had been employed as skilled artisans, as bankers, agents, merchants, clerical workers in commerce and finance, and as professional persons. Consistently have killed artisans formed from one-third to one-fourth of the Negro workers admitted since 1923. Those employed in commerce and finance have formed from 9 to 19 per cent of the total workers, while the proportion of professional workers has been from 4 to 19 per cent of the total. In this field lies the seed for much of the social maladjustment noted in subsequent discussions, for the foreign-born Negro brings into the American occupational picture skills and experiences for which little or no opportunity is provided for Negroes in the United States save in the limited occupational field of racial services. Yet, in marked contrast to the white immigrant population, Negro immigrants have shown fewer persons having no occupations in recent years.

The occupational distribution of Negro aliens leaving the United States indicates that between two-thirds and three-fourths of them are classified as laborers, servants, and " miscellaneous " workers. The ratios of departures among the other occupational groups, particularly the industrial and professional ones, are considerably lower than are their ratios to the total admissions.

Literacy

The test for literacy as stated by the Immigration Act of 1917 specified that the immigrant shall be required to read " not less than thirty nor more than forty words in ordinary use, printed in plain legible type " in the particular language or dialect in which he desires the examination to be made. The passage in current use is a Biblical one—" He hath also prepared for him the instruments of death; he ordaineth his arrows against the persecutors. Behold, he travaileth with iniquity and hath conceived mischief, and brought forth falsehood. He made a pit, and digged it, and is fallen into the ditch which he made ". The passage has been criticized because so many of the words are not in common use, and are not so easily explained. However, on the basis of this test Negro immigrants are more literate than the Negro population they join in the United States. Of the 6,528 persons 16 years of age and over admitted in 1923, 6,438 or 98.6 per cent of them could read and write. Of the 130 Negro aliens 16 years of age and over admitted in 1932, 129 or 99.0 per cent of them were literate. During the ten year period 1923-1932 of the 233 exemptions from the literacy test clause (section 3) of the 1924 immigration law, 231 were exempted because they were going to join relatives.

Closely correlated with literacy is the ability to speak English. Among the foreign-born Negroes 1,859 or 1.9 per cent were unable to speak English at the time of the last census. This percentage has not declined since 1920, and is higher than the proportion of Negroes similarly handicapped in 1910—0.2 per cent. This increase in persons unable to speak English reflects the increase in immigration from the French and Spanish-speaking areas of the Caribbean within the last quarter of a century.

This inability to speak English is largely confined to the Portuguese, French and Spanish-speaking populations, located in the New England and Middle Atlantic states, and Florida, areas accounting for approximately 99.0 per cent of the 1,859 persons, non-English speaking Negro immigrant aliens.

Geographic Distribution

The Negro immigrant of today arrives in the East and remains there. Ninety per cent of the Negro foreign-born population resides in the New England, Middle Atlantic and South Atlantic divisions of the United States; chiefly in the states of New York, Massachusetts and Florida. In 1930, 65 per cent of all the foreign-born Negroes in the United States were residing in New York City. This has not always been true of the distribution. (Table XII) In 1850, Louisiana, New York and Massachusetts, in the order named, had the majority of the foreign-born Negroes. Slave importations into Louisiana accounted for a great many of the 925 Negroes listed as foreign-born in that year.[4] By 1880 Florida, with 2,189 foreign-

4 On May 8, 1804, William C. Claiborne wrote from New Orleans to the Honorable James Madison, then Secretary of State: "The emigration from the West Indies continues great; few vessels arrive from that quarter but are crowded with passengers, and among them many slaves. I am inclined to

born Negroes, Michigan with 1,758 and New York with 1,692 were the chief areas of concentration. Since 1900, however, the three divisions named above have consistently contained more than seven-tenths of the entire foreign-born Negro population, the Middle Atlantic division, and particularly New York state, increasing in importance as the area of greatest concentration.

Between 1920 and 1930 there were absolute losses in the number of Negro immigrants located in the Southern states. The Midwestern and Mountain states also declined in importance as areas of concentration. New England, long the center for the Portuguese-speaking and the British West Indian immigrant, showed a loss for the first time during the century. Michigan and Illinois became favored areas because of their opportunities for skilled industrial employment. The shifting of the immigrant population has been directed mainly to New York and Harlem—the New World Mecca of Negro peoples. (Table XIII)

Another index to the concentration of the Negro immigrant is reflected in the intended future residences specified upon being admitted. Of 27,520 immigrants admitted between 1923 and 1932, 85 per cent specified New York, Massachusetts and Florida. In 1932, of the 183 Negroes admitted, 89 specified New York and 16 Massachusetts as the states of intended future residence.

The tendency for the Southern states to decline as an area of Negro immigrant occupancy appears to be significant. The three Southern divisions—South Atlantic, East South Central and West South Central—contained 37.2 per cent of the foreign-born Negro population in 1900. By 1910, the proportion had dropped to 22.5 per cent despite the tremendous in-

think that, previous to the 1st of October, thousands of African Negroes will be imported into this province; for the Citizens seem impressed with an opinion that, a great, very great supply of slaves is essential to the prosperity of Louisiana". Robertson, James Alexander, *Louisiana Under Spain, France and the United States, 1785-1807*, Arthur H. Clark Co., Cleveland, 1911, Vol. II, p. 63.

crease in immigration during the decade. But in 1930, only 14.7 per cent of the foreign-born Negroes were residing there. Furthermore, Florida, an area that received 13.6 per cent of the immigrants between 1923 and 1932, provided 31.2 per cent of the departing aliens during the same period. There are, of course, several reasons why this decline should be so large. In the first place, Negro immigrants do not like the South because of its dual racial set-up, to which the foreign-born Negro not only objects, but in the midst of which he frequently becomes a much-buffeted third party, accepted by neither whites nor native Negroes. This is particularly true in areas of large settlement in Florida. The Negro immigrant then occupies the position similar to that of the white immigrant in areas of " one hundred per cent Americanism." Furthermore, it is part of the alleged tradition of the new as well as the old South that it is hostile to immigrants. Its chief inducement to Northern capital and industry—a minimum of labor difficulty—was offered on a platter garnished with " an adequate supply of native-white labor ". In such communities, where the number of foreign-born Negroes was sufficiently large to make them highly visible, the foreign-born Negro worker ranked even lower in the occupational scale than the " black devils "—the native Negroes. (Table XIV)

Part and parcel of the situation, as a social determinant, are the economic conditions. The rise and decline of the cigar and tobacco industry was an important factor in the declining importance of Florida as a center for Negro foreign-born persons. Not only was there a lessening demand for operatives and laborers in these factories, but for the service workers of the trade, such as " Readers ",[5] as well. The collapse of the tobacco manufacturing industry in Florida and New York has seriously affected the status and distribution of the Spanish-speaking emigrants from the Carribbean area.

5 Persons employed by workers in hand-made cigar manufactories to read to them while they work.

A large number of West Indian Negroes was brought into the Southern states for emergency work during the war. In 1919, a large number was brought in from Barbados. From the Bahamas came 3,259 Negro laborers to work either on the truck farms on Florida's East Coast, or to be employed by private contractors on government construction work at Charleston, South Carolina. Also imported were 13,095 Puerto Ricans to meet the emergency labor needs of the South. In those days, Negro immigration into certain Southern ports was regarded as a problem. The official report of the Commissioner of Immigration [6] for 1919 states:

> The West Indies, including Cuba, Jamaica and other islands, have become an important source of immigration in recent years, the total admissions during the past 20 years being approximately 215,500. The peoples chiefly represented in the movement are African (black) who came mainly from Jamaica and the Bahamas, Cuba and the Spanish speaking islands. As in the case of Mexican immigration, many of those coming from the West Indies are seasonal laborers who find employment in Florida, but the development of steamship connections between the islands and Northern ports has resulted in a considerable movement of Negroes who stay more or less permanently in New York, Massachusetts, and other Eastern states.[7]

The fact that New York, Miami and Boston are the major ports of entry for Negro immigrants is undoubtedly a factor in their being the three oldest and largest areas of settlement for the foreign-born Negro. Yet, there is a tendency for the nationalities among Negro immigrants to be distributed in

6 *Report of the Commissioner General of Immigration*, 1919, p. 253.

7 The peak year for all Negro immigration was 1924, when 12,243 persons were admitted. Immigrant Portuguese Negroes reached their peak in 1914, and 1,711 arrived, the next peak year being 1921, when there were 1,364. Canadian Negroes have had a fairly consistent flow, chiefly into Michigan, and reached an all-time peak of 494 in 1924. Negro immigrants from Central America came in largest numbers during 1918 and 1919. South Americans and West Indians reached their peak in 1924, numbering 375 and 10,630, respectively.

various sections. The Spanish-speaking tend to concentrate in New York and Miami; the French-speaking in New York; the Portuguese in New England—particularly in Providence and New Bedford. The British West Indians concentrate heavily in New York and Boston; while the few from Africa are widely dispersed over the country. Climate, which is supposed to be a determinant of immigrant location, is apparently of minor importance to the Negro immigrant, who finds in the congenial climate of the South the least satisfactory social and economic conditions.

Urban Concentration

Negro immigrants have always flocked to the cities. In fact, their arrival during this century has paralleled the growth of the Negro population in urban centers of the North. Approximately 80 per cent of the West Indian, other than Cuban, immigration is from the cities of the islands. Their occupations upon arrival are city occupations, and the realization of their economic hopes is expected in the cities of the United States, particularly in the largest cities.

As a newer immigrant, the Negro between 1910 and 1930, increased in all of the cities having a population of 100,000 or more in 1930 and having 100 or more foreign-born Negroes in 1910, save Tampa, St. Louis, and Lynn, Mass. In this respect, the foreign-born Negro has a higher degree of large city concentration than does the native-born Negro, the percentage living in cities having a population of 100,000 or more, being 81.3 per cent of the former and 24.2 per cent of the latter. In these cities reside 87.4 per cent of all foreign-born Negroes living in urban areas. These proportions are somewhat higher than those of the white population, 30.3 per cent of whose total and 53.4 per cent of whose foreign-born lived in these cities. (Table XV)

On the other hand, the settlement of any race in a particular locality may be a slow and gradual process. The Portuguese, for example: " . . . first came to New Bedford in their own sailing vessels. As they returned to that port year after year a permanent colony was gradually formed, until, today, most of the Portuguese and the Bravas or 'Black Portuguese' from the Cape Verde Islands, who are coming to the United States, are destined for New Bedford, Fall River or some of the smaller towns on the Cape ".[8]

Other factors tend to influence the distribution of Negro immigrants. Take, for example, the tendency Carpenter has called the "ethnic idiosyncrasy".[9] The West Indian Negro immigrant apparently has a distinct bias for settling in the city, and will not be moved. This bias tends to increase with the recency of the immigration. One Trinidadian interpreted this tendency in a very sprightly manner by saying:

> These people have sat in what we at home call cities, day after day, night after night, and dreamed of going to a "real" city. A taste of Trinidad for some of them was enough to spur them on to see New York or Boston—and to live there. Why, it would be harder to get these people to live in the country than to get Edward back on the throne. You don't know what the feeling is until you have day-dreamed in the semi-tropics.[10]

There is also the matter of ethnic cohesion or the tendency of peoples of similar nationalities or races to congregate in national or ethnic units, and to occupy contiguous territory, a fact adequately demonstrated by the Negro immigrants whose mother-tongue is other than English.[11]

The high urban residence of the Negro immigrant is probably one of the group's most outstanding characteristics. Not only does he tend to cluster in the largest cities, but in all

8 Report of the Commission on Immigration on the Problem of Immigration in Massachusetts. House Document # 2300. Mass. Commission on Immigration, 1921, p. 33.

9 Carpenter, Niles, *Immigrants and Their Children*, 1920. Census Monograph, VII, 1927, pp. 145 ff.

10 Manuscript document No. 17.

11 See pages following on the clustering of the Cuban, Puerto Rican and Martiniquian immigrants.

urban areas. In 1930 there were 91,677 foreign-born Negroes residing in urban areas—93 per cent of the total foreign-born Negro population. Only 5,702 or 5.9 per cent lived in rural non-farm areas and 1,241 or 1.1 per cent on farms. Meanwhile, the relative numerical importance of foreign-born Negroes in the urban Negro population has tended to shift perceptibly since 1910. In that year, of all cities, New Bedford and Lynn, Massachusetts, had the highest percentages of Negro foreign-born in their populations. New York, Boston, Cambridge and Detroit had more than 10 per cent foreign-born in their Negro population. By 1920, Miami, Florida, had risen to the front ranks with 51.9 per cent of its Negro population foreign-born. Boston, Cambridge and New York had increased in relative importance as had New Bedford and Fall River. By 1930, the Florida real estate boom had sent a larger number of native-born Negroes into Florida, and the emigration of more than one thousand Portuguese from New Bedford had changed its ranking. Lynn and Fall River had but a fraction of their once high proportion. However, Boston, Cambridge, New York and Miami stood out as the leading alien Negro centers.

Such cities as New Bedford, Tampa, and Detroit, are distinctly immigrant-type-areas. The Negro immigrant from the Cape Verde Islands, Azores and Portugal has gone chiefly to New Bedford, Lynn and Fall River, while the Cuban Negro has settled in Tampa and New York. Detroit's immigrant group is largely British-Canadian in its composition. New York, however, is an amalgam of all immigrant groups, the British West Indian predominating, closely followed by the non-alien groups from Puerto Rico and the Virgin Islands. Chicago and Philadelphia also show a varied cross-section of all groups, with the British West Indian predominating. Each of these areas shows evidence of different nationality traits and cultures, and presents problems of social adjustment based upon the persistence and survival of these ethnic contacts.

As this concentration accompanies the urban movement of the native-born Negro, it assumes tremendous importance in terms of what Johnson has called " Negro personality changes ". Personality is defined as " the organization of an individual's habits and behavior patterns in the process of adjustment in which he is set to the institutions and customs which constitute this culture, and to other individuals who share this culture ".[12] Wide cultural differences already existing between the urban and rural patterns of Negro life become increasingly significant and more varied in areas of great immigrant concentration. When the immigrant populations bring their culture traits into these areas a new problem arises. One is then forced to ask: What are the conditions out of which these immigrant cultures arise? Why does the Negro immigrant come to the United States? What traits and culture patterns does he bring with him?

12 Johnson, Charles S., " Negro Personality in a Southern Community ", in *Race and Culture Contacts*, E. B. Reuter, editor. McGraw-Hill, New York, 1934. Ch. XIII, pp. 208-227.

CHAPTER V

THE ADJUSTMENT OF THE NEGRO IMMIGRANT

A. The Language Groups

Despite the fact that the Negro immigrant creates no special inter-racial problems for the white population, he does impress his cultural characteristics upon the Negro community with such definiteness that group adjustment problems do arise. The native-born Negro has been working out a process of adjustment to his total social environment that has permitted at least partial accommodation. This has been particularly true in the Southern states. The foreign-born Negro arrives, bringing the social habituations and adjustments of his own environment. When the two meet there evolve new problems of individual and group adjustment. These problems are not of race, except in their nomenclature; nor of color, except as color in the United States is related to the ideas of class and caste developed under the old habituations; nor are they of language, except in the relatively small groups of non-English speaking Negro immigrants. Rather they are problems of complete social readjustment in terms of diversified and unreconciled mores, that include the acceptance of a permanent badge of race to which the immigrant is even less adjusted than his native-born brother.

1. THE NON-ENGLISH SPEAKING IMMIGRANTS

To the Latin mind, the word " Negro " means a full-blooded black. If this term in its North American significance were applied to the Latin colored population of New York, there would be so few such persons that such a racial distinction would be relatively useless. Racial discrimination as practiced here is most amazing to this group of foreign-born. Their ideas of the racial role receive severe and revolutionizing shocks. Nevertheless, in the United States individual members of this group—French, Spanish or Portuguese-speaking though they may be, and though lacking any intra-group evaluation of race or color—become "colored", "Negro" or "African Black" as they encounter new standards, for races. Included in the non-English speaking Negro immigrants are the French-speaking émigrés from Haiti, Martinique, Guadeloupe, the French Guianas, St. Martin, Malgoches, Senegal and Somaliland; the Spanish-speaking ones from Puerto Rico, Cuba, Panama, Hondouras, Mexico, Santo Domingo, Venezuela and Colombia; the Portuguese-speaking from the Cape Verde Islands and the Azores. As early as 1920 the "colored" element in this group was so important to the success of Marcus Garvey's "Back to Africa" movement that special sections of his *Negro World* were printed in French and Spanish.

The French-speaking

Marked and varied are the differences between the various French-speaking people of color. The African Senegalese, Somalis and Malgoches have many differences between them particularly as to native language and racial stocks. The Antilleans, Martiniquians, Guadeloupians and Saint Martinians have many different culture traits and animosities. Yet, all of these people, residents and sometimes citizens of the United States, are united in a common "patrie" by the culture of France. The French language and the French culture remain to them the most important language and the most impressive culture in the world.

French colonials in the United States give evidence of being less race-conscious than the American, British or Haitian Negroes. As one Martiniquian expressed it, "We have a tremendous amount of race pride. We are profoundly cognizant of the great men of the Negro race, and we are proud of their history and the glorious part they have played in the history of France. These men and France have made us race proud. We have not had to become race-conscious—that is, until we came to America. Suffering and adversity make for race consciousness ".[1] Every French colonial from the Antilles is proud of the fact that the Empress Josephine was a Creole born on the island of Martinique, and that some of the ablest generals of France were of Martiniquian or Guadeloupian origin.

Though the French colonial group is widely scattered throughout New York, it maintains a close cohesive bond. Most of the Martiniquians and Guadeloupians came to New York between 1919 and 1929. Some came as family units, others as heads of families who later sent for their wives and children or sweethearts, and others as seamen and adventurers. They do not mingle extensively with the American Negro population, but frequently intermarry with the English and Spanish-speaking West Indian groups. On 111th Street between Eighth and Madison Avenues, the southern end of Harlem, live as many as thirty families. On Saturday nights they will congregate at certain homes to dance, play cards or to discuss politics —chiefly French politics. Almost any Saturday night one can find a dance at some Martiniquian's apartment. They work hard during the week and from Saturday to Monday they celebrate by dancing the beguine, the meringue and the rhumba, stopping only to eat, drink and talk. Over a week-end, life for the French Antilleans seems to be a continuous series of parties, dances, picnics, holidays and feasts.

The major organized social life of this group centers around the activities of the Franco-Colonial Club. This is a combination burial society, cooperative insurance society and social club. On or about the fourteenth of July each year this club commemorates Bastille Day with a dance. In former years this was the foremost social event of the year, attended by every French colonial, resplendent in top hat, white tie and tails. In 1936 this affair—held at the Park Palace, 110th Street and Fifth Avenue—lacked the patriotic fervor of former years, it being more of a get-together of old friends. The attitude of France in the Ethiopian crisis is given as the cause of this dampening of ardor.

1 Document No. 8, *Latin Negroes of New York*, p. 7.

Each year the French veterans' society, *Les Anciens Combattants,* gives a Bastille Day Ball, the date being set so as not to conflict with the Franco-Colonial affair. This year, however, the colonials did not attend *Les Anciens Combattants'* dance, which was given at the Hotel Pennsylvania. Again, the Ethiopian situation was given as a cause. Race and nationality were estranged.

International questions, particularly those affecting darker peoples, are being given increased attention by all Negro groups. The extent to which progressive and radical social thinking is developing among Negroes is most evident in Harlem. Here many French colonials are accepting the doctrines of Socialism and Communism. The Martiniquian, who is frequently described as being " more French than the French ", has lost much of his patriotism. The workers are distinctly leftist in economic philosophy. As early as 1925, two of the most radical members of the fur workers' union in New York were two French-speaking Negroes from Haiti. Today, the newspaper, *Le Crides Negres,* published by the Negro workers of Paris is more widely read among French colonials than *Le Courrier des Etats-Unis* and their home papers. Meanwhile, the majority of those who work are employed at personal and domestic tasks and in factories, even as the American-born Negroes. Two French employment agencies in the city assist them in securing jobs.

In the main, however, the French colonial is more bourgeois than his American-born brother. He has the Frenchman's reputed taste for good food and exquisite wine. In recent years a few of them have become American citizens, for economic reasons. In general, however, they are proud to remain French citizens. Like Frenchmen of the same class, the ideal of personal liberty is very dear to them. Coming from self-governing colonies that elect representatives to the French parliament in Paris, they resent and ridicule the American way of disfranchising Negroes in the South. Belonging to many of the same clubs as their white compatriots, they " can do almost anything we desire to do". Having little personal contact with Americans, white or black, except in work relations, many of this group "look upon American whites as a group of only partially civilized persons whose chief pastime is lynching helpless Negroes. The more thoughtful ones know better, but conclude that the American Negro is a coward, and must more or less deserve his fate".[2]

Believing himself more integrated into the French culture than the native-born Negro is in the American culture, the French colonial has little regard for the so-called American way. He appreciates the American materialism, but he would use it toward other ends. Thus, he wants to make money, he lives cheaply and amuses himself cheaply. Rare is the individual who is not able to visit "home" once every two or three years.

Haitians, of whom there are approximately 500 in New York, are scattered, and have few clubs or social organizations. As other Negro foreign-born, they are slow to become naturalized citizens. They mingle freely with other Negro groups, and also resent the prevailing prejudice against colored peoples. These émigrés are from urban rather than rural areas of Haiti and are more literate than other non-English speaking Negro immigrants.

Haitian workers in New York are usually engaged in industry, trade or the professions. Few, if any, of these persons are found in domestic service. Many of the male workers are found in the fur shops and electrical concerns, while female workers are employed in clothing factories, dressmaking establishments and lingerie shops. A few individuals conduct classes in romance languages.

Within recent years there have been continuous efforts to interest the American Negro population in Haiti and its commercial possibilities. Such organizations as the *Utilities d'Hayti* have endeavored to import and market such Haitian products as honey, coffee and rum. These organizations, however, have had only mediocre success.

2 Work, Monroe M., *op. cit.*, p. 75.

The Haitian family in New York loses many of its customary habits. Economic conditions are slowly but surely Americanizing the Haitians at home and abroad. The family, formerly the seat of all cultural and recreational activities, becomes affected by new employment habits. Catholicism, the state religion in Haiti, loses effectiveness in the United States as the Haitian's children are refused admission to certain parochial schools.

Haitians are taking advantage of the American educational facilities. Before the American occupation of Haiti, there were only a few graduates of American institutions. Since then, more than fifty students have been sent over by the government. Each summer a group of twenty students comes to study at Teachers' College, Columbia University. Various philanthropic foundations and religious groups have aided many Haitian students to study in this country, preparing them in such fields as education, the medical arts, radio engineering, religion and the trades.[3]

Perhaps the most singular contribution from the French-speaking colonies is the native songs and rhythms, chief among which is the " beguine ". As a dance the beguine was a European craze in 1932-33. The music has a more spirited cadence than the rhumba and is danced in two ways: one an earthy, sensuous series of body contortions, twists and jerks; the other a synchronized, graceful step similar to the American fox-trot. The former is a most exacting physical experience, while the latter is relatively non-tiring. The beguines are said to be the true folk songs of the Antilles. The cadence, characteristic of the gaiety of the French Antilleans, is *toujours carnaval.* Songs of love, work, hate, revenge, politics and scandal are all sung in this cadence. In Martinique one hears the beguine in the country, city and market place. A woman being deserted by her lover, for example, improvises a song telling all he did to her

3 McKay, Claude, *Home to Harlem,* New York, Harper and Brothers, 1929. Here is related an interesting conversation between a native-born Negro and a Haitian. See pp. 127-139.

which she sings in the market place, hoping to shame him into coming back to her. A servant discharged from a household comes out with an improvised song of the family's intimate affairs. A young girl from one of the " best families " who " goes astray " is " sung " on carnival day much to the shame of the proud family. The beguine is such an effective instrument of social control that during hotly contested political campaigns natives are forbidden to sing it on the street. In New York the beguine no longer serves as an instrument of social control but as the native music of an immigrant people.

The superstitions and magic regarded as typical of the Antilles are also to be found among these immigrant populations. The presence of so many " spiritualists " and " mediums " of all types and varieties in Harlem is working evidence of the continuation of this belief. It is a practice among the French Antilleans, for example, for the woman to help the lover make up his mind about her. A Martiniquian girl in New York was in love with " my friend who detested and despised her. The girl was not disturbed in the least. She knew she could pay to have him fixed, and she did. She went to see an old lady who is well versed in the black arts, and was given something to put in her bath water that would make her irresistible to the man she wanted. It apparently worked, for they were married today ".[4]

Many of the superstitions prevalent among this group are not " voodoo " in the common sense of the word, but beliefs that are decidedly French in origin. In them there is the intimate mixture of the demoniacal and the sacred. A few examples of superstitions heard in New York are:

The love philter: Take a four-leaf clover, dip it in holy water and make a prayer. Get the person by whom you wish to be loved to smell it.

To stop bleeding: Say aloud: " Consommatrum-ressurexit-beta-barroch ".

4 Document No. 8, p. 12.

To cure burns: Say three times: (translated) " Fire of God lose that heat—Es counareth ", then apply some kind of fruit jelly.

To discover thieves: (translated) Write on a piece of paper the names of those living in your house, then put these pieces in a vase of water saying: "Aragoni, labilasse, parandomo, eptallicon, lamboured; je te conjure de ma faire connaitre le larron!" If the thief's name is on one of the papers it will come to the top. If several names come to the top, there are accomplices in the crime.

Antidote for fear: Take a pin that was attached to the shroud of a dead person and wear it.

Surviving in a modified form is the " veillee " or wake. As will be found in any of the Caribbean Islands, and in the rural South, friends of the deceased's family gather at the home to eat, drink, dance [5] and tell stories. In the islands such ceremony might continue until time for the funeral. Economic conditions have modified the custom in the United States.

The Spanish-speaking

The pull of tobacco and the push of sugar are partly responsible for the large Spanish-speaking population in the United States. Earlier in the century the demand for experienced labor to develop the farm commodity and to manufacture cigars lured many thousands of Puerto Ricans and Cubans to these shores. Within the last ten years the collapse of the sugar industry in Cuba and Puerto Rico has been responsible for driving many a citizen from the over-populated islands. According to the Puerto Rican Service Center, there are today approximately 100,000 Puerto Ricans in New York alone. In the southern section of Harlem they form the largest urban Puerto Rican colony in the world.

Any attempt, however, to divide this population into "whites" and " Negroes " is an extremely difficult one. A staff member of *El Nuovo Mundo,* the Spanish language daily, estimates that

5 Dancing is not part of the American " wake " custom.

about 50,000 of the Spanish-speaking population in New York are of obvious Negro ancestry, the majority of them being from Puerto Rico, Cuba, and Santo Domingo. The Spanish-speaking group did not wait for the theories of Gobineau and Mendel, and the more recent theories of racial purity to mould their ideas of racial mixture. As realists, their ideas were turned to the pattern of things as they were. Mixtures of white, red and black human beings were to be expected; if white, red and black human beings lived together; and there was neither the need nor the desire for questioning the fact. Hence, racial consciousness is less evident among this group than among any of the other foreign-language-speaking groups.

The majority of the colored members of the Spanish-speaking group are to be found among the Puerto Ricans, who live between 100th and 116th Streets, Lexington and Morningside Avenues in Harlem. Spanish is spoken everywhere—by all types, by all conceivable racial mixtures. Outstanding is that mixture of Spaniard, Indian and Negro, fused into a new bronze racial type. From time to time one may see a very dark Negro who will be speaking Spanish more loudly than the rest. They say he does not wish to be mistaken for an American Negro.[6] All are Latins.

One hundred and twelfth Street and Fifth Avenue! The music of numerous week-end house parties. Another party, and another. The strains of Suavecito or Siboney greet you from one; the languorous lament of the rhumba *Barinquin* charms you from another. Black meets brown and white. All Spanish. One hundred and thirteenth Street. A Puerto Rican nationalist orator—brown of skin—harangues crowd of brown, black and ivory-skinned people, in passionate Spanish. He is certain to be saying, "We must fight 'Yanqui' imperialism. Free *la patria* of the odious influence of the Anglo-Saxons". Ten thousand

6 Similar tactics are employed by other Negroid types in the United States. East Indians with Negroid features have been known to wear their turbans whenever possible for the express purpose of indicating that they are not Negroes.

Puerto Ricans protest-paraded for this cause in Harlem last September. Here then is a group, neither white nor colored but both, geographically esconced in mid-Manhattan, between the two American colors, north of *the* Fifth Avenue and south of *the* Harlem, that is part and parcel of neither.[7]

Ideologically, the Puerto Rican group is sufficient unto itself; economically, it is far from self-sufficient. Today no special occupations characterize their employment pattern. The hand-made cigar trade is rapidly disappearing. Readers who were employed in the industry have gone. Many are employed in factory trades, others in sugar refineries. Women find employment in the lower-paid clothing factories. Seldom are they employed as domestic servants. For ten years now Puerto Rican welfare groups have been trying to effect satisfactory economic adjustments for this "slice of the Old Spanish Main". Yet, "there is untold tragedy in the coming of many of these people —disappointed hopes, unrealized ambitions, unattained jobs, a crushing poverty in a city where competition is keener and living costs higher than at home".[8]

There are many societies and clubs in "La Barriada Hispana", some of which are counterparts of American organizations. The Holy Name Society of the Catholic Church (La Sociedad del Santo Nombre), Masons and Odd Fellows function among this group even as do the International Benevolent Protective Order of Elks of the World, the virile order of Negro Elks, through Logia Hispana de Elks de New York no. 1000. Among the other clubs having both white and colored members are: the Club Latino de Ajedrez (a Cuban chess players' organization), the Caribe Democratic Club, the Peruvian Social Sporting Club, Liga Puertorriguenai Hispana, Inc.,

7 Middle-class Puerto Ricans live in Washington Heights in the vicinity of the Hispanic American Museum. This group is largely "white" in the American sense of the word, and is composed of business and commercial persons, employees of the Consulate, and professionals. See Chenault, Lawrence R., *The Puerto Rican Migrant in New York*, New York, Columbia University Press, 1938.

8 Pamphlet of the Puerto Rican Service Center, Inc., 1936.

Comite pro Puerto Rico, the Tampa Workers' Club, Vanguard Political Club and Perla del Sur—all engaged in social or political activities.

In the recreational life of the Spanish-speaking community the colored population has played an important role. Not only does one note the presence of colored entertainers and musicians in its orchestras, but, also, the touch of African rhythm in its melodies. The singing and playing of "Lamento Esclavo" (the theme of which is "I am black, I was born black, but I dance my dance without shame") by a sextet of native Cubans and Puerto Ricans was one of the most popular features at a leading cafe in the district.

Within this group, color prejudice or color consciousness does not exist as a social handicap. In the main, its members find it difficult to comprehend or compromise with American race prejudice since so many outstanding cultural and political leaders in their native lands have been of mixed bloods.

They rightly boast of their poets and musicians, and of the fact that, in her immortal Martin de Porres, Peru has produced the one colored saint in the Catholic Church. However, this group is less a part of American Negro life in New York than is the French colonial. And, while there have been no open conflicts between the Spanish-speaking immigrants and the American Negro there has been no close working relationship between them, despite the fact that several of the outstanding persons in the Negro community are Puerto Rican or Cuban born.

Tampa's foreign-born non-English speaking Negro population is the child of the cigar industry, which shifted there from Cuba. The majority of the older workers, therefore, are skilled laborers. The wages offered these workers exceeded as both real and money income their wages at home and permitted an improved standard of living. At the outset there was apparent conflict between these new immigrants and the native-born population, each creating, following and supporting its area of national or racial unity.

The status of this largely Spanish-speaking group has been determined very largely by the trend of economic conditions in the cigar manufacturing industry. Until 1922, these workers virtually monopolized the field. A ten-months strike in that year seriously impaired the monopoly, however. The Cuban workers refused to work unless their demands were met. The employers trained and hired experienced native-born whites and Negroes. These new workers remained in the industry until the NRA codes were established, and the industry was reorganized. Meanwhile, there arose the proverbial problem of paying Negro workers less wages than white workers, and the one-time monopoly disappeared with the decreasing importance of the industry. Tampa's intra-racial, or intra-cultural problem has been significant in that the economic consequences have shown one of the few instances within the Negro group where foreign-born workers have been replaced by the native born—a situation unusual in America's highly competitive labor markets.

The Portuguese-speaking

The fishing and whaling industries were responsible for the large number of immigrants from the Azores and Cape Verde Islands to New Bedford, Massachusetts, the largest area of Portuguese concentration. Until the establishment of cotton mills in the area, fishing and whaling were New Bedford's chief industries.

In 1920 this foreign-born group in New Bedford formed more than two-fifths of the population classed as Negro by the Federal Census. The Portuguese from the Azores consider themselves far superior to those from Cape Verde, whom they now look upon as " Portuguese Negroes ", though neither group considers itself Negro. Azoreans are fair of complexion, largely olive-skinned with straight black or brown hair. The Cape Verdeans range in color from brown to black, with hair varying from the long straight black to the short and " different " variety.

Both groups live in what is known as the South End of New Bedford, but each in its own section. The Azoreans live in the mill section where they are employed as operatives and laborers in the various textile mills. The Cape Verdeans, regarded as less literate and less progressive than the Azoreans, live around the water front, still finding the fishing industry a major employment. Some own small packets and schooners and earn their living from fishing up and down the Acushnet River and Buzzards' Bay. A few work around the docks as longshoremen, while others are unskilled workers in the cotton mills. A larger number of the Cape Verdeans are employed in a large cordage factory in New Bedford—in fact, so many are employed in this plant that it is frequently referred to as " Brava College ". The Azoreans have taken advantage of the training available at the New Bedford Textile School and have become skilled textile workers.

A number of Azoreans are following the professions of law, medicine and dentistry, and have built up lucrative practices within their group. Few of the Cape Verdeans, however, follow the professions, so few, in fact, that native Negro lawyers, dentists, physicians and undertakers have established practices among them with some success.

Portuguese immigration has long been a source of cheap labor in New England. The Black Portuguese virtually monopolized employment in the cranberry bogs, leaving the mills, the oyster boats and the docks of New Bedford to go to the fruit-laden bogs of Plymouth, Barnstable and Nantucket and other sections of Cape Cod.

But there is an exclusiveness among the Portuguese and Negro groups that brings to mind that famous Boston parody:

> Here's to good old Boston,
> The home of the bean and the cod,
> Where the Lowells speak only to the Cabots,
> And the Cabots speak only to God.

For there is almost no social intermingling between the Cape Verdeans and the native Azorean population, very little between the Cape Verdeans and the native Negroes, who feel themselves superior to the Portuguese, and none between the native Negroes and the Azoreans. Both foreign groups are Roman Catholic in their religious faith, and worship in separate churches where the services are conducted in Portuguese.

Meanwhile, New Bedford has attained unenviable significance because of its foreign-born Negro population. With 25.2 per cent of the population illiterate in 1920, and 18.7 per cent illiterate in 1930, New Bedford has for two successive decades maintained the highest illiteracy rate for Negroes in all the cities of the United States having a population of 100,000 or more.

2. THE ENGLISH-SPEAKING IMMIGRANT

The English-speaking immigrant, upon his arrival in the United States, both possesses in himself and arouses in others a strong sense of inferiority or superiority in social status. This is particularly true in such areas of great concentration as New York, Boston, Cambridge and Tampa. To move from an area where class and caste are catholic, to a bi-racial set-up where the Negro group is only partially accommodated to the whole social environment, creates problems of individual and group adjustment that, though not quantitatively manifest, are qualitatively operative. The "middle class" Negro immigrant is frank to say that it is only to his financial advantage to come to the United States, that at home his position is socially superior though economically inferior to that of the American Negro. On the other hand, the immigrant "peasant" whose position was one of manacled inferiority in his insular home, readily realizes the breakdown in the old class and caste values, and proceeds to set up new ones that likewise create conflicts in the new environment. These airs of vaunted superiority and conscious inferiority play an important part in the process of adjustment.

Numerous West Indians have come to the United States in order to crash these color-class barriers. Others have come because after suffering economic reverses and being unable to maintain their social position at home, they could neither perform the menial employments necessary for survival, nor mix with folk who were considered their inferiors. In the United States this group constantly refers to the glories of its past or of its remote present social standing across the waters. Similarly, they express more extreme resentment to any manifestation of discourtesy than the native-born Negro is wont to do. Such designations as "George" and "boy" are so emphatically resented that some employers refuse to hire West Indian Negroes because they do not make good servants, while many others prefer them because they keep the personnel tone at a high level.

Thus there arise within the Negro group distinct forms of prejudices which, if they were not intra-group in nature, might be incorrectly labelled racial prejudices. On the one hand, there has developed the customary group-accepted set of stereotypes or ideas or emotions about West Indians who are thought of as a unit. The individual West Indian Negro is frequently seen only through the eye of this group-stereotype. Let us examine some of these idea-forms.

Stereotypes

Stereotypes may be the product of accurate, objective observations, but it is more than likely that they are based upon a limited and faulty knowledge of the other group, distorted by the minds of the persons through whom they have been transmitted, and subject to the appraising group's subjective interpretations. Popular notions of West Indian traits are expressed with the utmost dogmatism. Thus, the following stereotypes about the West Indian Negro immigrant come into being:

1. He is very "smart"—(intelligent), and better educated than the native American.

2. He is craftier than the Jew, and is not to be trusted in financial matters.
3. He is over-sensitive and quick to defend his " dignity ".
4. He is hot-tempered.
5. He is so British or so French that he does not have time to be himself.
6. He feels that he is superior to the native-born Negro, and is overbearing in demonstrating it.
7. He is either too proud or too lazy to work.
8. He is clannish.
9. "All of them (the ' foreigners ') are just alike."
10. He beats his wife, and treats women as if they were chattel.
11. He is always looking out for himself, first.
12. He is a " trouble-maker " with white people.
13. He is always seeking to make an impression on someone.
14. He lacks race-pride.
15. He is too race-conscious.
16. He talks incessantly.

Substantiating evidence for these stereotypes is obtained from many sources. Woodson, for example, maintains that medical students from the West Indies have a distinct advantage over native-born Negro students because of their better training. Unlike the native-born, the West Indian student does not have to spend too much time relearning what he has learned, nor is he handicapped " by the inability to get the thought from the printed page ".[9] The growth and survival of these stereotypes depend upon the degree to which these foreign groups become fully assimilated in the native pattern. That this has not been fully accomplished is to be noted in a resolution adopted at the National Negro Congress held in Chicago during February, 1936. It was proposed at this meeting:

That the Congress go on record as condemning any form of discrimination practiced against foreign-born Negroes in the United States;

9 Woodson, Carter G., *The Negro Professional Man and the Community*, Association for the Study of Negro Life and History, Washington, 1934, p. 83.

Due to the fact that foreign-born Negroes have integrated themselves in American life by taking an active part in the economic, educational and political aspects, be it resolved that the Congress go on record as opposing any attempt at deporting foreign-born Negroes or dropping them from relief;

That the Congress go on record as seeking to bring about a better relationship between the foreign-born and native Negroes;

That the Congress go on record as supporting foreign-born Negroes in their struggle for economic and political freedom in their respective homes;

That the Congress try to bring about an International Congress in order to establish better relationship among Negroes throughout the world.

The mere introduction of this resolution, and certainly its adoption, serves as evidence that the integration of the foreign-born Negro has not yet taken place. And so long as the West Indian Negro must compromise between the adjustment processes of the old and the new environment, this maladjustment will continue to exist. For in the Negro community the foreign-born Negro is viewed as a threat to the native-born Negro's status. In New York the native complains that he can no longer get work because the West Indians are so "clannish" that once one gets work he proceeds to bring in a full crew of West Indians. It so happens, however, that the inter-insular prejudices prevent just such solidarity. The native complains that he cannot secure work-relief because of those "damn monkey-chasers"; that "they" have ruined the Baptist Church, captured the Episcopal Church and monopolized politics. The West Indians in turn are defensively resentful, constantly looking for insults, discrimination, and evidences of segregation.

In combating discrimination and segregation the Negro foreign-born are frequently able to employ stratagems not available to the native-born. Chief among such stratagems is the use of their foreign citizenship status. The native Negro maintains that the British Negro immigrant frequently breaks down all of the former's efforts at destroying racial segregation and discrimination with his " I am a British subject! I shall appeal to my consul ", whenever he runs afoul of the American segregation practices. Such individual protests, maintains the native-born Negro, while getting satisfactory personal results, do little to aid the concerted racial approach for eliminating segregation practices. An indirect outgrowth of such personal protests was the Georgia amendment of her racial integrity law in 1927 to define persons of color as [10] " all Negroes, mulattoes, mestizos, and their descendants, having any ascertainable trace of either Negro or African, West Indian or Asiatic Indian blood in their veins, and all descendants of any person having either Negro or African West Indian or Asiatic Indian blood in his or her veins ".

James H. Hubert, executive director of the New York Urban League, observed in this connection that many West Indians are applying their feelings rather than their brains to working out their relations with the native-born Negro in New York. Because the American Negro is maltreated the British West Indian boasts of getting " better protection as a British subject, hence he refrains from becoming a registered voter ".[11]

The Negro immigrant is aware of this difference. He is a product of, let us say, British culture, which is regarded as more " refined " (having more superficial nuances) than the American culture. One educated British West Indian expressed it by saying " There is something really raw and unrefined about the basis of the American social structure that stands out glaringly to one who has lived abroad. It is the crudest, most unrefined country I know ". The immigrant realizes that the American Negro is told to stay in his place; that the training of the American Negro very frequently is directed to that end. The foreign subject, especially the British, is taught from earliest infancy to stand up for his rights. Hence he becomes a great litigant, frequently with exaggerated notions of his dig-

10 Work, Monroe N., *op. cit.*, p. 75.

11 *The West Indian Committee Journal*, "Are We Forging Ahead?", Vol. I, No. 5, 1928, p. 14.

nity. Both the Pullman Company and certain railroads hesitated to employ West Indian Negroes as porters because of the rather vainglorious resentment exhibited when they felt that they had been insulted by passengers. This in turn led to outcries against alleged discrimination and segregation of the Negro immigrants. *The Montreal Star* published a letter from one West Indian who complained because of the Canadian Pacific Railroad's unfair practice of importing colored men from the United States as pullman porters when there were "plenty of capable colored West Indians here who are better qualified".[12] Similarly, the Secretary of the Faculty of Medicine at McGill University[13] suggests that West Indian Negroes think there is discrimination against them there because they are told that the requirements for a degree cover a longer period than at Scottish universities, though it is a difference that affects all students alike.[14] When such situations arise the West Indian alien goes to his Consulate, firm in the conviction that it is his inherent right to do so, and that justice will be had.

In the problem of race discrimination and segregation the foreign-born Negro is forced to make drastic adjustment. Forming a racial majority at home, and not being accustomed to such broad discriminations on a racial basis, he revolts against the oriental bazaar of segregation in the States. While color, class and caste lines tend to converge in the Caribbean, it is also true that their racial separation begins there. Color there is a factor in, though not a final determinant of, class status. Because of his resentment for the segregation pattern of the United States the foreign-born Negro is a relentless prota-

12 Greaves, *op. cit.*, p. 73.

13 *Ibid.*, p. 71.

14 Some of the highest ranking Negro physicians in the United States are McGill graduates. Yet among the British West Indians much prestige is attached to studying at Edinburgh or some other Scottish university. Until recent years degrees from American medical colleges carried little prestige among West Indian peoples. Even today the degrees are much more effective psychologically for practice in the United States than for practice in the West Indies.

gonist for all causes fighting the social, political and economic disabilities of the Negroes in this country. As he participates and succeeds to leadership the foreign-born Negro faces the same type of problem faced by the foreign-born white,—he frequently is refused leadership even when qualified. Yet the West Indians' major contribution to Negro life in the United States as stated by one of them, is in itself a conflict-producing one—" The insistent assertion of their manhood in an environment that demands too much servility and unprotecting acquiescence from men of African blood—the unwillingness to conform and be standardized, to accept tamely an inferior status and abdicate their humanity ".

Though stemming from sharply distinctive, and, at times, conflicting cultures, traditions, aims, customs and thought-schools, the non-English speaking and the English-speaking immigrants when meeting on United States soil are forced to find a new basis for social adjustment. That basis is race. Spiritually and culturally the immigrants bonds are more closely knit with Spain, France, Portugal and Great Britain than with the United States. Their arrival here is not always a metaphorical hand-washing to out the damned spot of their home land, rather it is thought of as an effort to preserve that which is regarded as most important in the past and link it with the profits—actual and potential—of this, their promised land. But this process involves additional struggle and accommodation. How is it accomplished?

CHAPTER VI

THE ADJUSTMENT OF THE NEGRO IMMIGRANT—(*Continued*)

B. Factors in Group Adjustment

The potential and actual antagonisms and conflicts indicated in the previous chapter play an important role in foreign-born-native-born Negro adjustment in the United States. Three factors tend to regulate the degree and tempo of this adjustment. Let us examine them.

I. CLASSIFICATION OF FACTORS

In the first place, *visibility* plays a vital role. The outward evidence of distinction, color, dress and language operate upon the Negro immigrant group as well as upon the white. It has been only within the past ten years that it has been impossible to spot the newly arrived West Indian through his dress. Accustomed to wearing tropical clothes, white shoes, flannel trousers and linen suits at home, he brought them with him to New York and Boston. Today, this male attire, formerly the butt of many a " monkey-chaser " jest, is an accepted summer fashion. The visibility of dress no longer makes the Negro immigrant conspicuous.

Language has never been a pronounced barrier to the Negro immigrant's adjustment but the various brogues and dialects of the West Indies continue to make the immigrant highly visible. Its persistence in the new environment is probably the least resolved of the externals that make for individual and group maladjustment. It becomes the standardized external of the Negro stranger by which he is prejudged and stratified. When the brogue passes out of the immigrant's normal expression it is perpetuated or revived in song and jest. Similarity of these brogues and dialects to the Gullah spoken by natives of South Carolina's sea-island section has led many West Indians to pose as migrants from Charleston or Savannah. Through such devices, it is believed, they become more acceptable to the native Negro community.

A popular song, " The West Indies Blues ",[1] current at the height of West Indian immigration, indicates how visibility through sheer numbers leads to ridicule and jest. The words, written in the parlance of the Jamaican immigrant indicate the nature of this visibility:

WEST INDIES BLUES

Got my grip and trunk all packed,
Steamship I'm gwine to take her,
So good-bye old New York Town,
I'se gwine to Jamaica.
When I git on de odder side,
I'll hang aroun' de waters,
I'll make my livin' sure's you born,
A-divin' after qua'ters.

Chorus: Gwine home won't be long,
Gwine home sure's you born,
I'm gwine home won't be long 'cause I've got no time to lose.
Gwine home I can't wait, gwine home
Mon, I'm late, I'm gwine home
I can't wait, 'cause I've got the West Indies Blues,
Got the West Indies Blues, Got the West Indies Blues.

Done give up de bestes' job,
A runnin' elevator,
I told my boss " Mon " I'd be back
Sometime soon or later.
When I git back to dis great land,
You better watch me Harvey,
'Cause 'm gonna be a great big " Mon "
Like my frien' Marcus Garvey.

1 By Edgar Dowell, Spencer Williams and Clarence Williams. Clarence Williams Music Publishing Company, New York, 1924.

Verses to the song were endless. The following parodies indicate how habits, customs and institutions of the foreign-born Negro were portrayed.

When I get on the other side,
I'll buy myself a Lizzie,
Climb up in a cocoanut tree,
And knock those monkeys dizzy.

Garvey, Garvey is a big man
To take his folks to Monkey-land,
If he does that I'm sure I can
Stay right here with Uncle Sam.

When you eat split peas and rice
You think your eatin' somethin',
But man you aint' taste nothin yet
Till you eat monkey hips and dumplin.

When a monkey-chaser dies
Don't need no undertaker,
Just throw him in de Harlem River
He'll float back to Jamaica.

When I get on the other side,
I'll buy myself a mango,
Grab myself a monkey gal
And do the monkey tango.

Today, however, the elements of visibility because of numbers exist only in the large foreign-born communities of New York, Boston and Florida. The various island brogues remain the outstanding points of visibility.

The second factor in these group antagonisms is *tradition.* In the foreign-born-native-born relations, the force of tradition is not emphasized by the native-born, but by the foreign-born. The latter is proud of the fact that he has always rebelled against oppression and race discrimination. He was released from physical slavery before the American Negro. The traditions of family and social position survive for immigrants who have maintained a preferential status in much more marked a manner than they do for the native-born Negroes. To the transplanted immigrant all of the social memories become rationalized traditions of other generations and lands.

Excerpts from the life history of a young Trinidadian reflect the impact of tradition upon the adjustment processes:

I was born in the island of Trinidad, British West Indies, the son of a prominent Pharmaceutical Chemist and Druggist whose grandfather was an Irishman. My mother was, prior to her marriage, a school teacher. She is the daughter of an East Indian who was born in Ragoon, India. Perhaps, as a result of this admixture of blood, Negro, Indian, Irish, there may be psychological reasons for my mental disquietude.

There was never any question of my being a gentleman. I was by the fault of a circumstance, of the "upper middle-class." From my earliest days, I had seen large signs bearing the firm name of Chemists & Druggists. I was at all times addressed as Mr. even by my elders and quite naturally by domestics who suffer intolerably from the devastating and disgusting effects of the class system that exists in the islands. I was rather accustomed to homage and deference.

In my home, there was always, love, happiness and dignity, of which I am indeed proud, servants and other superfluous comforts. Our friends were people who assisted in moulding the affairs of the government of the islands: a Barrister-at-Law, King's Counsel, and, at one time, Mayor of the capital, Port-of-Spain; an M.D., a graduate of Edinburgh University, Scotland, and also a former Mayor; the most prosperous Solicitor and Conveyancer, Queen's Royal College; a Merchant; a Barrister-at-Law, and many others.

From my very childhood, I had known these gentlemen to be close friends of my family. It is obvious that my immediate associates were sons and daughters of these families.

I was tutored at home until the age of six. I attended the best elementary schools, receiving an island scholarship by competitive examination which enrolled me as a student at St. Mary's College. St. Mary's is conducted by the Congregation of Holy Ghost Fathers from Blackrock, Ireland. This is a mixed college. Apart from the island scholarships offered by the government annually, attending college is solely limited to those whose parents, gentlemen and ladies, may be safely considered the more fortunate.

I was assured of finishing in England. It is expected that a gentleman must "finish" in England. My ambition was to have dinners at Gray's Inn. America at this stage was important to me, but only geographically. America was a place where people spoke in nasal, slangy tones; where people said "I guess" or "I reckon" for "presumably"; where all black men and women served in menial capacities—porters, cooks, dishwashers; where white men only were honoured by being granted the privilege of sweeping the streets, of operating street cars, of being butchers, bankers, bakers, and other mediums of public service.

America was a place where everyone mingled on an equal footing; where ladies would do their own shopping, going to grocery stores with their shopping bags; where everyone and anyone would address you by your surname in a most familiar manner, or be called "boy," and most frequently "nigger". A thought of attempting to exist under such barbarous conditions never entered my mind. I would have called a white boy "niggardly" without the slightest hesitation if his conduct so demanded. I was truly one with mankind, with humanity. I was extremely conscious of one fact—I was the son of ——————

My father's untimely death opened my eyes to the more important things. Business at this time was not at all favourable. I acted upon an impulse, guided by my always precocious attitude and perspicacity. On a Sunday afternoon, I was invited to a reception for a young Barrister who had visited New York. His was a broader interpretation of life in America. He saw a struggle. Indeed, he saw black men as porters, but he had also seen black men who, by their individual efforts, strength of personality and purpose, had become lawyers, doctors and dentists.

In England, it is unethical for gentlemen to work while they are students. In America, men do work, earn good salaries, study and succeed. I saw a more encouraging side of a country to which I was hitherto indifferent. I was young. I was ambitious. If others were successful, I could be also.

From the point of view of the native-born Negro, tradition is operative in terms of the stereotypes previously mentioned. One of the most unique rationalizations is that of comparing the West Indian with the Jew. Both are supposedly particularly efficient in operating business enterprises; both, they say, will cheat you upon the slightest pretext. The West Indians are argumentative, aggressive and possessed of great proselyting zeal for any cause they may espouse. They are profound respecters of the law, and are too frequently inclined to be litigious. However, all of the aforementioned stereotypes tend to fade in direct relationship to the decline of visibility, tradition and competition as regulators of group adjustment.

Competition is the third factor and is the matrix of the problem. Competition between foreign-born and native-born Negroes ordinarily takes place without being observed even by the individuals most concerned. It is only in periods of crisis when Negroes are seeking to control the economic and vocational aspects of their group life that the forces with which they are competing become identified with persons and groups. Under such circumstances actual conflict evolves. As adjustments and changes are effected the conscious competition tends to subside. This competition is most clearly indicated in the economic aspects of the relationship.

As has been previously stated, the development of the Panama Canal, and the opening of new travel lanes between the West Indies and the United States were largely responsible for the increasing flow of Negro immigration. The earlier immigrants, finding work which paid well and seemed permanent, invited and brought their friends and relatives from the islands. They advised with caution, however, for the occupational scheme to which the new comer must adjust was markedly different from that of his native land. Thus, the majority of the immigrants have come to the United States with training in some skill—carpentry, brickmasonry, shoe-making, wheelwrighting, baking, cigar making, tailoring, or sugar refining. They have easy access to such jobs at home. In the United

States these jobs are more difficult to secure. They come into a system where the positions they must accept are in the lowest brackets of economic security and prestige.

The foreign-born worker does not accept this change without a struggle. His new job is seldom in his old line, it is always more hurried and harried than it was when he was a worker at home. Security on the job is relatively unknown—the job exists from week to week, and planning becomes impossible. Yet this very atmosphere creates a new personal type. Eventually, the immigrant does not worry, because sooner or later he will either find something else, go into a business of his own, or return home. (To this might be added the additional possibility of the 1930's—going on relief.)[2] But it is the foreign-born Negro who contributes so largely to the business operations of the Negro community. For this group, and the Southern Negro migrant as well, has taken advantage of the Post Office as a method of saving and for sending money back home. According to a New York Post Office official, in 1936 four Post Office substations located in Harlem, Stations I, J, L and College, had more postal savings depositors than any city and than most states in the United States. Thirty thousand depositors had more than four million dollars in these savings accounts. At College Station, in the heart of Harlem, in 1936 there were 15,000 depositors of $1,300,000, an amount in excess of that saved in the Post Office of Pittsburgh, Pennsylvania.

Men who are accustomed to performing skilled tasks are seldom contented to do unskilled labor, except under conditions that promise surer economic stability or larger financial returns. The immigrant would feel more confident performing tasks to

2 "Going on relief" no longer represents a drastic change in status in the Negro community. It is not to be confused with accepting charity from either public or private sources. The former may be demanded, fought for, as a government-made right. The latter involves supplication, even humility, and loss of individual status. It is one of the era's most significant changes in group folkways.

which he is already adjusted than tasks in which he must reorient himself. A new job under new conditions was certain to facilitate economic and personal disorganization.

The disorganization continues with the employment of women outside of the home. The demand for factory workers in New York during the World War provided many jobs for the foreign-born Negro woman in the New York garment industry. Today the West Indian woman in the garment factory is more frequently found employed at the skilled tasks than is the native-born Negro woman.

Many of the unskilled workers secure employment as waiters, porters, elevator operators, factory workers, and in various branches of government service. They attend trade schools and learn new skills, profiting by their background of industrial education that has been such a controversial issue in the United States. But while the vast possibilities for self-improvement aided the unskilled worker, it frequently produced a different effect upon the skilled worker and the so-called "middle class" alien. The skilled worker frequently lost his skill in the monotonous routine of a service occupation. The West Indian white collar worker, forced to become an elevator operator, or a shipping clerk, found that he not only earned less money than the longshoreman from his native island, but was also forced to a lower plane of living. He could not improve his status so easily as could the unskilled worker. His mode of living in every instance was insecure unless he took advantage of his education and training and became engaged in some form of private business enterprise among Negroes. This he did to such an extent that he became a prominent factor in the professional and commercial activities of the Negro areas he occupied. James Weldon Johnson summarizes this tendency in Harlem as follows: [3]

3 Johnson, James Weldon, "The Making of Harlem", *Survey Graphic*. Harlem Number, March, 1925, pp. 635-639.

Often companies of half dozen men combined to buy a house—these combinations were and still are generally made up of West Indians—and would produce five or ten thousand dollars to put through the deal.

When the buying activity began to make itself felt, the land companies that had been holding vacant the handsome dwellings on and abutting Seventh Avenue decided to put them on the market. The values of these houses had dropped to the lowest mark possible and they were put up at astonishingly low prices. Houses that had been bought at from $15,000 to $20,000 were sold at one-third those figures. They were quickly gobbled up. The Equitable Life Assurance Company held 106 model private houses that were designed by Stanford White. They are built with courts running straight through the block and closed off by wrought-iron gates. Every one of these houses was sold within eleven months at an aggregate price of about two million dollars. Today they are probably worth about 100 percent more. And not only have private dwellings and similar apartments been bought but big elevator apartments have been taken over. Corporations have been organized for this purpose. Two of these, including The Antillian Realty Company, composed of American and West Indian Negroes, represent holdings amounting to approximately $750,000.

It is estimated that in New York as high as one-third of the Negro professional population—particularly physicians, dentists and lawyers—is foreign-born.

The industrial workers, however, have employed additional devices for economic security which operate in two directions—one toward the development of collective bargaining interests and practices among Negro workers, the other in fostering racial boycotts of concerns not employing Negro workers. While in neither device has the foreign-born Negro been the initiating or the sole motivating power in New York City, in both of them he has been an aggressive and emotional force in keeping them alive.

John R. Commons [4] holds that immigrants from countries having a low economic standard, when once moved by the spirit of unionism are the most dangerous and determined of unionists, since they have few obligations, little property and but meagre necessities that compel them to capitulate. For additional reasons, however, the foreign-born Negro becomes the aggressive labor leader in New York. Not only has he nothing to lose, but he also has something to regain. Such a loss of occupational status as he has had is an experience not consciously experienced by the native Negro. Furthermore, the foreign-born Negro is more accustomed to fighting aggressively, individually if not collectively, for his rights. It is therefore significant that the West Indian woman was largely responsible for the entrance of Negro women into the least exploited branches and factories of the needle trades; that Haitians were active in the labor union fights of the fur industry during the late 1920's; and that a Jamaican, David E. Grange, a vice-president of the International Seamen's Union, was described as the stormy petrel of the recent longshoremen's " outlaw " strike. Ashley Totten, a Virgin Islander, has been a consistently active officer of the Brotherhood of Sleeping Car Porters, giving organizational strength and support to the leadership of native-born A. Philip Randolph.

Likewise, the foreign-born Negro has played an active and aggressive role in the development of left-wing economic organization in the country. The many varieties of socialism and communism have always found more ready expression among groups of alien cultures. They have accepted it more readily, not because they are inherently more " radical ", to use the term in its colloquial sense, but because such movements provided them with status and tended to cross-cut the cleavages in the foreign-born relationships. The aggressive writings of W. A. Domingo, William Bridges, Hubert Harrison, George Frazier Miller, Richard B. Moore, and Cyril V. Briggs were effective

4 Commons, John R., *Races and Immigrants in America*, The Macmillan Company, New York, 1920.

moulders of economic opinion within the foreign-born and native-born groups. Bridges wrote editorially in the brief-lived but little restrained radical magazine, " Challenge ", the following impassioned prose assaulting the intra-racial color line and directed toward uniting the American Negroes and the West Indians:

> There is no West Indian slave, no American slave; you are all slaves, base, ignoble slaves.
>
> There is no more love in the hearts of the British statesmen when passing laws to curtail the liberties of their black subjects than there is in the hearts of Americans when passing similar laws to abridge the liberties of theirs.
>
> West Indian Negroes, you are oppressed. American Negroes, you are equally oppressed. West Indians, you are black. Americans, you are equally black. It is your color upon which white men pass judgment not your merits, nor the geographical line between you. Stretch hands across the seas, and with the immortal Patrick Henry say: " Give me liberty or give me death . . . "
>
> West Indians, the only things you are wanted for and permitted to do that white men do is worship the King and sing " Britannia Rules the Waves," no matter if Britannia rules you more sternly than she ever rules the waves.
>
> Americans, the only thing you are wanted for and permitted to do that white men do is to be loyal and sing " The Star Spangled Banner," no matter how many Southern hillsides are spangled with the blood of many another innocent Negro.
>
> " Negroes of the West Indies and America unite! Slavery is just as bad under a king as under a president.
>
> We don't want white wives; we don't want to dine in the homes of white men; we don't want the things they have acquired; but by the eternal God that reigns on high, listen to the rhythmic voice of the New Negro ringing at the court gates of kings and presidents like a raging tempest wind, furious as a curse of Hell, valorous, determined, unafraid, crying, " Give Us Liberty or Give us Death ".

The masses of foreign-born workers, however, have joined hands with American Negroes in supporting movements aimed at securing greater employment opportunities for Negroes. Thus, the slogan, " Do not buy where you cannot work ", becomes an effective method for regaining the occupational mobility lost by emigration. This movement combined with the so-called " black nationalism " efforts now current in Harlem is an outgrowth of the Garvey movement. It represents the struggles of Negroes both foreign and native to reconcile their differences, which are mainly in the area of secondary characteristics, and to unite on the larger issues of economic security and political participation.

2. FORMS AND PATTERNS OF ADJUSTMENT—RELIGION AND THE CHURCH

The native Negro is relatively homogeneous in his religious activity, being first a Baptist and then a Methodist. The foreign-born Negro, however, is found, for the most part, in the Lutheran, Christian Moravian, Wesleyan, Protestant Episcopal, Baptist (Jamaican) and Catholic churches—and " not averse to having a white pastor,"[5] since he had been accustomed to one in the islands whence he has come. The Census of Religious Bodies for 1926 listed the number of churches among Negroes in congregations with which foreign-born Negroes usually affiliate as follows:

	Number of Congregations
African Orthodox Church	13
African Orthodox Church of New York	3
Christian Church	1,044
Lutheran Congregations (United Lutheran)	3,650
Wesleyan Methodist	619
Moravians	127
Episcopals (Protestant and Reformed)	7,368
Roman Catholic	16,940
Seventh Day Adventists	1,981

5 "American Negro Churches of Manhattan," *A Study by the Greater New York Federation of Churches*, 1930, p. 7.

The establishment of the African Orthodox Church in 1921 grew out of a desire of a Bishop McGuire to organize a church where Negroes could worship in accordance with ancient religious authoritativeness. The founder had been for thirty years an Episcopal minister. He severed this connection and affiliated with the American Catholic Church from which connection he established the new denomination.

Other extreme examples of the religious life of the foreign-born Negro include the Black Jews of the Synagogue of the Commandment Keepers, headed by Rabbi W. A. Matthew, a native of Lagos, West Africa, who was "born in the Hebraic Faith." Since the Italian-Ethiopian War there has grown up in Harlem a branch of the Coptic Church, the native Christian church of Ethiopia.

The Episcopal and Catholic churches, however, have the bulk of the immigrant membership. The smaller churches are poorly organized and not in keeping with the new environment. The larger churches survive and flourish not only because of their religious forms and appeal, but also because they provide a central meeting place for old friends from the native land. According to Dunbar [6] the Church tends to perpetuate traditional practices. For example, one congregation, the membership of which is at least 75 per cent foreign-born, has been celebrating for several years the Harvest Festival, an innovation of its British West Indian members. In the month of October it is the custom in the British West Indies to bring the choicest produce of the harvest to the church. On Harvest Sunday the Church is decorated with fruits and vegetables of all kinds. The minister says special prayers and appropriate hymns are sung. On the next day the provisions are sold or distributed to the poor. This native custom becomes in New York a bazaar and financial rally period, providing income for

6 Dunbar, Barrington, S., "Factors in the Cultural Background of the American Southern Negro and the British West Indian Negro that condition their adjustment in Harlem." M. A. Thesis, Political Science, Columbia University, 1935, p. 23.

the church and reviving pleasant homeland traditions for the members.

Religion and the church are the last bulwark of the Negro immigrants' traditional system. Religious attitudes remain strong even in the second generation of immigrants and are manifest in the degree to which children are sent to Sunday School, the influence of the rector or the priest, and the importance attached to such customs as are part of their parents' religious practices. The most modern church in Harlem is the Community Church (later affiliated with the Unitarian denomination) organized, pastored and, to a great extent, attended by foreign-born Negroes. But at the same time the majority of the churches keep alive the tradition of the homeland. An excellent example is provided by this announcement of a Coronation Ball, in which the values of the homeland are combined with interests in the current setting. Even the subscription price is given in English monetary values.

More than 5,000 persons attended this coronation ball honoring the new king and queen—George VI and Elizabeth. The Union Jack and colonial flags were flown with the Stars and Stripes, and the singing of " God save the King " preceded that of " The Star Spangled Banner " in what was called " a highlight in international amity." The affair was attended by Sir Gerald Campbell, British Consul-general to New York, and eighteen members of his staff. The influence of the church and its sponsorship of the program is reflected in the following newspaper picture of the rector of St. Ambrose's Parish, who, " looking beatific, but acting like a regular guy, conducted the colossal coronation ball with dignity and efficiency. He was just as efficiently assisted by more than a score of tailed ushers who saw that everyone enjoyed himself.

" Rockland Palace was a riot of colors and bunting. Most eye-hitting were the Union Jack and Colonial flags, which were set in a blue background with white stars. While plenty of good liquor flowed freely among the exuberant celebrators, not one

Coronation Pageant and Ball

Under the Distinguished Patronage of the British Consulate in N. Y. C.

¶ You and Your friends are most cordially invited by the Officers and Members of

St. Ambrose Parish
New York City

to attend their

Grand Coronation Pageant & Ball

WHICH WILL TAKE PLACE AT

ROCKLAND PALACE, 155th St. and 8th Ave.

New York City

On Wednesday Evening, May 12th, 1937

(The same day as the Coronation in England)

VERNON ANDRADE
and his Popular Orchestra will play

Subscription Tickets 3s. 1½d.

Boxes, 12s. 6d. :: **Loges, 8s. 4d.**

Invited by ....

of the 5,000 was inebriated or boisterous—which was a tribute to the tone of the affair." [7]

The church more so than any other institution has tended to keep alive homeland values, frequently taking as its responsibility the fostering of extra-religious functions that would otherwise increase the visibility of the immigrant group. Thus, the mourning attending the death of George V was widely observed in Harlem churches. The *affaires de coeur* of Edward VIII were widely condemned by the ecclesiastical leaders. Special coronation services for George VI, were held at one of the Baptist churches and a coronation tea was poured at the Wesleyan Methodist Church. Through such activity the church becomes a conserver of the culture as well as an organization for facilitating the immigrants' adjustment and preventing complete personal disorganization.

Persistencies of the Old Cultures

Evidence of conflicts between the old and new cultures have been indicated throughout this study. It should be noted, however, that the immigrant's objective behavior changes much more quickly than the more subjective traditions and beliefs. The objective behavior requiring approbation of the community at large disappears, quickly in the face of social controls. The customs, beliefs and traditions of the ingroup persists in many instances only slightly modified by the new environment. The problem involved in an analysis of these persistencies is one of discovery and isolation. Miss Hurlbutt has adequately defined this area of exploration as the *invisible environment* of the immigrant.[8] The environment of the immigrant is a dual one—the new environment and the old environment. As time goes on the persisting environment of the old world recedes. If the process is not cruelly and artificially forced, the recession will be natural and inevitable and may result in growth and a

7 *The Amsterdam News*, May 22, 1937, p. 7.

8 Hurlbutt, Mary E., "The Invisible Environment of the Immigrant," *The Family* (October, 1923), Vol. IV, No. 6, pp. 150-164.

healthy reorganization of personality. Immigrants attempt "to reproduce in the new world the modes of social expression and organization familiar at home. The genuine reproduction is of course impossible; we get monstrosities neither American nor old-world but having a tincture of both—makeshift institutions, cheap and ugly and unsatisfying even to the immigrant, but meeting at least his habitual human needs as nothing in the American community can." [9]

In addition to the persistencies mentioned elsewhere, the cultural elements of Negro immigrants seeming to have the greatest survival value are those relating to death, courtship and marriage, royalty, food, and, cutting across all of these, superstitions. Even these have been modified to meet demands of the new environment. Folk games, tales, and songs become part of the new play pattern, and survive with any degree of vitality only among such socially isolated groups as the Cape Verdeans in New England, and as stories told to pre-school children.

Foods

Despite the fact that they evolve in a poverty economy, the food habits of the Antilles have a persistent survival in the new environment. In Harlem numerous varieties of native foods can be purchased in either the West Indian and Puerto Rican stores or at the Park Avenue Market. To the Harlem cuisine the immigrant has added the use of condiments—chives, garlic, timbric, peppers, curry and lime juice. He has introduced into the food culture of the Negro community native vegetables and fruits, yams, West Indian pumpkins, Guatamalean black beans, pigeon peas, mangos, pawpaws, ginger root from which ginger beer is made, choyos which look like large green peppers, plaintains, papaya, guava, eddo, alligator pears, breadfruit, cassava, black pudding, red fish and tannias.

Maintaining these habits, however, frequently presents difficult financial problems. Some of the everyday foods to which the West Indian Negro has become accustomed are now priced

9 *Ibid.*, p. 162.

beyond his limited means. " The price that the market man asks for a couple of rosy-cheeked Hayden Mangos, little fellows just the right size to snuggle comfortably in the hand, is the price of a basketful down home. So until he gets used to the American ways, if he decides that he ever will, he sticks to the same old diet of rice and beans, with fried eggs and tomatoes, when he has the eggs and tomatoes." [10]

According to Miss Glenn, of the New York Department of Markets, Weights and Measures, the West Indian frequently throws away " enough food to make an excellent second-day dinner for an American Negro family." Reared in the semi-tropics where a blazing sun and lack of refrigeration combined to discourage the use of " left-overs ", the West Indian family has a positive distaste for any food not freshly prepared.

Beef is a stock commodity in the West Indian islands. Not only is it shipped from the cattle-raising countries of South America in a frozen, semi-dried or corned state, but it was also native, for at one time oxen ran as wild on these islands as did the hogs in America.[11] Today fresh beef is used for stew, roasts and beefsteak. One recipe for West Indian beefsteak, a " dish for an epicure," is described as follows:

> The slices are cut as thin as steak can be cut then they are rubbed with just a little washed garlic and left to soak all night in plenty of sour orange juice. Next day, seasoned with salt and pepper, these steaks are fried in a frying pan, boiled rice is put into the pan afterwards to be mixed with the rich steak gravy.[12]

Pork in the form of chops, ham, or bacon is quite in demand. According to grocers and post office officials in the area, it is almost impossible to keep on hand a sufficient supply of hams weighing about ten pounds, so great is the demand from

10 Glenn, Viola, " The Eating Habits of Harlem," in *Opportunity*, Journal of Negro Life, Vol. XIII, No. 3, March 1935, pp. 82-85.

11 The term " buccaneer " which finally came to mean " pirate " is said to have originally referred to those who captured the " boucans " or wild bulls of Haiti and used them for food.

12 Glenn, *op. cit.*, p. 84.

foreign-born groups for this size ham to send to the folks back home.

Among the Spanish-speaking group "arroz con pollo"—chicken with rice—is a traditional dish. "Fungy" or "cuckoo", a thick paste made of yellow meal and okra served hot with meats and fish continues to be a favorite and inexpensive dish, as are black pudding and souse. Trinidadians, proud of their creole cooking, spend an inordinately large amount of time preparing *pelau*—a savory mixture of chicken, rice, green peppers, onions and a few pieces of salt meat,—and calla-lou a spicy fish-meat vegetable hash made of okra, tania leaves, peppers, crabmeat, a bit of ham and lots of pepper. Add to these fish-cakes, bulljol, talkanee, mango chutney, dal-pouri, and sancloche and one has an idea of the increasing variety that exists in Negro foods in the United States because of this immigration.

As the natives of semi-tropical countries increase the demand for their native foods, the average high price is being lowered. Meanwhile the market is expanding because others have tried the dishes and find them palatable.

Funerals and Wakes

The wake of the West Indies, is perpetuated in the United States. There friends sit up all night with the relations of the dead, praying, feasting and socializing. In some islands the "wake" is an occasion for much merriment for the younger groups, ranging in type from the simple telling of Anansi stories to dancing and drinking parties. No body is kept in the home longer than three days. Celebrations may continue for the whole period prior to the funeral. After the burial services friends and relatives return to the home of the deceased and are served food and drink as befits the class of the family. In New York City the "wake" continues to be a period of celebration for some islanders, although the corpse is now embalmed and kept in an undertaking establishment. Friends are still served at the home after the funeral. The element of merry-making is determined by the moral standards and religious beliefs of the decedent's family. The occasion is always the perfect setting for reunions and reminiscences. But one of the most unique characteristics of the adaptation is the hope that if some one dies, the demise will occur on Friday or Saturday, in order that the social obsequies may be performed without interfering with a work-a-day life of friends, who would like to take part in the ceremonies.

MARRIAGE

Customs of marriage undergo only slight revision in the foreign-born family of culture, particularly if both parents are foreign-born. There must be a wedding. The old customs of courtship in which the young native upon becoming interested in a young lady "addressed" himself to her parents, stating his intentions before being permitted to call, have passed. But, perhaps, no event is more solemnly and more glamorously staged than the romantic customs of the wedding. All of the formal traditions of the church wedding, followed by only the wealthy in the United States are included in the nuptial ceremony. As one writer has expressed it, "The big question in West Indian circles is not whom you marry but how you marry" . . . An ordinary American marriage might mean only the girl and boy's dropping two nickels in the subway and slipping downtown and becoming Mr. and Mrs.[13] But your true Jamaican marriage, your true Barbadian marriage, your true Virgin Island or Trinidadian marriage means prosperity for everybody. . . . The florist, the dressmaker, the shoe salesman, the caterer, the jeweler, the tailor, the butcher, the baker and the candlestick maker all get their share when the bride of island lineage is given in marriage." [14] Receptions are attended by from two to five hundred guests, and, to a much greater extent than is true among the native-born Negroes, the strict regulations of formal attire and etiquette are observed.

13 Many of the second-generation marriages are just this type, it being the only way to avoid the parents' desire for a "real" wedding in keeping with their parents' *past* status.

14 Matthews, Ralph, "Wedding Bells Ring Loudest in Harlem," *The Baltimore Afro-American*, May 2, 1936.

THE SYMBOL OF ROYALTY

Devotion to the symbol of royalty among the British West Indians remains an active cultural persistency even after naturalization. During the illness of King George V in 1928-29, special prayer services for his recovery were held in numerous Harlem churches. Upon the occasion of his death in 1936 the Church of St. Martin held a special memorial service attended by Sir Gerald Campbell and several British societies. Reactions to the abdication of King Edward VIII were largely in defense of British traditions, and not typical of the romantic angle taken in the United States. What was romantic to the American Negro was scandalous to his West Indian brother. The coronation of King George VI likewise was the occasion for similar festivities. However, as problems of political import became more important the symbol tended to tarnish. When Great Britain dropped her sanctions against Italy, Dr. P. M. H. Savory, co-publisher of the *Amsterdam News,* and a well known Harlem physician and business man, who " led a delegation of fifty West Indian Negroes to the British consulate to protest against Great Britain's retreat from her sanctions stand, said that the replies given by Consul-General Sir Gerald Campbell were completely unsatisfactory." [15]

At the meeting where the above statement was made one person declared that, although he had remained a British subject during his thirty-year stay in the United States, he will now renounce British allegiance " as a result of Britain's betrayal of Ethiopia."

Folk Tales and Songs

The significance of folk tales, songs and games is particularly noted in the homes and at the private social functions of the foreign-born. The romance of the old and distant environmental experiences does much to cement the relationships between parent and child. The famous Anansi stories of

15 *The Amsterdam News,* June 27, 1936.

Jamaica,[16] based upon the conception of the spider Anansi as the trickster hero of the Gold Coast, and comparable with the Brer Rabbit stories of the United States, survive as a device in this relationship. Folk games have almost entirely disappeared in the new urban environment, despite the fact that the Christmas and New Year holidays and the August first Emancipation Day,[17] once the days especially devoted to game playing, are still observed in the States. The Emancipation Day Celebration in the United States maintains the same form as typified the occasion at home, but differs tremendously in its content. The 103rd anniversary of the Emancipation Proclamation in the British West Indies celebration on August 1, 1937 launched an ambitious and far-reaching program of political, economic and social reform. The agenda included discussions of and action upon the following subjects:

The United States and Negro peoples	*The West Indies and Great Britain*	*The World and Negro peoples*
Lynching.	Labor troubles in Trinidad.	Ethiopia's seat in the League of Nations.
The Scottsboro Case.	British controlled clinics, in Bermuda.	
Problems of foreign-born Negroes in New York and other cities.	The constitutional crisis in Barbados.	Germany and her claim for African colonies.
	Crown colony government in the West Indies.	
	Segregation by steamship companies.	
	Development of a Negro colony as haven for 60,000 West Indians in British Guiana.	

Folk songs are usually heard at small parties when folk are " feteing " and where native rhythms are interspersed throughout a program of contemporary dance tunes. " Sly Mongoose "

16 Beckwith, Martha Warren, " Jamaica Anansi Stories," *Memoirs of the American Folk-lore Society*, 1924, pp. xi-xii.

17 The one hundredth anniversary of West Indian emancipation from slavery was celebrated in 1938.

is one of the most popular among the Trinidadian and Barbadian groups in New York. The words of one verse follow:

Sly Mongoose, dog know your name
  Sly Mongoose, ain't it a shame
Went right into the white folks kitchen
  Snatched up one of their big fat chicken
Put into your waistcoat pocket
  Sly Mongoose.[18]

Younger children may not be taught their alphabets in the following manner, but they are told that their parents might have learned them as follows:

K 'tan fe kallaloo
  nice when it boil.
L is fe Lizard
  him a well 'poil!
M 'tan fe Monkey
  'top!—a wha do him face?
N is me Nana
  she hat trim with lace!

The Cape Verde islanders are scattered through eastern Massachusetts, Rhode Island and the seaport towns of Connecticut. They seldom intermarry, and seldom mingle with the native populations. In these groups, whether it be a colony of Fogo Islanders, Boa Vistans or Brava Islanders, folk stories

18 The mongoose is a member of the rodent clan, about the size of a squirrel. The story of its invasion of Barbados is given by M.L.N. as follows: "The rats were getting into the sugar cane fields, gnawing the cane from the roots and ruining the crop. The English brought in the mongoose to kill the rats. Now, when the rats got wind of the coming of these destroyers they called a council of war and decided to send their females out to make friends with the mongoose. As a result it was found that the Mongoose was breeding rather than destroying rats. It was also discovered that the mongoose's favorite dessert was fowl of all sort. He stole live poultry and sucked the eggs. He was a very sly animal and created such a problem by his vicious ways and rapid increase that the matter of extermination was brought before the local Assembly for action. It is said that only a dog is feared by the mongoose, and only then if he is attacked quickly.

are retained, although these stories appear to originate only among the Fogo Islanders. The characters of their stories center around the Wolf and his nephew—Lob' and Tobinh'.[19] Mrs. Parsons found extreme similarity between some of the riddles and stories collected from this Portuguese Negro group and those obtained in the Sea Islands of South Carolina and tales recorded in the Bahamas.[20]

Another carry-over of old world customs is the present popularity of the Trindadian calypso. Once a year, just prior to Lent, the island of Trinidad carnivals. During this carnival certain characters compose, play and sing the Trinidad music known as calypso. These are impromptu songs of jerky rhythms and insinuating tunes which tell in a Caribbean patois of local and world news events, and celebrate such subjects as women and drink.

Calypso specialists have put to song the visit of President Roosevelt to their island, as well as the events leading up to King Edward VIII's abdication from the throne of the British Empire.

For more than five years recordings of calypso songs have been for sale in Harlem, but in recent months a boom has occurred in the calypso market. Today, these records, which must be censored by British officials before being sold in the native Trinidad are " hot " in New York's music shops.

Superstitions

Few of the second generation of the Negro foreign-born population know of " Duppies " or " Jumbies "—the ghosts and spirits of the West Indies. These beliefs in ghosts and spirits have become less haunting in the new environment, yet the immigrants themselves have maintained numerous superstitions and beliefs which are to some degree overtly practiced or worshipped in our larger cities, even if under the guise of

19 Parsons, Elsie Clews, "Folk-lore from the Cape Verde Islands," *Memoirs of the American Folk-lore Society*, Vol. XV, Part I, 1922, pp. xi-xvi.

20 Parsons, *op. cit.*, Vol. XVI, 1928, pp. xiii-xxii.

some esoteric cult. As these beliefs survive mainly in individual relations the extent of practice and their current significance may not be stated quantitatively. City patterns have taken these beliefs from the realm of the exoteric. The only extensive evidence exists in relation to the playing of policy, or " the numbers " in which the dream is a most important symbol. But this is such a catholic device in all areas that its origins, or that of any of its features, are inseparable on the basis of nationality contributions.

" Jungle-Town ", a former slum area near the Brooklyn Navy Yard, which is now cleared away, was in 1930 described as " a world of primitive beliefs and practices as unchanged by the centuries as the deepest savannahs of the Matto Grasso region, where the British scientists are exploring man's ancient arts and stratagems against evils." [21] In this settlement of Haitians, Martiniquians, Barbadians, Virgin Islanders and Trinidadians were said to be practiced in the complete repetoire of old world sorcery—all save that of human sacrifice. In the back room of some flat, chicken blood from a fighting bantam rooster would be shot in your arm to give strength. From another could be obtained pharmacopoeia and talismen of all kinds, for all purposes—including tiger bone dust, cat whiskers, and enchanted feathers.

Here was repeated the oft-told tale of Old Tulia which may be heard occasionally in Harlem. Tulia, some millenia ago, murdered her child. The gods as punishment turned her feet backward and made her body bloody red. There was a curse on any man crossing her trail, and women meeting her were made barren. Any one seeing her reversed footprints must flee in the direction they were turned. Tulia had a low menacing cry which if heard demands that the hearer go to the " obeah " man to overcome the spell. But streets are paved in modern

21 Hill, Edwin C., " Primitive Superstitions in the United States ", *Human Side of the News, Washington Herald,* Washington, D. C., May 18, 1930.

cities and the cement of time and social circumstance have covered old Tulia's footprints.[22]

Crime as an Index of Culture Conflicts

Any appreciable conflict of mores brought about by immigration is supposed to be reflected in the prison population and arrest statistics of the new environment. In most cities having large aggregates of foreign-born Negroes, the nationality of persons arrested is not further classified by race or color. The following data from the Department of Correction of New York City on the prison population of New York indicate the number of West Indians present in the prison population at the time of each year's census. The statistics for West Indians, while not classified by color, are " by a very great majority the statistics of West Indian Negroes, who are more commonly known by that nationality title than are the whites ", states our official informant.

More reliable data, however, are available for New York State and are reflected in the various censuses of admission and population of Sing Sing Prison, for the " depression period " 1929-1936. It will be noted that though Negroes of foreign birth formed 14 per cent of the State's Negro population in

22 For interesting and definite pen pictures of cultural persistencies and their operation in the United States, see the following works by West Indian Negroes:

(a) McKay, Claude, *Harlem Shadows*, Harcourt Brace, New York, 1922, pp. 6, 8, 11, 53.
Home to Harlem, Harper & Brothers, New York, 1928, pp. 96 ff.; 1927, pp. 134, 291-292, 306-317.
Banjo—Harper & Brothers, New York, 1929, pp. 5, 6, 45-46, 76, 77, 110, 183, 199, 200, 202, 203.
Ginger-Town, Harper & Brothers, New York, 1933, pp. 38, 41-42.
Banana Bottom, Harper & Brothers, New York, 1933.
A Long Way from Home, Furman, New York, 1936.

(b) Walrond, Eric, *Tropic Death*, Boni and Liveright, New York, 1926, pp. 35-58, 237-283.

NEGROES AND WEST INDIANS IN THE PRISON POPULATION OF NEW YORK CITY
1930, 1931, 1934, and 1935

	Total		Negro		West Indian	
	Number	Percent	Number	Percent	Number	Percent
1935						
Total	79,732	100.0	16,233	20.4	1,324	1.7
Male	71,744	100.0	12,472	17.3	1,228	1.7
Female ..	7,988	100.0	3,761	47.1	96	1.2
1934						
Total	77,173	100.0	15,544	20.1	1,321	1.7
Male	70,558	100.0	12,456	17.6	1,226	1.7
Female ..	6,615	100.0	3,088	46.7	95	1.4
1931						
Total	59,828	100.0	8,997	15.0	709	1.2
Male	55,859	100.0	7,535	13.5	659	1.2
Female ..	3,969	100.0	1,462	36.8	50	1.2
1930						
Total	66,696	100.0	18,108	27.15	953	1.4
Male	59,007	100.0	16,391	27.8	763	1.3
Female ..	7,689	100.0	1,717	22.3	190	2.5

1930, at no time during the years covered by the data did they reach their population expectancy among Sing Sing prisoners. On the other hand, the native-born Negro population admissions during this period have been from three to even seven times higher than its population expectancy.

Thus, even when assuming that the West Indian statistics from the Department of Correction are representative of Negro

PRISONERS ADMITTED TO SING SING PRISON BY COLOR AND NATIVITY OF NEGRO PRISONERS, 1929-1932 AND 1936

Year	Total admissions	Negro admissions	Per cent Negro of total	Negro admissions: Native-born	Per cent	Foreign-born	Per cent
1936 ...	2,464	719	29.1	645	89.5	76	10.5
1932 ...	2,461	563	22.7	—	—	—	—
1931 ...	1,393	333	23.9	288	86.5	45	13.5
1930 ...	1,088	235	21.7	208	88.6	27	11.4
1929 ...	1,098	244	22.2	225	92.2	19	7.8

Source: Correspondence to the author from Office of the Warden, Sing Sing Prison, Ossining, New York.

West Indian arrests, one is forced to conclude that in New York City and New York State, at least, the foreign-born Negro comes into contact with the law, and is arrested less frequently than his native-born brother.

The Foreign-born Press

Although human associations and cultural adjustments are based primarily upon language there has not been a significant need for a foreign-born Negro newspaper. Except for the now defunct *Negro World,* former organ of the Universal Negro Improvement Association, there has been no outstanding Negro weekly devoted mainly to the interests of foreign-born Negroes. Numerous magazines have appeared, but these have been short-lived. One reason for the non-existence of such a press is the ease with which important news from the homeland is gleaned from the insular, press which does not treat news from the racial angle but publishes news of importance concerning all peoples. Another reason is found in the diversity of immigrants, who, though grouped as West Indians, maintain loyalties to specific islands. The relatively small number from each island would render the establishment of a foreign press unprofitable.

Two factors tend to affect this possible deficiency in ethnic contacts. First, at least two major Negro newspapers in the United States are owned, controlled and edited, in part, if not entirely, by foreign-born Negroes—the Boston *Chronicle* and the New York *Amsterdam News.* Furthermore, in the Negro newspaper within recent years an increasingly large amount of space has been devoted to foreign-born news. The *Pittsburgh Courier,* the New York *Amsterdam News,* the Boston *Chronicle,* the *New York Age* and the *Chicago Defender* have been outstanding in this respect. The development of this feature in the Negro press has not been due entirely to the presence of a large foreign-born population. The Negro's expanding interest in foreign affairs as they affect the darker races throughout the world has been a natural outgrowth of (1) events following the World War treaties and their handling of minority and colonial peoples' problems, (2) the various Pan-African Congresses, (3) the Garvey movement, and (4) the migration of colonial Negroes. The writings of such men as W. E. B. DuBois in *The Crisis* and the *Pittsburgh Courier,* of J. A. Rogers, George Schuyler, George Padmore and writers for the Socialist and Communist parties in various journals have promoted interest in the problems of Negro peoples throughout the world. Today international news of Negroes is sympathetically and extensively reported through the Negro press.

3. ETHNIC COMPOSITION AND BIOLOGICAL EFFECTS OF IMMIGRATION

Fertility and Fecundity

The rate of increase of the native Negro population, its racial type and its ethnic composition, has undoubtedly been affected by the immigration of other colored peoples. And though conclusive evidence in this field is completely lacking there is reason to believe that differentials in the Negro populations' fertility and fecundity noticed between such areas as New York, Boston, and Providence may find partial explanation in the nativity of Negroes residing in those areas. Anthropologists have held that there are no distinct differences in the biometric norms of Negroes from the West Indies and the native-born ones.[23] But certain factors in the social environment indicate that the presence of a foreign-born Negro population does exercise some influence upon the quantitatively measurable indices of social adjustment, and upon the vitality rates—fertility, birth and death, illiteracy and delinquency, especially.

We have already noted that the Negro illiteracy of New Bedford, Massachusetts exceeds that of any other city having a population of 100,000 or more. In Providence, R. I. where foreign-born persons largely Portuguese-speaking, classified as Negroes, form 12 per cent of the population, there were 460

23 Herskovits, M. J., *The American Negro,* Knopf, New York, 1928, pp. 41 ff.

children per 1,000 Negro women between 15 and 44 years of age in 1930. This was the highest ratio for any of the 147 cities having 5,000 or more Negro inhabitants in that year. Now immigration in itself may not be the causal nexus for this unusual fertility, but it is reasonable to conclude that the factor of social selection by affecting the group's response to the current mores and changing conditions [24] has not operated among the Negro population of Providence in such a way as to foster a decline in fertility. Such factors as the influence of Catholicism, the sex ratio, the economic level of the group, and the impact of cultural influences upon the immigrant group are important selective influences in Providence.

Yet, similar trends are not noted in other areas of foreign-born concentration. The number of children per 1,000 women classed as Negroes in the urban United States in 1930 was 268. In New York City the fertility index was 242, and lower than that of the white population. In Boston it was 286, and also lower than the white population. In Miami it was 322 and higher than that of the whites. But in every urban center to which native-born Negroes migrated in large numbers between 1920 and 1930 there did the index of fertility increase during the decade. Likewise, every southern urban area that experienced an emigration of Negroes, and a lower rate of increase during the decade, showed a decline in this index. Kiser of the Milbank Memorial Fund made a study of fertility among Harlem Negroes in 1933.[25] Though the samples were regarded as too small " to afford conclusive evidence of social class and nativity differences in the fertility of urban Negroes " the total rate of live births per 100 Negro wives of child-bearing age was 85 for native Negro women of white collar classes, 97 for native Negro women of the skilled classes, and 160 for all foreign Negro women—chiefly from the West Indies and of the laboring classes.

24 MacIver, R. M., *Society, A Text Book of Sociology,* Farrar and Rinehart, New York, 1937, pp. 463 ff.

25 Kiser, Clyde V., "Fertility of Harlem Negroes"—*The Milbank Memorial Fund Quarterly,* Vol. XIII, No. 3, July, 1935.

However, the differential rates for mortality, fertility and illiteracy for those areas where the Negro populations include a relatively high percentage of foreign-born persons, indicate that no adequate interpretation of the causative or correlative factors involved can be made without giving due weight to the social adaptation of the immigrant group.

Intermarriage

The effect that immigration is having on the ethnic composition of the Negro population is shown in the fusion of immigrant and native stocks. The mixed parentage population (those with one parent native, and one parent foreign-born) increased from 29,334 in 1920 to 39,909 in 1930. For decades between 1900 and 1930 the per cent increase of this foreign stock population was as follows—3.0, 20.1, 51.1. Mixed stocks formed 0.3 per cent of the total Negro population in 1900, but 0.7 per cent in 1930. The mixed parentage population is usually the result of a foreign father and a native mother union. In 1930 the number of cases where the father was the foreign-born parent totaled 2,458.

Little data are available on the subject of marriage between native-born and foreign-born Negroes. Conflicts over authority in the family often arise in the marriage of American Negro women and West Indian men. The men insist on maintaining the ideal of male superiority which American women resent. This conflict is resolved either by accommodation or separation. The American man, however, less frequently, marries the West Indian woman. Frazier believes that this problem of culture adaptation as well as that of illegitimacy could receive additional light through "comparative studies of the family among the Negroes in America and the West Indies." [26] In the West Indies a large number of children are born out of wedlock, because of the absence of church marriage among the lower economic groups. But it is also true that in the United States

26 Frazier, E. Franklin, "Traditions and Patterns of Negro Family Life in the United States," *Race and Culture Contacts*, E. B. Reuter, Editor. McGraw Hill, New York, 1934, p. 196.

the Negro woman's role as breadwinner has made her the dominant and more important figure in the family. Thus, the adjustment to the problem is difficult. Frazier cites this case as an example.

In 1922 I was married to a young Jamaican who at that time was a chiropodist. A boy was born after a year. We lived together two years and then separated because we found it impossible to continue to live together. He had been brought up in Jamaica where the men were lords and the women worked as slaves. For example, he believed in dressing up and going about in other women's company while his wife and children were to go along on barest necessities and live in seclusion. It became necessary for me to live with my mother as he would not provide for me and my child. After two years of separation I got a divorce on grounds of non-support and desertion. I went back to my professon when I became separated from him in order to provide a living for my son and myself.[27]

But an important factor accounting for the preponderance of foreign males in mixed marriages is that in the city native-born women outnumber native-born men, hence many must accept foreign-born husbands or go unmarried. Thus, opportunity and propinquity seem to influence the proportional distribution of these marriages.

The Second Generation

The second generation of Negro immigrants now numbers over eighty thousand persons. Except among the Spanish and Portuguese-speaking groups these children of immigrants have lost most of the social characteristics of their parents, reacting more favorably to the traditions and institutions of the Negro community. They react against the standards, interests and attitudes of the foreign group, promoting thereby conflicts between the two generations as well as between the two cultures. In the main, the conflicts are those of mental attitudes

27 Frazier, E. Franklin, *The Negro Family in Chicago*, University of Chicago Press, Chicago, 1932, pp. 122-132.

rather than of physical behavior. This is partly due to the fact that the vast majority of foreign-born persons come from English-speaking countries, bringing with them family and culture traditions which if not exactly identical with American customs, are certainly not incompatible with the tenets of the social *milieu* in which their children grow up. However, situations best calculated to bring about such clashes are

1. An overly strict discipline of children.
2. Inability of parents to reconcile methods of parental control with the greater freedom youth is demanding.
3. Inability to reconcile methods of child-rearing, based upon the woman's constant presence in the home, with the new setting where many mothers work away from the home.
4. Inability of children to appreciate the psychological differences involved in the " old country " traditions of these parents and their own.
5. Efforts of parents to check the Americanizing of their children.

Though the children of Negro immigrants quickly lose their identity as immigrant offspring they frequently find themselves amid conflicting situations. Many of them, oppressed by feelings of inferiority in such areas as New York and Boston, break away from the homes of their parents and eventually repudiate their origins.

Assimilation in both its economic and cultural aspects does not differ greatly for the immigrant children and those of the second generation. The older generation may encounter psychological friction in endeavoring to change its habits, but education and experience quickly modify habits, customs and traditions for the younger group. Frequently the clashes between the older and younger immigrants of a family group occur when the parents have not been able to secure the economic footing that would permit a ready and facile adjustment to the demands of the new environment. But, they, as do the youth of the second generation, learn to sing " America ", and pointedly state the shortcomings of the United States much more quickly than their forbears.

CHAPTER VII

THE ADJUSTMENT OF THE NEGRO IMMIGRANT—(*Continued*)

4. LEADERS AND ORGANIZATIONS

In his effort at readjustment in the new environment the Negro immigrant consciously attempts to reconcile his heritages by modifying them in terms of the new situation. The social disorganization that attends migration must be replaced by a social reconstruction that will enable harmonious functioning. Thus, the process of organized reconstruction tends to develop new leaders and new movements. Because of the persistence of deeply rooted traditional class-color, and nationality prejudices among the immigrants, and the rapidly developing antagonisms of the native-born in areas of immigrant concentration, the reconciliation was not easy. The class-conscious colored bourgeois immigrant was prone to treat his proletarian fellow-immigrant with *hauteur* and disdain, demanding the recognition accorded his position at home. The masses of immigrants were not inclined to continue this obeisance. Leaders and organizations, therefore, tended, and probably quite unconsciously, to develop with too much emphasis upon the old system. The " middle class " Negro was mistrusted and not followed. With the one there was a residue of fear, with the other there were evidences of unmistakable contempt. Negro organizations, largely of the mutual benefit variety, evolved. Street-corner speaking became the device through which loyalties were analyzed, interpreted and resolved into group-action. The minister, the physician, the lawyer and the soap-box orator became group leaders, either because of the prestige of their positions or because of their vocal audacity in a new societal setting. The aforementioned professional persons represented the highest degrees of occupational attainment in the United States. The sphere of their influence may not have exceeded the bounds of their local communities, but it facilitated the process of adjustment.

It seemed inevitable, therefore, that the first stage in the adjustment should have been through organizations in terms of old and accepted interests. Thus the ——— club, composed of "middle-class coloured" immigrants from the West Indies met for a formal evening of dancing and card playing on one floor of a Harlem building at the same time that a mutual benevolent association of immigrants from the same island met on another floor. The latter group was, in the main, the peasant group. A young immigrant upon attending one of these meetings expressed amazement that none of his class was there. The older attitudes persisted in the newer organizations. The new groups were born of circumstance and need, and were, in all probability, promoted by imitation, or aroused by propaganda. They were the direct result of old patterns of life and community. Its members were drawn together by the bonds of tradition, neighborliness, and kinship. Leadership was developed in terms of the old pattern.

The street-corner speaker, however, found for himself a new rôle. In the insular homes there had been much talking and much analysis of the various political and social problems among the peasant classes, but little recognition was given either the leader or his followers. In the United States the voice was not only heard, but was recognized, followed, and even feared in public office as well as in private thinking. This recognition aided and abetted the very movements that otherwise might have remained unknown and inchoate.

Marcus Garvey and the U. N. I. A.

It is reasonable to expect that the type-movement of immigrant organizations would have followed very closely the evolution of such organizations among other immigrant groups had it not been for the rise of Marcus Garvey and the Universal Negro Improvement Association during the height of Negro immigration. This movement not only reconciled the differences of the mass of immigrants, unifying at certain levels the native-born and foreign-born populations of the United States, but it became the first mass-movement aimed at repatriating persons of African descent and nativity on African soil. Ridiculous though the idea may appear, it became the asylum for and the messianic hope of the Negro masses throughout the world who were dissatisfied with their status as Negroes. The leader of this movement, Marcus Garvey, was a Negro immigrant. The core of his organization was the West Indian group in the United States and Jamaica.

Garvey's leadership was that of a demagogue. His ability to organize a movement reported to have had at least 4,000,000 members,[1] at least 45 per cent of whom were in the United States, was utilized in a leadership of fear and hope.[2] His was a type of leadership that underlies all mass movements of a political and social nature. It endows the leader with positive and negative values which are the object of the desire or fear of others, and which he can at will change, grant, withdraw, impose or take off. The mere existence of this leadership rested upon the partial assimilation of Negro peoples throughout the world, and especially in the Americas. The results from such leadership are of little consequence to the followers, since the leader eventually acquires prestige—resulting from the half-emotional, half-intellectual attitude of the members of the group toward the leader. In time of chaos or unrest such leadership is most evident. Garvey was the perfect symbol. Peasant-born and without high status in his own country, Garvey developed the *Universal Negro Improvement Association and African Communities League* to redeem Africa for the black man. Initiated by the West Indian group it became the first Negro mass movement, with the additional unique feature of

1 W. E. B. DuBois pointed out that the paid-up membership never exceeded 300,000.

2 Thomas, W. I. and Znaniecki, F., *The Polish Peasant*, Knopf, New York, 1927, Vol. II, p. 1330.

being essentially nationalistic. The U. N. I. A. developed with all of the symbols, beliefs, and mythical social distinctions essential to the mass movement.

Garvey was a black man natured and nurtured under the tripartite color system of his native Jamaica. Wherever he went, writes Eric Walrond,[3] " whether to Wolmer's, the college patronized by the upper class mulattoes in Jamaica, or to Europe or to Central America as student and journalist, he was constantly reminded that he was black and that it was futile for him to rise above being a ' hewer of wood and drawer of water ' ". The conditions of this system aroused in him a deep resentment against mulattoes and whites as well as a determination to escape the pressure of the color bar. As early as 1914, after much European travel he attempted to raise the status of the Jamaican black masses by establishing the U. N. I. A. in Jamaica. By 1916 he had become interested in the United States and arrived in Harlem in the spring of that year.

As the story is told by James Weldon Johnson,[4] Garvey spent some time travelling around the United States and returned to New York in time to attend a mass meeting being called by Hubert Harrison, an outstanding West Indian lecturer (later editor of Garvey's *Negro World*), in order to organize the Liberty League. Garvey was asked to speak " and his magnetic personality, torrential eloquence, and intuitive knowledge of mob psychology were all brought into play ". He swept the audience with him and pledged support for Harrison's movement. But Garvey was not of the kidney to support anybody's movement; he set up the Universal Negro Improvement Association instead. It was natural that he should first appeal to the West Indians. Prejudice against them was rife. They rushed to his standard. He was one of their countrymen starting a new and wonderful movement of which no American Negro had ever thought. It was wonderful! It was thrilling!

3 Independent, January 3, 1933, " Imperator Africanus ", pp. 8-11.

4 *Black Manhattan*, Knopf, New York, 1930, p. 251 ff.

"They would show these damned American Negroes what British West Indians could do." [5]

The American Negroes, on the other hand, especially those in New York, reacted to this trend by calling the U. N. I. A. a "West Indian movement", which was actually true in New York City and Boston and to a certain extent in Philadelphia. Yet Garvey got the Spanish, French, and English-speaking Negro immigrant groups in large numbers to join with him. He established *The Negro World* as his publication and published sections in Spanish and French. He brought delegates to his mammoth conventions from the various states, Africa and the West Indies. He appealed to the fears and hopes of masses that had been victimized by the West Indian color-class system. His steamship company was *The Black Star Line;* his nurses were the *Black Cross Nurses;* his army the *Great African Army.* Christmas became symbolic of the Negro's birth among the nations of the world; Easter became the symbol of the resurrection of an oppressed and crucified race, the Negro.

In the U. N. I. A. all officers were given status in the best European court tradition. There were dukes and lords, Knight Commanders of the Distinguished Order of Ethiopia, and Knight Commanders of the Supreme Order of the Nile. There were gorgeous and resplendent uniforms, regalia and insignia, and strict court etiquette. The parades were so spectacular that they threatened the life of such older parading Negro lodges in New York City, as *The Independent Benevolent Protective Order of Elks of the World* and the *Knights of Pythias.* When his Supreme Highness the Potentate of the U. N. I. A. held his first annual court reception at Liberty Hall in August, 1921, it was an event of great social importance for the followers of the movement.

But the movement incited intra-racial antagonisms within and without the nationality groups. Though newsboys could not sell *The Negro World* on Harlem's streets because of the atti-

5 Brooks, Samuel L., "Marcus Garvey, An Analysis", *Interstate Tattler,* Vol. V, No. 27, February 21, 1925.

tude of the circulation offices of other Negro weeklies, Marcus Garvey cigars were available and sold well in neighborhood stationery stores. The native-born Negroes could not understand the economic principle underlying the operation of a steamship company, but the West Indians could and supported the movement. Garvey wanted all Negro peoples to join, but his emphasis upon the glories of blackness alienated many of the mixed bloods, both native and foreign-born. Afro-Utopia became less real. The appeal to racial idealism coupled with the exhibition of aristocratic trappings was too much for the less race-conscious Negroes to accept. One analyst believed that many of the West Indian and southern Negro followers came into the movement largely because of the titles, forms and illusory grandeurs. In the main, however, the movement both undermined the national patriotisms of the native and foreign-born groups, and arrested the conscious assimilation processes of the immigrants.

Perhaps no persons fought the Garvey movement more vehemently than did W. E. B. DuBois, editor of *The Crisis,* and A. Phillip Randolph and Chandler Owen, editors of *The Messenger*—both racially militant Negro monthly magazines. DuBois attacked with a vast compendium of facts and a facile pen. To him Garvey was essentially " an honest and sincere man with a tremendous vision, great dynamic force, stubborn determination and an unselfish desire to serve ", who also had " serious defects of temperament and training . . . dictatorial, domineering, inordinately vain and very suspicious . . . no business sense . . . no flair for real organization and with general objects so shot through with bombast and exaggeration that it is difficult to pin them down for careful examination ".[6] Yet he was, according to Dr. DuBois, an extraordinary leader of men who, with singular success capitalized and made vocal the great and long suffering grievances and spirit of protest among the almost leaderless West Indian peasantry, a

6 " Marcus Garvey ", *The Crisis,* December, 1920, pp. 58-59.

peasantry whose natural leaders, mulatto and black, had crossed the color-class line leaving them, with only the rudiments of education, grovelling at the bottom of the English colonial system.

To the radical *Messenger* group and others, Garvey was a nuisance, the "mudsill of Jamaican society", a "Supreme Negro Jamaican Jackass" [7] who represented the views of the ignorant West Indians only. This group urged the West Indians to become naturalized and fight the problem in the American way. This way was neither defined nor delineated. Propaganda against West Indians was so highly pitched that threats of bodily harm were made against a Trinidadian operating a department store in Harlem. While many foreign-born Negroes were vehemently and passionately opposed to Garvey's doctrine as it ultimately developed, others, as W. A. Domingo, a former officer of the U. N. I. A., pleaded for less emotionalism and fewer tirades against the man. All save Garvey's staunchest followers regarded him as dangerous to the racial welfare. The height of passionate recrimination, however, was reached in the following pen picture of Garvey.

"A Jamaican Negro of unmixed stock, squat, stocky, fat and sleek with protruding jaws and heavy jowls; small, bright pig-like eyes and rather full dog-like face. Beastful, egotistic, tyrannical, intolerant, cunning, smooth and suave, avaricious; as adroit as a fencer in changing front, as adept as a cuttle-fish in beclouding an issue he cannot meet, prolix to the nth degree in devising new schemes to gain the money of poor ignorant Negroes; gifted at self-advertisement, without shame in self-laudation, promising ever, but never fulfilling; without regard for veracity; a lover of pomp, tawdry finery and garish display; a bully with his own folk, but servile in the presence of the Klan; a sheer opportunist and a demagogic charlatan." [8]

7 *The Messenger*, Editorial, Vol. V, No. 1, January, 1923, p. 126.

8 Bagnall, Robert W., "The Madness of Marcus Garvey", *The Messenger*, Vol. V, No. 3, March, 1923, p. 638.

To these and other maledictions Garvey, upon his arrest for using the mails to defraud, replied—" There has never been a movement where the leader has not suffered for the cause, and not received the gratitude of the people. I, like the rest, am prepared for the consequence ".[9] Sentenced to five years in the Atlanta Federal Penitentiary for selling stock through the mails, Garvey was deported after serving nearly three years of the term.

Yet, Garvey and his movement, more so than any other individual or organization, succeeded in arousing a deep mass interest in the problem of darker races throughout the world. Almost as if overnight the provincialism of the American Negro's outlook on his economic plight disappeared. The development of " black nationalism " was the logical result of the meeting of two culture groups with a common racial bond —each proscribed and partially assimilated. Subject races consciously or unconsciously create some form of nationalist movement to substitute for those supplied to them by other races. The Back-to-Africa Movement, therefore, was based upon elements of racial individuality and embodied sentiments which spring out of the life experiences of Negroes, whether they be foreign or native.

This fact Garvey himself realized. In one of his later writings he maintained that " the very light element of Negroes don't want to go back to Africa. They believe that in time through miscegenation the American race will be of their

9 For full and interesting interpretation of Garvey see: Garvey, Mrs. Amy Jacques, *Philosophies and Opinions of Marcus Garvey*, N. Y. Universal Publishing House, 1923. Frazier, E. Franklin, " The American Negro's New Leaders," *Current History*, 28: 56-9, April 1928; " Garvey A Mass Leader," *Nation*, New York, 123, 147-8, August 18, 1926; " The Garvey Movement," *Opportunity*, 4, 346-8, November, 1926. DuBois, W. E. B., " Marcus Garvey ", *The Crisis*, December 20, 1920, pp. 58-59; January 1921, pp. 112-115. Hartt, Rollin Lynde, " The Negro Moses ", *The Independent*, February 26, 1921, p. 205. Talley, Truman Hughes, " Garvey's Empire of Ethiopia ", *World's Work*, January 1921, pp. 265-270.

type"[10] To the masses of West Indian immigrants and Southern migrants the pragmatic value of the symbol of blackness was limitless. Therefore, despite the manifest weaknesses of the organization it succeeded without benefit of the lighter colored population. As a mass-movement it satisfied the vanity and longings for something to give meaning to the lives of thousands of immigrants. The movement was essentially one of escape. It survived because it gave those newly urbanized groups status in a white world where they were nobodies.

The far-reaching effects of this movement are to be noted in Kepner's analysis of labor difficulties in Central America.[11]

> Although workers have grumbled often there has been little organized direct action in the banana zones until recently. Following the World War, when strikes were rife in many parts of the world, reverberations of these conflicts resounded in parts of the United Fruit Company's domain. In Costa Rica, for example, there were a number of strikes, ineffective for the most part. Except for one which was inspired by Marcus Garvey's racial movement, these strikes were spontaneous outbursts of indignation or strivings for better conditions, rather than culminations of the efforts of outside agitators. During the twenties no union organization existed in the banana region among banana, railway or dock workers. The backbone of these sporadic walkouts was broken when the company, by playing white and black workers against each other, persuaded sections of the strikers to return to work.
>
> For several months during the winter of 1918-1919 a strike of considerable magnitude prevailed on the United's Panamanian properties. The workers, who had no strong labor organization, had been aroused by the propaganda of Marcus Garvey and his *Negro World*, which infused labor struggles with racial antagonism. The company's officials, realizing the potential power of workers when aroused by unjust conditions, made certain concessions in the hope of breaking the strike and forestalling similar suspension of work in the future. These concessions, which the officials recognized to be no more than just considering the pre-

10 Garvey, Marcus, "Aims and Objects of a Movement for Solution of the Negro Problem Outlined," New York, 1924.

11 Kepner, *op. cit.*, pp. 180-181.

vailing cost of living, included some advance in wages and the issuing of hauling equipment without charge. Workers thus learned that wages need not be determined solely by the company's need for their individual services. They discovered the possibility of developing collective bargaining power.

Garvey as a leader made vital blunders. He assumed that the rôles of mulattoes and blacks in the United States were comparable with their status in the West Indies. By appealing to blacks, as such, he created an imbalance by driving a wedge between the mixed bloods and the blacks. Furthermore, in so doing he did not utilize the experience of the American Negro in dealing with problems of race. Not that the native Negro's experience was a successful one, but that it hurt the native Negro's pride to be overlooked when counsel and advice would have been most helpful to Garvey. Above all, the discipline of European culture and civilization, all that which was Europe and America in the Negro, particularly the thoughtful Negro, rebelled against the African scheme. The immigrant became less dependent upon tradition and more concerned with immediate success as Garvey's movement in the United States decayed with his enforced retirement. Schisms and splits developed, and the grandiose U. N. I. A. became the relic of a conflict era.

With the coming of the depression and the expansion of Father Divine's socio-religious program in Harlem, discussions arose over what Garvey would do were he in the United States in 1937. Writing in a Negro weekly, A. M. Wendell Malliet stated that

Garvey's hold and spectacular leadership would have created a situation in Harlem and Negro America like that which has developed in Germany under Hitler. Garveyism would have emboldened the mob and engendered intraracial and interracial strife. Garvey's personal leadership would have encouraged the masses to take things in their own hands whenever a situation was sufficiently provoking—if Garvey were in Harlem today.[12]

12 "If Garvey were in Harlem Today, Would Divine Vanish?", *New York Amsterdam News*, Vol. XXVIII, No. 27, June 12, 1937, p. 13.

Other Groups

Since 1925 the major group life of the immigrants who wish to maintain ethnic contacts has been through the various beneficial, social and cultural societies they have organized. These institutions have, in the main, been the direct outgrowth of circumstances and need. Thus one finds approximately 30 benevolent associations and mutual aid societies organized by immigrant groups from Anguilla, Antigua, Guiana, Dominica, Grenada, Montserrat, British Jamaica, St. Lucia, Turks Carios Island, Trinidad, and the British Virgin Islands. Numerous social clubs organized on the basis of color-class plus status in the United States; literary clubs, particularly among the British West Indians; cricket clubs and tennis associations. In addition, there are such politically centered groups as the Afro-American Voters Coalition, to foster naturalization and political participation; Utilities D'Haiti to promote the sale of Haitian products; Caribbean Fisheries to foster the development of commerce and trade in sea foods; several Virgin Island societies to promote the civic, political, economic and social welfare of the Virgin Islands and their people whether at home or abroad; the Consolidated Tenant's League to promote the housing interests of Negro residents; the West Indies Communities' Development League to encourage colonization in British Guiana; The Council on West Indian Affairs; the Jamaica Progressive League; and, The United Aid for Persons of African Descent. In March, 1933, the West Indian Federation of America was organized, stating as its immediate objectives the federation of and self-government for the various West Indian colonies; to stimulate an interest in West Indian affairs among British West Indians in America; and, to foster such industrial and commercial enterprises as may be considered necessary for the economic welfare of the group.[13] Fraternal

13 Similar societies exist in Boston and Cambridge, Mass., among which are the Jamaican Associates, the Barbadian Associates, the Bermuda Overseas Club, the West India Society, the Holy Name Society of Cape Verdeans, the U. N. I. A. and eight cricket clubs.

orders particularly prominent among West Indian immigrants are the Ancient Order of Free Gardeners, the Ancient Order of Foresters and the United Order of Mechanics.

The West Indian Committee of America proposes in its platform to stimulate the development of West Indian business enterprises; to give charitable assistance to West Indians in need; to aid them in securing satisfactory employment; to provide a clearing-house for all West Indian affairs; to publish a journal of West Indian opinion, " owned, controlled and edited by West Indians ", to encourage naturalization; and to promote cordial relations between West Indians and Afro-Americans.

Although these new groups were formed to satisfy specific needs their social function is not limited to their explicit and conscious purpose. Of equal importance are the social contacts between their members. Even when the abstract political and economic rationalizations have waned in importance, the association of the members becomes the most permanent bond for holding them together. The nature of their sessions is indicated in these parallel accounts of meetings held by the Jamaican Associates of Boston, Massachusetts, and the Cape Verdeans Smart Set Club of Providence, Rhode Island as reported in *The Chronicle*,[14] a Negro weekly paper of Boston, Massachusetts.

Occasionally many of these clubs combine for some special event—such as the coronation parties in New York. The affair sponsored by the All-Blue Club was supported by clubs representative of many other Caribbean groups including the Isthmica, Club Aristocrat, L'Arc en Ciel, Emanon, Altaire, Zodias, Concordia, Golden Glen, Clair de Lune, Karma, LaVivia, Lilac, Ajax, Solidaritée, Aster Social and Literary Club, Dutch Guiana League, Trinidad Athletic League and the Cosmopolitan Tennis Club.

The new setting provides new opportunities for leadership as the integration of the foreign-born Negro in New York is not yet complete. Any national or international situation involving

14 *The Boston Chronicle*, issues, March 16 and June 8, 1935.

CAPE VERDEAN NIGHT HELD

The Cape Verdean Smart Set Club connected with the Providence Y. W., observed its annual Cape Verdean night at the Y. W. on Thursday evening, March 7. There was a large gathering, with representative Cape Verdeans being invited as special guests. The guest speakers were Miss Gladys Doherty of the Y.W.C.A. staff; Miss Isabel Pifer, Aveline P. Araujo of the "A Vos Caboverdeana;" and Manuel Ledo of the International Longshoremen's Union.

The program included a welcome address by Miss Dorothy Reis; "Boa Festa" by Miss Isabel Fortes; Solo Mrs. Jennie Lopes; Song, "Moon Glow", Miss Mary Braz; Portuguese Folk Dance by a group of club girls; Song, Miss Candida Ramos; Song, "Amor", Mrs. Jennie Lopes; Song, Miss Adelina Lima, and several selections by the Strong Ensemble. Dancing for everyone followed the program.

The cabinet of the Cape Verdean Smart Set Club represented to the audience by the club president, Mrs. Viola LeMar, consisted of Mrs. LeMar, president; Celia Lima, vice president; Isabel Lima, secretary; Mary Lopes, treasurer; Hortense Ynoz, program; Dorothy Reis, social; Mary Lopes, membership chairman; Clara Babbitt, Adelina Lima, Ida Evans membership board; Anna Babbitt, reporter.

JAMAICAN ASSOCIATES

The final meeting for the season of the Jamaican Associates was held at L'Ouverture Hall, 1065 Tremont St., last Tuesday evening. Eric Jackson presided.

Quite a goodly number of the membership turned out and during the routine business George Tell was asked to report on his visit to the open meeting sponsored by the Roxbury Civic Club at St. Marks. Mr. Tell who was a delegate, gave a brief but somewhat unfavorable account.

Kenneth B. M. Crooks, Instructor of Chemistry at Hampton Institute, Va., was made an honorary member of the Society, and gave a short interesting talk on "prevailing conditions in the South".

After introducing the subject of "The Benefits of Cooperative Banking", the president gave the floor to Alfred Haughton, editor of the *Chronicle*, who spoke on the South End Cooperative Bank and Credit Union. A lively discussion followed.

On the suggestion of a Burial Fund brought in by the Board of Directors, Mr. Tell explained the matter in detail. It was decided that the matter be taken up in September.

OUTING IN AUGUST

The president called for suggestions as to a day and date for the annual outing and Sunday was the favored day. Power was given to the Entertainment Committee to decide between August 11 and 18.

The session closed with the serving of refreshments followed by dancing.

problems of race tends to be the cue for the resurgence of group animosities and interests. Street-corner speakers, who in Harlem are largely foreign-born, have been held responsible for much of this current animosity. The Sino-Japanese conflict, Garvey's program, the Scottsboro case and the Italian-Ethiopian war, have been their chief plaints. Their constant haranguings encouraged the formation of "The Committee of Twenty-five Native-Born Colored Americans" who banded themselves together to eliminate "this un-American gang from our midst".[15] In support of their determination, this newly formed group maintained that these "foreign-born agitators" fomented the Harlem riot. They "never have a kind word to say of our institutions or of our accomplishments. Their mentality is focused abroad. Ignorant of the inevitable consequences of their acts, they destroy what they seek to build. They have no program of progress. The native-born Negro, as well as the responsible citizen of foreign birth, should wake up to this community menace, take steps to clean house and sweep this riff-raff from Harlem's streets". The reactions of this Committee indicate the development of new attitudes leading to activities which do not comply with the socially recognized and sanctioned schemes of behavior.[16]

It is significant, however, that the antagonism of the native-born committee becomes vocal only in times of increased social maladjustments. Street-corner speaking has been a symbol of Harlem's social disorganization ever since the World War. And though the mere presence of these speakers indicates integration in process, it also represents a conflict phase in immigrant-native adjustment. But as adjustment is effected, special interest groups of the foreign-born Negro tend to be organized around three factors; (1) economic and political adjustment in the United States, (2) mutual benefit organizations, and (3) organizations to foster and perpetuate desirable conditions in,

15 As reported in *The New York Age*, August 8, 1936.

16 *Cf.* handbill distributed by the *For America Association*, p. 169.

and relations with the homeland. Leaders of the first two groups tend to be those who have most successfully adjusted themselves to new economic and political conditions. Success in these fields automatically gives them prestige with the third special interest group, in which they serve as the titular if not the functional leaders. The transference of leadership and values in this intra-group situation is no different from the pattern followed in the inter-racial movements of the United States.

5. NATURALIZATION AND CITIZENSHIP

The improvement that the Negro immigrant in the United States experiences with regard to physical condition, and the availability of food, clothing, shelter, is catholic to all immigrants. However, the social recognition as an individual which was obtained in his homeland does not exist in the States. This social situation is his *bete noir* of American citizenship. It explains in part why the Negro immigrant becomes naturalized at a very slow rate, since, until he is thoroughly assimilated, he finds little social advantage in naturalization. Furthermore, becoming naturalized attracts the unfavorable criticism of his fellow-countrymen who have kept their nationality. Being a subject of King George VI, or a citizen of the British Empire, or a Frenchman, is no mean distinction in a country where Negroes are socially mobile only unto themselves, and where the frontier practices of segregation and lynching are still part of the culture.

However, the extent of naturalization among foreign-born Negroes is not to be regarded as an adequate measure of the degree of assimilation. The two-fold process of naturalization involving bestowal of the rights of a native citizen upon a foreigner, who, in turn, renounces his former national fidelities, frequently means only that and nothing more to the Negro immigrant. In many instances, he renounces more political rights than he gains by becoming an American citizen. This phase will be discussed later. For the time being, let it be observed that it has been only in recent years that any major efforts have been made toward increasing the naturalization of foreign-born Negroes. Theirs is truly a citizenship with reservations.

Young has aptly observed that "A Negro born and reared in any place on earth may become a naturalized American citizen by complying with the same regulations as an European immigrant. Our courts are forbidden to issue naturalization papers to Chinese, Japanese, and other Orientals. Indians born in Canada have been refused the privilege of citizenship, although Mexicans, be they pure bloods of the same racial stock, have been made citizens on application as though they were white. The Ainu of Japan, biologically white, are in effect Orientals before the law. These are but a few of the capricious contrasts which may well bewilder the student of race relations if he allows himself to be misled by anthropological classifications which have no standing in the eyes of the law or by his false expectation that common prejudices always find recognition in the statute books".[17]

The earlier naturalization laws adopted between 1790 and 1854 limited the privilege of citizenship by adoption to "free white persons". It was not until after the adoption of the Thirteenth, Fourteenth, and Fifteenth Amendments, that the law extended the right of naturalization to Negroes—classified as "aliens of African nativity" and "persons of African descent". Since 1870, no extension has been made in the law.

The present laws governing naturalization require:

1. That the alien be either white or of African descent.
2. He must have been legally admitted for permanent residence.
3. He must have resided in the United States for at least five years prior to his application, and for the last six months in the county where he applies.
4. He must be of good moral character.

17 Young, Donald, *op. cit.*, p. 195.

5. He must be " attached to " the principles of the Constitution of the United States.
6. He must be able to speak the English language.

None of these requirements makes any especial hardship for the Negro immigrant.

Extent of Naturalization

Since 1890 data on the citizenship of foreign-born Negroes have been available through the Federal Census. The returns for 1890, 1900 and 1910, however, referred only to the citizenship of foreign-born males 21 years of age and over. Data for both sexes were not available until 1920. In 1930 there were 7,919,536 naturalized citizens in the United States of whom 24,815 (three-tenths of one per cent) were Negroes; 15,024 males and 9,791 females. Practically all (94 per cent) of the naturalized Negroes were over 21 years of age, the remaining 6 per cent deriving citizenship through their parents' naturalization. Of the foreign-born Negro population 21 years of age and over, in 1930, 25.6 per cent were naturalized, 10.5 per cent had their first papers, 55.2 per cent were aliens and the citizenship status of 8.7 per cent was unknown. Comparing these facts with the foreign-born white for the same period, we find that among them 60.4 per cent were naturalized, 9.6 per cent had their first papers, 25.6 per cent were aliens and the citizenship status of 3.6 per cent was unknown.

The per cent of foreign-born Negroes and whites naturalized at the various censuses since 1900 is shown in the following table.[18]

18 Statistics on naturalization by color are not available for 1890. The percentages cited by Davie, Maurice R., *World Immigration*, p. 541 are for all foreign-born males. See: *Eleventh Census of the United States*, 1890, Population, Vol. II, p. lxvi.

PERCENTAGE OF FOREIGN-BORN NEGRO AND WHITE POPULATIONS OF THE UNITED STATES, 21 YEARS AND OVER, NATURALIZED

By Sex, 1900–1930

Year	Foreign-born Negroes		Foreign-born Whites	
	Male	Female	Male	Female
1930	28.3	22.3	62.0	58.4
1920	13.9	18.3	49.0	52.9
1910	19.8	—	46.2	—
1900	32.2	—	58.0	—

Source: Fifteenth Census of the United States, 1930. Population, Vol. II, p. 405 ff.

Race, however, appears to be only an incidental factor in the naturalization rate of Negroes. It is to be expected that their rate of naturalization will increase as the year of their immigration recedes. In the main, unhampered by the language difficulty, the Negro immigrant faces only the barrier of racial proscription. Coming from areas of inferior economic opportunity and some social discontent, it would be expected that a higher rate of naturalization would prevail. The explanation of such differences as are found between Negro and non-Negro groups must be sought in the attitudes of the Negro group and in the degree of social and economic status attained while here.

For the Negro immigrant from the French or British West Indies, particularly, the label of democracy is found to be fictional. Accustomed to class lines that he has learned to respect even though he may hate them, he can find little of immediate solace in a system that brands him as inferior even before he is known. Acceptance of an inferior social status, that is urged upon him abruptly, is not easily done even if the economic conditions are materially improved. The marked decline in the percentage of foreign-born Negroes returned as naturalized which occurred between 1900 and 1910 was due to the tremendous increase in Negro immigration, which began in 1903 and which continued through 1920. Between 1920 and 1930 there was a decrease in the number of Negro immigrants, which, in conjunction with the ever-increasing assimilation of the Negro immigrant resulted in a naturalization peak of 28.3 per cent for the Negro male, which was lower than the 1900 percentage of 32.2.

Unfortunately, data on naturalization by country of birth are not available for the Negro foreign-born population. It is interesting to observe, however, that the per cent of Negro aliens naturalized is lower than the rates for the 27 leading nationalities recorded by the country of birth for foreign-born whites. The Negro being a newer immigrant has not been in the country so long as have many of the persons from countries having a higher rate. It is significant that the highest percentages of naturalized Negro immigrants in 1930, were found in the states of Ohio, Illinois and Indiana. In these areas, more than two-fifths of the foreign-born Negroes were naturalized; in the states of New York, Massachusetts and California approximately one-fourth; and in Florida, the most accessible state to the Caribbean, approximately one-eighth. More than one-half of the total naturalized population resides in New York State. (Table XVI)

It frequently happens, however, that a change in the ebb and flow of economic activity may determine the volume of naturalization for any group. During good years, or in the upward trend of business cycles, the naturalization rate tends to mount near the end of the period. Likewise, the emotional strength of such a movement as Marcus Garvey's Universal Negro Improvement Association, active during the days of greatest Negro immigration, may hinder the naturalization process through its emphasis upon a new black empire. Similarly, the efforts of a Father Divine whose movement is not interested in the question of political citizenship, may deter the movement through its emphasis on a religious citizenship. Over and above all these, however, the question of one's "bread and butter" ranks first, whether it be attained through direct or indirect channels. Thus, politics, and the quest for individual security as found in governmental positions open only to citizens, become potent forces determining the rate of naturalization.

Boston, and New York offer the best examples of how such forces can influence naturalization movements. For some years now a slow and steady pressure from the naturalized foreign-born Negro has been exerted upon the non-naturalized, largely through the *Boston Chronicle,* a Negro weekly, published by foreign-born Negroes and *The New York Amsterdam News.* In New York an increasing political strength accompanied by the election of some foreign-born Negroes to office, one as a magistrate, plus the fact that the leader of one of the most active Democratic Clubs in Harlem is himself foreign-born, have been both a push and a pull for citizenship. No less effective a naturalization instrument has been the fear accompanying depressions when non-citizens may be excluded from relief programs. The *Washington Tribune,* another Negro weekly, commented as follows upon the proposed dropping of foreign-born or unnaturalized persons from WPA.

It is expected that this step will affect the jobs of 120,000 persons on emergency work relief, chiefly in New York and New Mexico, and will include many Negroes from the West Indies and Africa.[19]

In 1937 the masthead of the *New York Amsterdam News,* Harlem's foremost weekly paper, carried this boxed statement

Become a Citizen—Prepare to vote. The Negro's strength in affairs which concern his very existence is gauged by his ballot. If you are not a citizen, become one. The United States Naturalization Service has division offices at 641 Washington Street, Manhattan, Canal 6-2100.[20]

In the Fall of 1936 the National Negro Independent Political League was organized in New York City " to encourage citizen-

19 *Washington Tribune, Washington, D. C.,* February 3, 1936, " Drive on Jobless Opens with Attack on Foreign-Born ".

20 *Amsterdam News,* New York, N. Y., Saturday, January 23, 1937.

ship among our non-citizens; encourage membership and assist them in getting citizenship papers ".[21]

But the problem cannot be expressed better than has been done by one naturalized citizen, now 74 years of age, who received his final papers some 44 years ago. Born in the British West Indies Mr. ——— came to the United States in 1884 and received his citizenship papers in 1892. Excerpts from the interview indicate most emphatically his views as a naturalized citizen, and as a person who has conducted a naturalization school:

> When I first came—I believed and still believe, that an alien intending to remain here and enjoy privileges, whether for weal or woe, ought to become a citizen of the United States. If he doesn't like it here, he ought to return from whence he came.[22] If a foreigner, whether he be white or black, were contented at home he would not leave it to come here and receive less.
>
> With all of the disfranchisement in the Southern states, I believe that this is the best country in the world for the Negro. Regardless of what they might say, West Indians in this country have received many benefits from citizenships.[23]

Mr. ——— is bitterly opposed to those West Indians in this country who, by claiming birth in some Southern State which doesn't keep birth records, vote and even receive Civil Service appointments without becoming naturalized:

> The first one I catch . . . I shall have him prosecuted . . . I shall never stop teaching the advantages of citizenship. . . . As long as I live, I shall do everything in my power to help West Indians, or any other foreigners coming to this country, to become useful citizens of the United States.

Citizenship for the foreign-born Negroes is something that Negro immigrants feel should be studied very carefully. When

21 *New York Age*, New York, September 12, 1936, "New Organization to Aid West Indians in Naturalization Cases."

22 The editor of a Negro newspaper is alleged to have made practically the same remark at a Harlem forum in 1935.

23 *Amsterdam News*, New York, N. Y., July 4, 1936, "Oldest Naturalized West Indian Proud of American Citizenship."

its rewards become apparent, they usually seek to qualify themselves for it. The method of adjustment to this "citizenship with reservations" varies North and South—in the North the emphasis being upon collective action, political and economic; while in the South, economic individualism has predominated. Yet, the foreign-born Negroes do come to the United States, and they do become citizens even as do other eligible groups. Social and cultural factors alone determine the rate and tempo of its occurrence.

Politics

Increasingly the naturalized Negro citizen is becoming an important power in the political life of such northern communities as New York and Boston. In New York, particularly, the force of his presence is keenly felt. The West Indian immigrants brought to the United States express an interest in population representation as well as a desire for political responsibility. They have made themselves a special interest group, holding the balance of power in many Harlem precincts. Today, in New York, the influence of foreign-born Negroes is more potent than ever. Not only have they been able to secure the election of one of their number to the magistrate's bench of New York City, but they have also received several appointive positions.

Furthermore, the only Negro presidential elector from New York State in 1932 and 1936 was a naturalized citizen of high civic and social standing. One of the foremost of New York's famous political clubs, located in Harlem, is headed by a West Indian Negro, one of the three Negro Democratic designees for the New York State Constitutional Convention of 1938. In fact, so effective has been their participation in politics that dissatisfied native-born Americans have circulated rumors to the effect that there is a conscious political effort on the part of West Indians to capture New York for themselves.

This activity of West Indian Negroes has led to mutual jealousies and recriminations and is alleged to be an important factor in preventing an eligible naturalized citizen from being named to an important federal office in New York. Furthermore, at the time of the last presidential campaign, fights were waged over Democratic leadership in New York State to prevent the West Indian from obtaining a stronger grip on the Harlem political machine. The situation seems to reach an impasse whenever important issues or desirable political plums are available. One observer reports that:

> The position is getting worse and worse daily. It is known that several public offices of honor, note and dignity have been recently allowed to get out of the hands of the colored people because of mutual intraracial jealousies. It has occurred that political offices, which could have been won at election, if there was united action, were lost to the whites because there was a common understanding that rather than allow it to go to a member of one or the other faction or group (the naturalized citizen) it would be preferable in their own blindness that the whites should win.[24]

In the tensely fought mayoralty campaign of 1937 appeals to nationality prejudices were used as the basis for electing a native-born Negro woman as one of the district leaders. The hand-bill shown on the following page was distributed among Harlem voters at that time. A fact not stated in the hand-bill, however, is that Mrs. Haynes did not support the district leader's program in the primary and, according to the rules of the game, was scheduled to be ousted.

To many of our immigrants politics has become a primary rather than a secondary interest. Campaigning and electioneering have been done with independence and variety. Street-corner speaking has been made an effective means of proselyting. Only the low rate of naturalization has prevented a greater participation in voting. This political activity may be expected to grow for some time. The Negro foreign-born population is relatively young, and has the potentialities for tripling the size of its naturalized members. As it has tasted and obtained power, it may retain its influence and develop more. On the other hand, a

24 Petioni, Charles A., "The Inter-racial Problem," *Education, A Journal of Reputation*, Vol. II, No. 2, May-June, 1936, p. 2.

decreasing volume of immigration may eventually render puerile and ineffective such foreign born-native born schisms as have developed in the past, and lead to a more militant and united political action.

> IS THIS FAIR?
>
> BRUCE ousts Mrs. Elizabeth Ross Haynes
>
> So He Can Have a West Indian Woman For Co-Leader!
>
> IS THIS FAIR?
>
> Leader Bruce is a West Indian!
>
> The State Committeeman Thomas B. Dyett —Is A— West Indian!
>
> The Majority of his Negro Job Holders are West Indians!
>
> ---
>
> Mrs. Haynes Must Be Thrown Out
> NOW — To Make Room For A Co-Leader
> Who Is A West Indian! ! !

Summary

The foregoing materials indicate that the Negro immigrant is not only a "problem" and a producer of "problems", but also an agent of social benefits to the native Negro population. It is evident that the immigrant is economically better situated than in his original or native home. Migration to the United States opened up new worlds, a broader vision, and a generally more satisfactory life. On the other hand, the very experiences which the immigrants and foreign-born have are sources of friction, for Negro immigrants are not seeking new ideas and new moral codes. Painful to native and foreign alike, though the adjustment may be, it does effect a more virile, a less narrow-minded Negro population in the United States. Two illustrations will serve to show this change.

During the summer of 1938 the British West Indies witnessed a series of labor strikes, riots and police shootings in Kingston, Jamaica. In October, the Rev. Ethelred Brown, Secretary of the Jamaica Progressive League of New York, was sent to Jamaica to represent that organization at the hearings to be conducted by the British Royal Commission appointed by Mr. Malcolm MacDonald, British Secretary of State for the Colonies. For the first time Jamaicans in New York have taken an active part in the politics and struggles of their homeland—and they are aided and encouraged to a great extent by the native agencies and institutions.[25]

The second example is an open letter to the " West Indian Readers " of the *Pittsburgh Courier,* written by Robert L. Vann, its publisher. In the feature spot of its September 10, (1938) issue, Mr. Vann appeals to these readers in a two column spread to support the cause of the Hon. W. Algernon Crawford representative of the *Barbados* (BWI) *Observer.* Says Publisher Vann " about the only independent mouthpiece the Islanders have ", *The Observer,* is facing extinction and the *Courier* is seeking through this letter to aid Crawford's campaign. The statement is indicative of the broader perspective through which the United States born Negro now views his racial setting, He continues

> You have come to this country for one reason or another, and you are now enjoying the fruits of your labor, regardless of when you work and regardless of what you earn. Whatever reason impelled you to leave the Islands is your business, but you cannot turn your back indifferently upon conditions which you found it necessary to leave. . . .
>
> . . . Dear brethren, the conditions in the United States can be neglected for a moment in order to help conditions in the Islands, which are a million times worse than the conditions you complain of in the United States.

And for the first time groups of foreign-born Negroes are admitting that such a statement is not far-fetched. That is progress.

25 *The New York Amsterdam News,* September 10, 1938.

CHAPTER VIII

THE NEGRO IMMIGRANT'S LIFE STORY

A PARTIAL explanation of an individual's behavior is found in his past experiences. The autobiographical statements presented in this chapter indicate the most important mental and material characteristics of a series of individuals who have become a part of the Negro population of the United States. The composite story of Negro immigration is well told in this collective autobiography of a Virgin Islander, who, though from one of the United States insular dependencies and not subject to immigration quotas, is regarded by the native-born Negro as a " foreigner ". In this story one notes: (1) the existence of an occupational and color hierarchy; (2) antipathies against the new British West Indian immigrants; (3) the organized struggle for freedom so different from that waged by the American Negro; (4) the psychological reaction to returned migrants, largely because of the external changes in clothes, manners and language; (5) the evaporation of class distinctions upon arrival in the United States, accompanied by an awareness that the folks back home must never know; (6) the ruses for 'keeping up" appearances and maintaining prestige; (7) the escape-mechanism afforded by New York's night life; (8) the disturbing variants of religious practices; and (9) the conflict with the native-born Negroes and the attempt to discard the visible indices of the Virgin Island culture.

The story is told by a Virgin Islander now holding a professional position in the United States.

A COLLECTIVE AUTOBIOGRAPHY

I am a Virgin Islander. I may belong to one of many classes. I may be a laborer of the sugar-cane fields and factories. I am a worker at many trades, a clerk, owner of many businesses and acres of land. I may be a government employee, a politician, or a professional man. I may be a black, a mulatto, a "buckra".[1] I may be an educator or a member of the professions in any part of the United States. Whatever I am or wherever I am, I am a Virgin Islander.

As a laborer, I plough the fields and plant stalks of sugar-cane. Through my care they grow into succulent long-jointed stalks. I cut, load, and transport them by mule carts and wagons, or perhaps, by locomotive-drawn cars to the factories. There I load the stalks on the carriers and send them through the great rollers. I turn the juice into syrup, the syrup into sugar and molasses, and the molasses into rum. I am in charge of the centrifugal machinery that crystalizes the syrup. As such, I occupy a more superior position than I would if I were laboring at the carrier. And as a worker at the carrier, I am more superior in social status than if I were to labor in the fields. I am a native. As such, I am better than my fellow field workers at the right. These are newcomers from the British West Indies. I look down with disdain and contempt upon these contracted laborers. I am superior for I can move from place to place and work for whom I will. But at times I forget my prejudices, join hands with my fellow-workers and fight for human rights and freedom.

Three times have I fought. In my struggles I have used the cutlass, the torch, the bill, and the strike. When the Crown in 1848 decreed that every newborn and every child not beyond the age of twelve shall be free, I incarnated myself into General Buddhoe, rose from the ranks of those left in bondage and said: "Like our children, freedom and liberty are our due. The masters plan to keep us in slavery. You who would be free follow me."

I fought and led my people to freedom. I started the "Fire-bu'n." It was in 1878. For my labor I was receiving measured rations and a mere pittance in wages. The owners of the estates lived lavishly. Many of the planters were Irish. At the time when they were refusing to pay me higher wages and give me freedom of movement, they were sending money to Ireland to finance the movement for Irish freedom. Unable to obtain higher wages, I applied for passports in order to go to the Spanish Main. But

1 Term applied to whites in the Caribbean, and in the Southeastern area of the United States, particularly Georgia and South Carolina.

the planters and government would not let me go. Then I burned the factories, the mansions of the rich, and the hovels of the villages. I re-incarnated myself into "Queen Mary" and wreaked vengeance upon the heads of those responsible. "Ourside or Ironside" was my battle-cry. I burned the houses of those who were not on ourside. I sat in the parlors of the buckras, and I rocked myself in their rocking chairs. I commanded: "Fan me, missus, fan me," and they fanned me as I, their former servant had once fanned them. But because I tend to shirk drudgery, and am prone, except in times of strife, to avoid extreme sacrifices; because of the ease with which I forget events of the past, and my failure to be vigilant, wrongs, once righted, stealthily crept up again upon me. I was no longer free. Today my weapons are the newspaper and the strike. The weapons of 1848, 1878, had given way to those of 1915. In the newspapers I castigated the officials, the middle-class and the planters. I struck. They turned me out of their villages. I trekked to the city. There my brother laborers shared their lodgings and victuals with me. I suffered. But through my sufferings I raised the price of labor. As a memorial to my sufferings I founded and dedicated Liberty Day. I celebrate November the first as a symbol of my freedom. Freedom, not from the drudgery of the fields and farms, but from fear and poverty. Liberty Day is not merely a day of Thanksgiving and joy, but one dedicated to the establishment of better social conditions; the removal of hatred and false pride.

I am a Virgin Islander. I do not work only in the fields, but also round about the town. I do domestic service—wash, scrub, and cook. Even though I scrub, wash, and cook, and get less for my labor, I, as a domestic worker, am superior to those who are field laborers. I rank one notch higher in the scale of things. I am a worker at the trades — carpentry, tinsmithing, tailoring, dressmaking, and goldsmithing. To me many apprentices come. I require that the apprentices do the ordinary chores around the shop and house. Yet, I must be careful of the type of tasks I require certain of my apprentices to do. Customs and traditions do not permit the sons and daughters of the middle-class to do the same type of chores as the sons and daughters of domestic workers and shop employees. Yet both can go to the same "boss". I work as a clerk, but as a clerk, belonging to, or becoming a member of the genteel class, I can seek employment only in stores that sell dry goods and sundry wearing apparel and materials. For I as a clerk in the provisions and meat shops am generally considered to be one class below I as a clerk in the dry goods establishment. I am also an owner of stores and shops. I am an ambitious, progressive Negro. I possess natural business acumen. I am able to make a success of my business and acquire property. With my hostler, bay gelding, and rubber-tired carriage, I drive up and down the town, over the Center Line Road with its tall and graceful royal palms. There I meet the white planters. My hostler says to me: "John, cock your foot, let buckra see you".

I am a Virgin Islander—a laborer, a master tradesman, a businessman, whatever I am, I can make one "heap of all my winnings" and risk it on foreign shores. I am an inveterate traveler. The size of the islands, their topography, limited natural resources and opportunities have made me so. Surrounded by water, I develop an adventurous and hardy spirit. I cannot expand the area of the islands nor increase beyond a certain point its economic opportunities. I set sail on the Caribbean, seeking greater economic and educational opportunities. New York City is my Mecca. I read and hear of the schools and colleges of this city and the States. Those who have preceded me at times return. Their transformation seems miraculous to me. With new suits and dresses, new habits and a new brogue, the returning ones often-times seem to be persons who have been born again. I long to be in such a land. Consequently, I set sail seeking new opportunities and the "pot of gold". For the glaring tales of the well-dressed visitors conspired to make me believe that gold grows on the trees of the sidewalks of New York.

I am in New York. Dazzled by the bright lights? Yes. Bewildered by the fast ways? Most assuredly. I long for those I knew, for the familiar spots that meant so much to me. Frantically I write letters, a dozen, two dozens a week. Anxiously I await the weekly arrival of the mail. Through the letters I live vicariously the events of the homeland. I feel the longings, the hankerings; the petition is always there: hurry up and send me the steamer fare. I walk the streets and avenues of Harlem. I look into every face. Recognizing one, I am filled with joy. We exchange experiences and news. In such moments, the differences due to class distinction disappear. I must settle down to the task of finding a job. Soon, I shall be rudely awakened. At home I was a clerk. My beginning salary might have been fifteen dollars per month. I was led to despise the tasks of the porter. I could not buy my own groceries and carry the packages and baskets from the shop to my home. Care not how small the salary was, I had a position. Now I have to work at a job, a menial job at that. Usually, my first position is that of being a porter or an elevator runner. I cannot write home and inform my friends of the nature of my work. If I should venture to say anything concerning the nature of my job, I must state that I am working downtown, New York, in one of the largest, best, oldest establishments. It is always good policy to let my friends do the surmising as to the nature of my job. To add the element of plausibleness to any of their suppositions, at times I use the letterheads and envelopes of "my firm". Gradually, my correspondence becomes less and less until I communicate rarely with any at home, except my immediate family. I can always depend upon family pride to keep the exact nature of my task a secret. As a matter of fact, at times, it is very much magnified.

But the foregoing hypocritical state cannot be maintained for long without deadly effect. I grow restless, dissatisfied, maladjusted. I think constantly of the job as one being both below my dignity and ability. I try to avoid, after the first meeting, the new arrivals. To compensate, I dance, dine and wine. I join the sporting fraternity. At home I look askance upon gambling. But, here, I try to gamble my way through life. I join the benevolent and political organizations of my countrymen. But among the membership of these organizations I do not find many of the middle-class. The bulk of the membership is made up of the former tillers of the soil, skilled, semi-skilled, and unskilled workers. It seems that while the sons and daughters of the upper classes fiddle and dance away their time, those accustomed to do honest labor with their hands, the dependable and hardy, with great love of home, are always working for the rehabilitation of the islands. Periodically, my conscience pricks me. Did I not make a vow that I would become one of the most educated of natives? At night I lie awake in bed. The sacred promise to return some day and take part in the amelioration of conditions and the breaking up of the senseless class distinction looms large before me. I picture myself as the ideal citizen, businessman, teacher, judge, yea even governor. I am awake. My humdrum, mechanical and monotonous elevator job calls me.

On Sundays, all day at times, while my friends strut and stroll up and down the avenue, I try to solve algebraic problems. I lie on the couch and dream. The fire of ambition burns within. I take upon my shoulders all the burdens of my people. I recoil; am filled with a feeling of despair and impotence. Something within drives me out at dusk into the street. I visit many of the religious sects conducting services in basements and places formerly occupied by saloons and stores. In none can I find that overpowering calmness, that majestic serenity, that can allay a troubled mind. I am unable to reconcile myself to these sects and their manner of expressing their religious experiences. It seems to me that there is too much crudity, too much boisterousness, too much secular activities carried on in these places supposedly devoted to the worship of God. Nor am I able to get any solace, experience any spiritual rebirth when I attend the better organized and more orderly conducted congregations. In fact, very seldom am I in the mood even to attend the services of the denomination in which I was christened. Before I came to the States I knew of only four organized religious denominations: the Roman Catholic Church, the Episcopal—a branch of the Church of England, the Lutheran—the State Church during the Danish regime, and the Moravian Church—the first mission of which was established more than one hundred years ago. The services of these denominations were conducted in a dignified, restrained manner. The ministers and priests were white. The secular activities of the denominations were rigidly kept out of the church edifices. When I entered one of these placed of worship I was filled with an appreciation of, and a deep reverence for, the omnipresence and omniscience of an unlimited and universal power. Now I find it difficult to reconcile myself to the multiplicity of sects in the States, the many temporal uses to which the church buildings are put, and even at times, to the officiating of colored ministers.

Just as I am dissatisfied with my religious experiences and growth, so I am with my educational progress. I enter one of the evening high schools. But in my haste to finsh my preparation, I transfer to a private college preparatory school. I find it difficult to settle down. At night I walk the streets and listen to the political discussions and harangues. Having no definite political bent, I listen to the speakers of all parties. I am impressed with the argument that the Republican Party has no perpetual mortgage on the allegiance of the Negro; that the Negro has long since paid the debt due to the Republican Party because of the services of Lincoln; that the Negro should be an unpredictable factor and support the party from which he can get the most. I am sympathetic toward the arguments of the Socialists. They point out that there are no great differences between the two major parties. They prove to me that a vote for the Socialist Party is not a vote thrown away; that I have more to gain by supporting them. I find more of my countrymen active in the Socialist and Democratic Parties, particularly the former. The Socialists seem to make special bids for my support. Being free from the traditional political prejudices, I find myself one time a Socialist, another time a Democrat. I attend one meeting, then another. Suddenly it dawns upon me that I am not here to dream. My aspirations begin to prod me on; my taste and ideals begin to come in conflict with the general interests and activities of the group in which I ordinarily find companionship and pleasure. I abruptly leave the city.

I matriculate at Howard, Hampton, Lincoln, Wisconsin, Columbia, Harvard, and Brown. Or perhaps, through travel and self-directed study, I become a recognized authority in the field of literature and African history and folklore. At school they think I am smart, a lover of books and a social failure. My fellow American students insist on fitting me into preconceived, stereotyped opinions. I win scholarships, medals and honors. They say I am a bookworm. I am supposed to know West Indians coming from other islands separated by a thousand miles of water from my own. I am supposed to speak with a certain accent, and that accent must be the Jamaican accent, regardless from which island I come. I am subjected to good-natured mimicry. At times an impetuous person may poke fun at me in my presence. If this should occur too frequently, like a sensitive child, I begin to avoid large groups, to spend my time reading, to keep away from many of the social activities, to apply myself diligently to the task of correcting the grosser differences between mine and my fellow students' method of accenting words. Withal, I am liked, respected, and usually elected to many of the important positions by the student body. If I stand out among my fellow students, it is because I have passed through a finer sieve. Usually, I am among the most ambitious and striving of my group. My fundamental training, generally speaking, is better. I tend to have a better perspective because I am impelled by a master desire. Things in the immediate present tend not to loom up large and important, thereby overestimated; things in the distance—education, prestige, admittance to a higher social class—do not appear small and inconsequential, thereby becoming under-estimated.

The general public also has stereotyped opinions about me. I am honest, true and jealous in love; dependable, impetuous and hot-headed; sly and vindictive; successful in most of my undertakings. The Spanish-American War is largely responsible for many of these preconceived notions. This War did two things: first, American Negroes for the first time on a large scale, went away from the mainland and came in contact with Negroes living in their own habitation and, generally, the type of Negroes with whom they came in contact were of that class of people which follows armies for many diverse reasons; secondly, it was about this time that West Indians in large numbers started to emigrate to the States. Undoubtedly, the Cuban Negroes with whom the troops came in contact possessed the proverbial Latin temperament — earnest, quick in action, proud and retaliatory in nature. The returning troops ascribed indiscriminately these traits to all West Indian Negroes, and the troops succinctly expressed both their contempt of, and admiration for, the West Indian Negroes with the phrase: "A West Indian Cuban Negro". If a West Indian should commit a crime in New York, and I am in Georgia, I am shown the account which is featured in glaring headlines in our colored newspapers, and made to feel that West Indians are hot-headed, vindictive and vicious.

In the early part of the century, especially in New York, the West Indian Negro was most successful in winning the affection of the America colored women. The stereotyped opinion was that he supported more adequately than the American Negro the woman of his love. Now, as then, I am branded as a jealous man. I do not tolerate the most innocent flirtation. It takes a brave girl to "go" with me. Such a one is labeled as the "girl who goes with the foreigner". She is constantly warned to be careful, for I am serious and jealous, do not think highly of her, or perhaps, I am ardent, passionate, sensual. Friends and relatives tease her continuously. When I take her as my wife, I have to allay the fears of her parents and promise that my jealous nature will never impel me to mal-treat her. They are afraid that I will one day establish my residence at the place of my birth and thus endanger the safety of my wife. For, the women of my home do not like their men folk to marry one that is not a native. And so, on and on it goes.

Marcus Garvey has also contributed to the formulation of some stereotyped conceptions of the West Indian Negro. If I propose a scheme beyond the grasp of my listeners and thereby seem fantastic, I am warned: "Don't be a Garvey." If I refuse to change opinions and manners, or ways of doing things, I am exhorted: "Don't be a Garvey." Presently, all the contempt, all the respects, all the jealousy, all the sentimentality once included in the phrase: "West Indian Cuban Nigger", are now conveyed by: "Don't be a Garvey".

I am a Virgin Islander. I usually return home. During my temporary stay, I enjoy many perfect days. I walk along the lanes and byways of my home. I roam through shrubbery and fields of grass. The ruins of buildings and lonely arches and columns grimly remind me of a civilization that hoped to be. I go to the crescent-shaped beach that runs along the roadstead. In this land that once furnished safe havens to the buccaneers, where the torch razed magnificent buildings, where men keep up constant fight for economic justice and political rights, I find solace. Over and above the turmoil there seems to soar a weirdness that soothes my soul and lures me into forgetfulness. But it is only a visit.

ON LEAVING HOME

More personal aspects are revealed in the following documents. Not only do economic forces impel migration to the United States, but colored peoples may easily encounter such a variety of social experiences at home as will dispose them to restlessness and migration.

Emelen Craig is a native of Lagos, West Africa, and came to the United States via England.

During my early years in Lagos, America was never a country in my dreams of travel. This is not an astonishing fact, for our education in the government and mission schools was so narrow that I think I only knew of the Gold Coast, Sierra Leone and England. People were constantly coming from or going to these countries. Going to study in England is the dream of every young Lagosian. My father, a lawyer in Lagos, sent me to England at the age of nine. At all the schools I attended I was always the only colored girl and it was not until the age of sixteen that I began to come into contact with other Africans studying in London. It was then I began to differentiate between myself and the English girls. I became very race conscious; proud of my country and I got a thrill from it. I longed to return home and to be able to help my people and free them from the trials of a subject nation.

At the age of eighteen I entered the Froebel Educational Institute in London, to take the three year teacher-training course, for the teaching of children between the ages of nine and twelve. When I received my diploma I was to go home with my mother who was to arrive during my final year. Before she arrived I received a most surprising letter from home; I read and reread it.

My father wrote that a friend of his had once sent his daughter to Columbia University, New York, and had thought much of it. Father wrote that the people at home were beginning to recognize American degrees as well as the English ones, and he wanted to know whether I would like to spend three years in America studying for my M.A. The M.A. would give me prestige and the people's confidence when I returned home. Of course, by this time, I knew of America. I was interested in it as I would be in some make-believe world; I considered it far from my sphere of life. I read the letter in great perplexity; I longed to go home for youth does not last forever, yet what an opportunity this was! I decided I would go. Try as I did I could not imagine New York nor could I imagine myself in it. I was thrilled and terrified by turns at the idea. I began to try to learn more of America. I studied American movies carefully; I spoke with people; I even read geography books! There was one thing I heard about America that stood out in my mind and fascinated me; it was the land of liberty. I had heard much of the Statue of Liberty and as anything in connection with freedom of man has always and will always fascinate me, I thought America was a wonderful place.

Paul Ponder is a native of Demerara, British Guiana.

I was born in a small town called Buxton on the east coast of the county of Demerara, British Guiana, the only British colony on the mainland of South America. I am the fourth child of a family of nine, all of whom are still living. My oldest brother, thirty-six years old, is a physician practicing in the States; another older brother is a sugar-boiler by profession; and an older sister (thirty-two) is a music teacher and dressmaker. Two younger brothers, twenty-eight and twenty-six respectively, and a sister, twenty-three, are engaged in the teaching profession; one sister, twenty, has just graduated from high school; and the "baby" sister, seventeen, hopes to finish high school soon. My brother held, for twenty-three years, the post of clerk of the town in which we were all born. He resigned last year on pension. The population of the town, plus that of its two "suburbs", is about eight thousand.

Exactly forty years ago there came a change in my life that was destined to lead me through my experiences. The first shock was the death of my father. This was followed very soon after by the death of my elder brother. My father left me some values by his will which I converted into cash—that brought me a few thousand dollars. Soon after I secured employment with my sister-in-law (then a widow) who carried on a dry goods store. Conditions did not work to suit my temperament so I chucked it and pulled out on my account. After a year's trial at storekeeping, on my own account, I grew restless and gave it up. Determined to go abroad my choice was the United States. In consequence I left the West Indies on the steamship Barnstable bound for Boston, Massachusetts. I embarked at Port Antonio (Jamaica) with quite a number of white Americans who had come to the Island from Boston and other New England points to escape the rigor of a North American winter. I was the only colored person on board. I traveled first-class. The steamer had no other form of accommodation. Naturally, I drew upon myself a deal of attention, particularly at table, as we went from one port to another, for the Barnstable was a fruit steamer which carried bananas between Jamaica and Boston. It was at Kingston that a white gentleman, who I learned afterwards was the " father " of the banana industry, asked me, " Where are you going, my lad? " I told him that I was going to America. " For what purpose? ", was his next query. " To see the sights ", I replied with a twit of smile. He laid a hand on my shoulder and said with a broad smile, " I hope you will enjoy yourself ".

Then he opened out into a lecture which stood by me. " My boy ", said Captain Baker, " everything will depend upon how you conduct yourself. Never anticipate opposition. Don't go into the country with a pre-convinced idea that every white man you meet dislikes you because you are colored. That, I might tell you, is one of the great failings of your colored brothers in the United States. They will not understand that the white man is their best friend and greatest benefactor. The colored people in the United States of America take it as a delight to run counter with every white man with whom they come in contact. They are wrong, but there is no immediate remedy for the situation. Time alone can right it. You must not make the same mistake." The Captain rose from his seat; I, too, got up. He extended his hand, and after giving me a hearty handshake he bade me good luck and left the steamer. The S. S. Barnstable cleared for the United States ports in a few hours.

William Scott, a native of Jamaica, has lived in the United States for thirty years. His story indicates the problem of the immigrant's visibility as it was evident in the early days of Negro immigration.

My family was exceedingly poor so when I finished my grade school education at the age of 13 I felt it necessary that I should hunt some sort of job to help out in my maintenance. Class system, which was then and still is one of the depressing evils of the colony, dictated that unless I could secure what I have since learned to classify as a white collar job, I would have been ostracised by my associates.

When I was a youngster my aunt washed, sewed, baked, sold almost everything she could in the house to pay my fees in the private school. The full term was four years, but I could only attend two and one-half years.

Just about that time an uncle, now pastoring in California, was attending one of the Negro colleges in the East. He sent me a catalog of the school and when I read of the great work of that institution and how it was possible for ambitious young men who were not afraid or ashamed to work to acquire an education there my heart was set on attending it. I wrote asking my uncle to advance my traveling expenses. He graciously sent me $80.00. My ship-fare was $60.00 and the balance, with what my aunt could scrape together, was used to outfit me for the trip.

In my village was a tailor who styled himself a " First Class American Tailor ". As my mind flashes back to that period with its ultimate results I am sure my aunt took me to him largely because of the name "American Tailor " rather than because of his ability. I was a fairly tall youngster for my age and one of the customs of my people is to keep a boy in a boy's place. I was too tall for short pants, and not quite tall enough for long pants so the tailor thought he would compromise. He made me some three-quarter pants that struck me midway between the ankles and the knees. My coat was an abbreviation—just two or three inches below the waistline. To this was added a Boler Hat, a cross between a derby and a felt hat.

Then came October 1, 1908, and after the prayers and admonitions of taking good care of myself, being a good boy, making a man of myself, etc.,—the kisses, the embraces, the farewells—my aunt placed around my neck a tape with a purse with $10.00 (a gold piece), the last of her possessions. She placed me in charge of the purser of the ship and we set sail for America at noon, October 1, 1908.

Thrilled as I was at this new adventure, the ocean voyage itself was meaningless, my heart was pounding with anticipation to see New York—to see America—this promised land of opportunity.

John Wright was born in the Bahamas and has been in the United States for more than a quarter of a century. Note the class-consciousness of his story.

Savannah Sound is unique in that it is the only settlement in the Bahamas where the Negroes are regarded as the intellectual, social and economic superiors of the whites. Here the Negroes are masters and white people servants. I recall very distinctly, in the days of my youth, how a white girl sought my association, but I persistently avoided her because I regarded her as my social inferior. My grandfather was a white man. He married my grandmother, a colored woman, and bettered himself socially. My father, a near mulatto man, married my mother, a black woman, and bettered himself intellectually, socially, and economically. Of course, considering the Colony as a whole, this is rather the exception than the rule.

Few vocational avenues were open to the ambitious youths of the Bahamas. Fishing and farming brought meager financial returns and offered but a scanty livelihood. My father raised pineapples on a large scale, employed many laborers, owned his own home (my mother's), had many acres of land, had a shop whose stock in trade consisted of flour, lard, pork, sugar, grits, meal, kerosene, tobacco and matches, and, under out-island standards, was considered well-to-do, but his repeated failures, after successive years of hard work, to receive satisfactory or even fair financial returns from the marketing of his crops, diminished any desire I may have had to till the soil. The trades were equally discouraging. I could be employed by the government as a schoolmaster, a policeman, a tidewaiter, or get a job as clerk in a store in the city of Nassau, but none of these arrested my fancy. The Bahamas offered me nothing to satisfy my high ambition. In those days the sponge industry flourished in Key West, and Miami was a young Magic City where money could be "shaken from trees". Home-returning pilgrims told exaggerated tales of their fame and fortune in the "promised land". As convincing evidence to their claims, they dressed flashily and spent American dollars lavishly and prodigally. Those American dollars had a bewitching charm for a country lad who worked for wages ranging from 36 to 50 cents a day. Moreover, the splendid appearance of those boys from the States stood out in striking contrast to us ill-fashionably clad country lads. It was the year 1911, and I was nineteen years of age. And so, having obtained reluctant permission of my parents, I took my journey to a far country and landed in Miami, Florida, on June 11th of that same year.

Henry Oliver, a native of British Honduras, rebelled at the imperialistic practices of his native government. It is apparent, however, that this rebellion was an after-thought, a rationalization evolving after settlement in the new country.

I was the last of thirteen children—eleven girls, two boys. My father's principal income was a paltry pension from the government for military service as a non-commissioned officer in the famous old West India Regiment. He fought in the wars of the Ashantis against British rule; was decorated by the late Queen Victoria for valor at Coomassie; and awarded the coveted military medal for long service and good conduct. After army service, he joined the Constabulary (Police) Force of British Honduras.

Upon retirement as an officer of the law my father settled at Belize, the capital. Like in most of Britain's mal-administered Crown Colonies, the native population of 12,000 was at the mercy of an unscrupulous coterie of 500 Europeans from whose ranks the Governor appointed his Executive Council, the dictator of native policies.

My father worked at odd jobs to augment his meagre pension. My brother married at an early age, the salary he received as principal of the Wesleyan school being barely enough to keep his wife and children from dire poverty.

I became a bread-winner for the family at ten, earning 50 cents per week as an errand boy. At twelve, I succumbed to the lure of the sea and became a deck-hand on a sailing vessel plying between Belize and Yucatan, Mexico, at $3.00 per week. At fifteen, I finished elementary school, winning a year's scholarship at the Wesleyan High School. The plight of my eleven sisters, my distracted mother and father checked, temporarily, my burning ambition to excel in the junior and senior examinations of Cambridge University—the major cultural objective of ambitious young natives in the British colonies and dependencies. After two years in high school I went out into the world to earn a living and give my family some measure of economic and social security.

My brother and the white superintendent of the Wesleyan Mission, who sought to convert me into an agent of imperialism, secured me a position in the Civil Service as typist-clerk in the Chief Magistrate's office at Belize, paying $15.00 per month. The peonage and political proscription practiced upon natives; the inferior status of native Civil Servants who were really running the business side of the government while the white departmental heads drew lucrative salaries and emoluments, made me an open advocate of the abolition of Crown Colony Government.

My militancy cost me my job. There is no room in the Colonial Civil Service for an outspoken, radical, independent native youth who dares challenge the " sacred " prerogatives of imperial masters and empire builders. Those for whom I fought deserted and betrayed me. I was forced into menial occupations because European employers and the rich native timber and fruit merchants feared my influence with their docile native employees.

Seeing the futility of my efforts, and realizing that I would eventually rot in jail or die on the gallows as other native patriots had done, I decided, for my family's sake, to seek a new land of opportunity.

Out of my meagre salaries I subscribed for American Negro newspapers and magazines, read everything I could find on American life and customs and traditions, and familiarized myself with the philosophies of Dr. Booker T. Washigton, Dr. W. E. B. DuBois, the late Monroe Trotter, Dr. Carter G. Woodson, Robert Abbott, and other native-born leaders and educators. The United States became my Mecca.

Came the War of 1914. I volunteered at 17 and saw active service in France, Egypt and Mesopotamia as a non-commissioned officer with the British West Indies Regiment. I was demobilized at Taranto, Italy, in 1919, and sailed for home. After a brief stay with my family I said goodby to British Honduras. I worked on several ships which touched at American ports, getting a perspective of the country, studying its cultural and economic advantages. In 1921 I took up permanent residence in New York City. Doing so was a vital turning point in my racial life.

EXPERIENCES UPON ARRIVAL

In most instances the immigrant Negro comes from a primary agrarian community into the secondary urban organization of modern industry. In many instances he comes to friends or relatives who, in many cases, have changed in America. Furthermore, he experiences quickly the feeling of "not knowing what it is all about" on the one hand, and having his bubble of liberty burst quickly, on the other. The nature of these experiences is shown in the following documents.

Our ship was scheduled to arrive in New York on October 13, 1908, and I wrote my uncle to meet me on that date. However, we arrived in New York about 2 P. M. on October 12th. Overwhelmed as I was by the colossal magnitude of New York's imposing water front, and excited over the immediate prospect of setting foot on this new land as I nervously scanned the hundreds of faces at the pier there to meet their friends and loved ones, I was unable to recognize a single face of my acquaintance. You can imagine my feeling of utter despair and profound dejection. Here was I, an immigrant lad just turning fifteen years, arriving in a strange land, among strange people, with no one to meet me at the pier. The Purser of the ship was very kind to me, he took me to his quarters and consoled me with the thought that my uncle would soon come. The hours soon passed and it was 8 P. M. Feeling that I might be detaining the Purser from his shore leave, I thought of the last letter my uncle sent me which was in my bag. In it, fortunately, he gave the name and address of a friend in Philadelphia.

After much persuasion and with assurance that I would be all right, he sent someone with me to the station. For fare I used the $10 gold piece my aunt gave me. Securing my ticket I stuffed it in my pocket with the many bills given me in change—for I hadn't the slightest idea how to count the money. I arrived in Philadelphia at 2 A. M. on October 13th—oh, what memories! I remember how I passed through the gates following the crowd not knowing where I was going. There was a street car taking on passengers, some of the crowd I was with got on the car—I got on too. I showed the letter to the conductor. Fortunately the car was going in that very direction. He put me out at the indicated corner and there I was at 2:30 A. M., with a letter in one hand, my folded portmanteau bag in the other, looking up at every house trying to find the number. An officer came by, arrested by my alien garb, heard my story and piloted me to the house. My uncle had told the folks of my expected arrival, so they took me in, fed me and put me to bed. That very afternoon my uncle, hurrying through from his summer employment to leave his bag en route to meet me in New York, was dumbfounded to find me sitting there. What a meeting! It was years since we saw each other—tears of joy flowed freely.

The next day, October 14, 1908, we started for the college for it was then late for my matriculation. We arrived at noon. My uncle ushered me to his room in the dormitory, then left me for awhile. I thought I would take a walk about the campus to get a line on my surroundings. The students were at that time just leaving the dining hall after lunch. Bear in mind my comic attire: three-quarter pants, abbreviated coat, Boler hat, etc. To my mind, I was in the height of fashion. The sophomores, whom I later learned were the campus "irritants" to incoming freshmen, soon began their work. One came up to me with this query, "Son, what part of the jungles did you come from?" Another got behind me and knocked off my Boler hat, another pulled my coat, someone unfastened my tie, etc. Unprepared and unaccustomed as I was to such unusual behavior, I gave vent to my indignation in the only way I knew then by saying, "Now, mon, I am getting vexed" (with characteristic West Indian brogue). This remark of mine so amused my tormentors that they continued their indignities just to have me repeat it. Pushing his way through the crowd that gathered about me, a tall, fine looking chap came up to me; he asked my name and told me his, informing me that he too was a freshman. Said he, "Don't let them know that you are getting vexed, they don't know what you are talking about, tell them that you are getting damn tired." With my brogue, I repeated after him, "Now, mon, I am getting domn tired now." Thus began my liberal education. That tall, fine looking chap is today the best friend I have in the world.

Another immigrant, who landed in Florida, related the following account which indicates how the color problem is introduced to the newly arrived immigrant.

Having passed the immigration and customs examiners, I took a carriage for what the driver called "Nigger Town". It was the first time I had heard that opprobrious epithet employed, and then, by a colored man himself. I was vividly irked no little. Arriving in Colored Town, I alighted from the carriage in front of an unpainted, poorly-ventilated rooming house where I paid $2.00 for a week's lodging. Already, I was rapidly becoming disillusioned. How unlike the land where I was born, I soliloquized. There colored men were addressed as gentlemen; here, as "niggers". There policemen were dressed in immaculate uniforms, carried no deadly weapon, save a billy; here, shirt-sleeved officers of the law carried pistols, smoked and chewed tobacco on duty. Colored Miami certainly was not the Miami of which I had heard so much. It was a filthy backyard to the Magic City. There were few paved streets and no sidewalks at all. Palmettoes grew in the sandy streets and rattlesnakes were not uncommon. (The population of Miami was only 5,000 then; it is more than 100,000 today.)

Failing to find a job after a week of diligently seeking one, I wept for my father's house, but had not enough money left to pay my passage thither. So I decided to go to Cocoanut Grove, a suburb five miles south of Miami. It was my first sight of a train. And now I experienced a new thrill as that giant locomotive rushed through space heedless of danger or uncertainty. Having entrained, it was goodbye Miami, and fifteen minutes later, Hello, Cocoanut Grove!

Here I detrained and, with exalted hopes, anticipated rapturous greetings by relatives and friends whom I had known in the old home town. But instead of the warm, cordial, friendly evidences of kinship, even my relatives treated me as a pilgrim and as a stranger sojourning in an unfriendly land. Some of the boys told me that "this is America where, if a man does not work, neither shall he eat".

Probably the most striking experiences upon arrival is the awareness of race that is soon discovered, as revealed in the following document. Note, also, the difference between the African and the Caribbean point of view on race mixtures.

Perhaps if I had not passed my first days in the United States in New York I might not have developed such a deep aversion for the country; or perhaps, if I had to spend the rest of my life here I would have developed a liking for it. The fact remains I had much disillusionment. I came to New York in a very friendly spirit, willing to like and admire all; to have an exciting and wonderful time, but very soon I learned that the United States is not much of a place for friendly Negroes. I was soon to understand that here one never forgets his color.

I had thought that in New York no difference was made between black and white; I thought they ran the same businesses together. I did not know of racial discriminations. So, as I puzzled my way around the college trying to learn these strange numbered streets I wondered where all the American Negroes were. No Negro professors! I was very miserable those days for I had no one to show me around and my financial affairs were not as settled as they should have been. Then one of the Negro girls I had met on the boat called me up and said she was coming to take me out. What a ray of sunshine in my hole of darkness. She arrived and said we were going to Harlem where she lived. I wanted to know what Harlem was. She said wait and see. And I saw! To me it was a strange Negro world filled with Negroes, no longer African, but with the definite stamp of Western civilization. What an over-crowded place! How inferior to those other areas I learned were for the whites! I asked my friend about the Negro's place in America; what I heard I had been suspecting, but, nevertheless, it came as a blow.

I saw Harlem in the daytime with its amazing vari-colored people; white Negroes; Negroes with blonde hair; white pallid faces with Negro features. I could not understand why they were any more Negro than white. In my home we had once prejudices against the mulatto, but I had seldom seen any. It was interesting how my prejudice took on a rational attitude in this country of black and white mixtures—yet I would never relish those conditions for my country. I still have a sneaking unreasonable feeling that black and white form an antagonistic mixture. But I have nothing against the American Negro; the blood mixture is not their fault. Anyway, who was I to judge them?

I was to find out that they had their little prejudices also. The ideas that many of them had about Africa astounded me; and the way many of them are so proud. In many groups I have been they have expected me to admire America and slander Africa, but that will never be the case. The more I see of the lot of the American Negro, the more I cling to Africa."

Frequently the initial shock of segregation is received through an institution or social device close to the individual. This document reveals how it is accomplished.

In the United States I was to gain some new experiences. In New York City there were separate churches for colored and white people. This caused me to conclude that there was something rotten in Denmark. "If", I argued, "the churches were places to create a right spirit in people, that they may live clean lives so that after death they may inherit Eternal Life, and if there is no jim crowism in the life hereafter, why should there be discrimination here in striving to reach the same goal?" I went to a Harlem church during my first week here. The collection plate was passed five times during that service. The dancing, shouting, and comments during the service were all new to me. I learned to know of such people as "Father Divine", Elder Michaux, Becton and his consecrated dimes. Religion appeared to be a big racket to me, so I left it alone. I found that discrimination existed in hotels, in the residential sections of the city, and in office buildings, where in many instances colored people must use the freight elevators. In general, I gathered that Negroes were not wanted except to do menial work.

Even the Virgin Islander, who is reputed to know more about American practices, is affected by the change.

My first set-back was when the pangs of segregation closed in on me. The Pennsylvania train arrived at Cape Charles; I boarded the steamer for Old Point, and not knowing the customs walked into the white section only to be reminded a moment later that my color was to determine where I would stay during the two-hour trip across the Chesapeake Bay. What an impression! Why were people of the two races separated? At home such is unheard of. Segregation would be very impractical in the Virgin Islands because of the overwhelming number of Negroes (apology, please, and don't ever use the word Negro again or we'll ostracise you.)

Another experience was to adjust myself in living in such close contact with so many students. It was my first time in a large boarding school. Many of the students were kind to me, but what most impressed me was the mechanical, business-like relationship which existed here. In the Virgin Islands people seem to be more intimate, know each other better; and none of the stiff "mind-your-own-business" attitude prevails. In occasional instances some students would attempt to make me feel uncomfortable by calling me "monkey-chaser" or "Barbados", but that soon went through the window, due largely to the success of several students from the Islands who had been here and had established a reputation for themselves.

Protective devices against the slurs and inconveniences faced are quickly established by the immigrant. The writer of the next document developed this rationalization after a very limited experience in the United States of America, during which he moved from the west coast of Florida to Boston, thence to New York. The movement is fairly typical of immigrants arriving at ports of entry located in the South.

My experiences with white and colored Americans upon arrival were a mixture of admiration, surprise, and embarrassment. Because of what I learned he and his progenitors did to lift native-born Negroes "up from slavery", I expected to find the white native-born more tolerant, sympathetic, charitable towards them. But the treatment accorded native-born Negroes in Dixie, and in the East, Middle West and North, as I observed it, made me cognizant that if there is any difference between the egotistic empire " blunderer " in the West Indies and Africa and his blood-brother, the white American, it is to be found in his methods of dramatizing racial prejudice and national fear.

The European is more polite, painfully polite, and superbly hyper-critical—he succeeds in almost making the native believe he is merciful so skillful is he in dismembering and subjugating racial entities. The white American, in his relations with the Negro, is nervously blunt, apologetic, and pathetically undiplomatic when thrown on the defensive. His inflexible rudeness and barbarism in Dixie is readily understood when thrown in bold relief against the background of ancient prison life in Great Britain and Europe, the environment from which came the scums and incorrigibles who planted the seeds of lynching and mob law in American life.[2]

The thought that racial life here would be easier and less painful than it was at home quickly faded before the daily atrocities meted out to native-born Negroes. Their relentless struggles to fight back inspired me. I was made aware that this was no Utopia, but a battleground only for the valiant and the martyr. The new realities did not awe me. I was impressed by the formidable weapons at the disposal of the native-born to be used in defense, which we did not possess at home.

Hunting a job, I was amazed to find that native-born whites were more considerate and sympathetic to the foreign-born Negro than his own racial relative. Ugly epithets were hurled at me by native-born Negroes at employment agencies and places of employment; landladies tried to " play me for a sucker " because they thought I was ignorant of living standards. I was handicapped, too, by the fact that most native-born Negroes hold the illusion that all foreigners are rich, and in possession of some magical power to do things impossible for the native-born. I was amused by others who presumed that, because I was from " across the sea ", I could tell fortunes and give them good luck.

Whatever fears I had as to my ability to successfully adjust myself to conditions here were dismissed after study and analysis of the mental attitudes and strategy employed by determined

2 Note the deductive fallacy of this statement.

groups of foreign-born, white and colored, to hurdle the barriers. Foolish pride was buried, and customs and traditions imported from home which I found unsuited to the new civilization were thrown aside.

I cultivated a sense of humor and found it a sustaining asset. When I was called a "monkey-chaser", I laughed as heartily as the offender. When the native-born poked fun at my accent I reminded them that there is little difference between the accents of a native Charlestonian, Haitian, or Jamaican. When they invited me to go back home, I asked casually, "What would the United States be like if all foreginers, white and colored, accepted the invitation?" Silence and academic discussion generally followed.

The newly arrived foreign Negro who comes to the States to better his economic condition first seeks to get himself acclimatized, then to get a job that he may pay back the friend or relative who assisted him in getting here. His next procedure is to save enough money to send back home for more friends or relatives. Prior to 1923 the average Negro immigrant, particularly the West Indian, was a marked man, often the victim of unscrupulous fakers. He was conspicuous, lacking in the "standardized externals", and highly visible. A general picture is provided in the following document which indicates that the West Indian Negro was conspicuous for the following reasons:

(1) His clothes were rather loose-fitting
(2) His pants were often three-quarters the length of the average American
(3) His accent was readily recognized
(4) His hair was not "slicked back"—since slicking was not known in the islands prior to 1926.[3]

On the whole his general appearance indicated right away that he was not one of the *city boys.* As a result on his taking a cursory glance at the city for the first time, he is soon met by a

3 This is one of the elements of visibility peculiar to Negro immigration as compared with the immigrants of white groups.

gentleman who approaches him, perhaps on 125th Street on Seventh Avenue, saying, " Say, buddy, I am just from down South and cannot locate Sam Jones, the boot-black, will you tell me where I can find him? " This foreigner, himself bewildered, soon entertains this man who has " just come up " in a rather lengthy and interesting conversation—the very thing the confidence-man desired. Hurriedly, piles of dollar bills are drawn from his pockets and this West Indian wonders if this is the land of milk and honey he heard so much about.

Of course, these are all fake bills; he begins to inform the foreigner that he doesn't want money, that he has plenty of it, etc. " Do you have a job? " asked the Southerner, " No ", replied the West Indian. " Then you give me $5 and I'll get you one ", said the former. Soon there comes along another *smart boy* who meets the two already in conversation. The trio soon get further into the topic of the day. The West Indian in spite of his " greenness "—a word used frequently to denote newcomers—smells the rat—a vernacular term—and soon leaves the gentlemen to carry on the discussion. He relates the story on reaching home, then passes it along to his fellow-countrymen, and soon all the West Indians are cognizant of these smart boys.

The following experience may be had by any stranger in New York. Such situations were frequent at the time of the migration of Negroes to the North.

There is quite a bit of discussion as to whether or not the West Indian Negro knew very much of the race problem before he entered the United States. This unforgettable experience was related to me by a very close friend. After being in this country for some weeks he became restless and wanted to take on the habits of the American Negro—he wanted to get a " real haircut ". Passing a barber-shop at 125th Street he noticed a sign which head: " *Hair Cut—50c* ". Not knowing, however, that tonics, massage, etc. called for extra money he stepped into the shop and sat in a chair. All the barbers eyed him. The barber of that chair came over and asked him if he was Spanish. " No ", he replied. " But you have just arrived? " he further questioned. " Yes ", he replied. The matter was dropped and the lad was excused for not knowing that white folks did not care to cut black folks hair in 125th Street on Seventh Avenue. After he had his hair cut, the barber leaned over slightly and in a very soft tone asked if he wanted tonic. "Yes", he replied. "Massage?" "Certainly." "Singe, sir?" "Surely", he further replied. On getting out of the chair he noticed that the barber struck the register for three dollars and some cents. Sensing that these extra things had to be paid for, in order to save his embarrassment, and not wanting to make his greenness too pronounced, he immediately without asking told him to send the shoe-shine boy to his home because he did not have enough money in his pocket. All that poor boy had in his pocket was fifty cents.

EXPERIENCES IN THE UNITED STATES—ECONOMIC, SOCIAL AND CULTURAL

The occupational attitudes of Negro immigrants undergo a profound revision when the working population begins seeking employment in the United States. While many of them are willing to take any job available, there are numerous others whose occupational experiences back home were far superior to those obtainable in the United States. This is particularly true of those persons who were formerly employed in the skilled and white collar occupations. The psychic income from employment in all fields save the professions is lost in the United States. The transition from schoolmaster to common laborer is well shown in the following document.

I was inducted into American labor one fine Sabbath morning while on my way to apply for an elevator boy's job I had seen in the newspaper want column. While passing through a side street in the lower section of Manhattan I watched and silently criticized the ungodliness of men working on a building construction on the Lord's Day. While musing, a foreman of the laborers' gang came up to me and in his native Irish accent said, "Want to work?" "Yes", was my reply. "Well, god damn it, take that collar and tie off and pitch in." Without stopping to think, I obeyed. I left my coat, collar and tie in the basement, got hold of a wheelbarrow and soon found myself loading it with bricks which I transported to the bricklayers. There were about two dozen of us in the labor gang. It was apparent that these workers were of all races and nationalities. After three or four hours I was shifted to the concrete gang, i. e., to transport concrete. How I did welcome that whistle at mid-day! I was so tired and my hands were so painful that I stretched myself out on a plank to rest. One fellow said to me, " Don't worry, you will break in ". I bought some lunch and went back to work. At five o'clock my day's work was done. . . . I went home, washed up and rested. My roommate, whom I saw once or twice per week—he was working on two jobs—asked me once during that week if I was working. "Yes," was my reply. That's all he wanted to know so I said nothing else. But when I had time to reflect I felt rather badly. I wondered at times if I was the same person who but lately had been a very successful schoolmaster with hundreds of children and their parents looking up to me as their idol, with someone to do every form of menial work that I required at my least bidding, and here I was, transformed into a day laborer, trucking bricks and concrete. I decided to quit, so I completed that week and got a porter's job in a hotel at $18 per week and meals. After being on the job for about four weeks I was fired for being too slow and inexperienced. One thing resulted from this in my favor, however, was that I decided to turn in the time checks from the first job. To my surprise I was paid $37.50 for that week's work of seven days, time-and-a-half for Sunday. It took me almost two months to earn a like sum in my home country. That amount for one week's work was a financial shock to me.

I landed a job in a wholesale firm through a young lady who worked for one of the bosses. This boss was a German. He invited me to his house and along with his wife entertained me royally. I was a kind of novelty on that job then. To see a colored man with a pencil behind his ears checking goods, receiving and shipping thousands of dollars worth of merchandise each week without making the slightest error, was something extraordinary to all the colored help and white clerks in that establishment. My salary was stepped up to $35.00 per week, and pretty soon I was entirely in charge of the place on Sundays, taking the keys home with me. I was even given the combination for the safe. One Sunday while there in some part of the building hoodlums stole thirteen bags of sugar from a lower floor. There was quite a furore by the police and some of the bosses. But I was not even scared of losing my job for my honesty was above reproach. When I finally resigned from the job to enter medical school I was given a fine send-off, and I still keep my reference from the Head of that concern.

Economic adjustments are made less easily by some immigrant groups, however. This seems particularly true of the middle-class British subjects, and of the French and Spanish-speaking colored immigrants who have been engaged in commerce and finance. Two cases illustrate this point.

A family of three from Spanish Honduras came to a Southern city some eight years ago. The father was a clerk in the offices of the United Fruit Company in Tegucigalpa. His contacts with the Americans led him to believe that he could make more money in the United States. He was making a good livelihood in Honduras, but he wanted to make more money and give an American education to his daughter. The company offered him a job as janitor in one of their offices, which he refused. He found that he was obliged to make himself a part of the colored group if he wanted to earn a living here. He was forced to drink the bitter tea of American race prejudice. He first taught Spanish privately, and then music in the public schools, but being very sensitive and a reactionary, he was constantly causing trouble everywhere he went. He always tried to sit above the screen in the trolley cars and busses and was constantly rebuked and always in trouble. He lost his reason trying to break through the solid wall of American race prejudice. He is now an inmate of a state institution for the insane, his family destitute.[4]

In New York there lives a Negro family which had to leave its native land because the father failed in business as a result

4 Manuscript document no. 3.

of the political and economic upheaval in Haiti which followed the American Marines' occupation in 1915. The father came to this country where he worked as a translator for several exporting houses in New York City, but his health broke down because of the rigour of the climate and he died. Before his death he sent for his oldest daughter, aged seventeen, who was in a convent in Haiti, and for one of his sons, aged nineteen, to come to the United States. The young girl was an expert seamstress and found employment in a fashionable lingerie and corset shop on Fifth Avenue. She got the job because the proprietor was an American lady of French descent. Her brother found work in a hat factory where he learned the trade. Everything went well for them for a few years. They made money and saved a bit. They intended to return to Haiti to go into business for themselves, but in 1929 the crash came and their mother in Haiti died. They no longer wished to return to Haiti so they sent for their sister and all three lived together. The two girls worked together in the various corset and lingerie shops on Fifth Avenue, but finally were obliged to go to the factories when many of the small exclusive shops reduced their personnel. At present they can find no regular employment. The brother, too, has shifted from job to job. When times were good he was offered many good jobs and opportunities to learn such trades as linotyping, printing, auto mechanics, garment operating, interior decorating. His nervous character closed the door of these opportunities. He detested manual labor. He could not make the necessary rational adjustments that the American environment calls for. He is very race conscious and has an inferiority complex more fatalistic than that of the average American Negro. He does not try to learn to speak or write English correctly. He reads only French papers and books. Having, as one might say, gone into himself, he has very few friends even among the Haitians. He detests jazz, believes that there is no culture at all in this country and that the Negro is doomed to eternal sufferings and despair. He has even lost his religion. The poor fellow really lives in a shell, not even his most intimate friends can give him any advice. He now works in the Bronx as an elevator operator. One week he works nights and the other week days. He is the sole support of his two sisters who work only now and then. All of them are unmarried and each one of them lives or rather exists almost without hope.

There are persons of the same class of people from Martinique and Guadeloupe who also have not been able to make the necessary economic adjustments without misery in the United States. Their uncompromising attitude against American race prejudices has led them to close the door of many opportunities that could not have been had in their homeland.[5]

On the other hand, standards of class and caste can be thrown aside as was done by this immigrant who is now an outstanding professional man in his community.

In the South I was hired by a building contractor who assigned me to a box to mix concrete. To me, this was hard work; it was drudgery. At home I was required to work only five or six hours a day, and that, for the most part, as timekeeper for my father. Now I must labor ten hours a day with a typical Southern slave-driver as an overseer—wages $1.50 per diem—but I toiled on that job for a year, the words of my countrymen still ringing in my ear: In America if a man will not work, neither shall he eat.

As a common laborer I worked at concrete-mixing, ditch-digging, palmetto grubbing, log-skidding, etc. On all of these jobs I came in contact and had experience with the American Negro. For the most part, I found the native-born to be a more skillful laborer. The foreigner knew what to do, but knew not how to do it. I regarded the native as a killer, and, therefore, feared him. But I also felt superior to him and unwittingly assumed an air of superiority towards him. The native laborer bitterly resents any show of superiority in any way, and, with oaths and curses, orders the foreigner to shut up or return to his native land. The foolish boasting of the foreign-born about what he was used to in his native land causes more friction among bi-

5 Manuscript document no. 14.

national laboring groups than anything else. Wealth and position in the colonies and hard labor in a strange land, added together, just do not make sense, opines the native. And, of course, they do not.

While sweating profusely one July day under a blistering noon-day sun the turning point in my life came. With a dozen other laborers I was skidding pine logs. Beside me worked a man who, though in all points my inferior in my native land, was easily my superior in the skillful manner in which he handled heavy logs on that job. "John", said he to me, "in our home town you thought yourself better than me, but just look at you now,—you can hardly make the grade." He spoke the truth and it hurt me. Pondering those words over and over in my heart, I resolutely determined to graduate from the level of a common laborer. And I did! A month later I was employed as a clerk, and still later as manager of a second-hand dry goods store at a salary of $4.00 a week. I had now been in America eighteen months.

Note the intra-racial stereotypes and judgments in the following document based upon two years' experience in the United States:

As a merchant I learned something of the honesty and race pride of the native-born Negro. The native has far more race pride than the foreigner. He will patronize business of color. Not so with the foreigner. He loves the white man and thinks whatever he sells is superior. He really believes (the ignorant ones) that ice sold by a white man is colder than that sold by his own color. That is the way he has been trained, and it takes many years of life in America to change him. Neither will he pay his debts. The foreigner is a bigger liar than the native. He knows the native will hardly go to the colonies to investigate the accuracy of his exaggerations. In business the foreigner is reluctant about mixing his money with that of the natives, and vice versa. The native (very naturally) wants to be at the head of all cooperative business enterprises. The foreigner must always play "second fiddle" to him or no "fiddle" at all. I was a merchant two years.

This alien found it to his economic and psychological advantage to hide his national identity. Again the stereotypes are accepted as valid group judgments.

As a sleeping car porter I concealed my national identity and made myself an American. This was during the summer of 1917 while I was in course of preparation for the sacred ministry. I did this for the purpose of knowing in very truth the prejudices of the native towards the foreigner. A great number of the men were college students, and our district office was Grand Central Station, New York. Having no foreign accent I was not suspected. I would join the boys in their scathing criticism of foreigners. We condemned them as being boastfully arrogant, of making monstrous claims to wealth in their native land, of possessing unblushing conceit, of suffering from over-active imaginations and having an unwarranted superiority complex. We admitted our fear of their superior ability to acquire knowledge, and property, and money, and we pledged our troth one to another to protect our birthright in business, in politics and in learning against the foreigner at any price. Those " monkey-chasers " are too damn smart, was an oft-repeated expression.

However, much is dispelled in America. To one who has been brought up in African and English society, " it seems very fine that anyone can climb up in life here, though, of course, money means a lot. Nevertheless, a grocer's son, by working his way, has as good an education as a professional man's son. . . . People here don't go around with a class stamped on them. Clerks don't look like clerks, servants look as good as their mistresses." [6]

CONFLICT AND RACE CONSCIOUSNESS

The documents included in this section represent some expression of conflict with native-born Negroes, white Americans, or some maladjustment arising out of the varying folkways. Frequently they express some vigorous statement of race or

6 Manuscript document no. 37.

nationality consciousness and pride. Invariably they are based upon direct sensory experiences so well demonstrated by the young student of foreign parentage who maintains that " I was never very conscious of my foreign heritage until after the great economic upheaval of 1929 which instituted the changes which completely revolutionized my life." He continues—

In the year 1929 I was sent to Howard University. It was there that due to the influence of a certain French teacher, I learned not to be ashamed of foreign things. Then, too, I met many students from the West Indies with whom I became more friendly than with the Americans. I was soon classed as a " monkey-chaser ", but I was proud of my ability to speak French and I had a great desire to go to France. I got into relationship with my relatives in Haiti and began to correspond often with my people in Canada. I was thrilled by my new readings. In French literature and the history of Haiti I discovered a new soul! The University life broadened me considerably. I learned to despise our educated minister back home. In fact, I did not believe anymore; I was exposed to Freud and McDougal. Then came the crash. I went to New York to live with my brother who was studying at New York University. He was quite out of sympathy with my foreign leanings so we soon quarreled and I moved to the International House to live. There I met all kinds of foreign students. I was friendly with all of the French-speaking students and became their interpreter and pilot. I found that I could go anywhere with them so long as I spoke French. I soon perfected myself. I went to French movies, clubs, churches, read only French books and newspapers. I lived at the International House for two and one-half years. I went to New York University for one year and then I went to C. C. N. Y. the next year, when I took sick in March and abandoned the year's studies. The following summer I went to Canada where I thoroughly enjoyed myself. I enjoyed the freedom. I was flattered and honored by the French Canadians because I spoke French. I spent an entire summer in New York as the tutor, interpreter, and escort of three charming Haitian ladies, my contact with them being the cause of my embracing the Catholic faith. A very dear Belgian friend acted as my god-father at the baptism. I made the acquaintance of almost all of the Haitian and Martiniquian and Senegalese people in New York and was considered as one of them. I went to their homes, learned to eat their food—particularly red beans and rice cooked with salt-meat. I was invited to their parties and there I learned to dance the 'beguine', and the 'rhumba'—the exaggerated and sensuous stage dance has very little in common with that dance. I began to meet also Spanish-speaking Negroes from Panama, Santo Domingo, and Puerto Rico, and Cuba, and I started to learn Spanish. I noticed that on the whole the Latin Negroes, that is to say, the French and Spanish-speaking Negroes, do not mix with those of Anglo-Saxon culture unless they happen to be of the same religion. The Latin Negro takes his recreation in his particular area, the Spanish quarter, where he finds his churches—French and Spanish—his restaurants, dance halls, and vaudeville and motion pictures in his own language, even his 'dupers' have followed him here. The Jewish lawyers, doctors, pharmacies, cater to him in his language; the signs *Se habla Espagnol* and *Ici on parle le francais* adorns the windows of most of the stores in this section. Here the Latin Negro is at home; he does not suffer much from the American race prejudice. On the job he speaks Spanish or French, the white American boss lets him by. In this respect the white Americans are really funny. If a Negro, no matter how black he may be, speaks either French or Spanish, he may enter where the lightest English-speaking mulatto or octoroon is refused admittance. From New York to New Orleans this is true to a certain degree (more or less) according to what class of white people one deals with; and I learned how to fight this prejudice.

I know how to rationalize as well as the average American, white or colored. Everyone does so in the United States. This compromising on moral issues is still the great American enigma.

I know and have seen quite a bit of the conditions in the British West Indies, the class system, the plantation workers, the poverty, the wretchedness and hopelessness of the lower class natives, exploited by the upper class Negroes and whites, separated from his blood brother by social barriers almost as great as between Negroes and whites in this country. He has truly found a warm spot in the so-called 'Nigger Heaven' that is Harlem. He does not hesitate to change his nationality, and send home for the rest of the folk and participate in politics, open up tailor shops, barbershops, and other small businesses, acquire property, etc. America has been kind to him.

At any rate, I have learned to appreciate the good points of the United States and I would be one of the first to hold up the flag and cheer were it not for race prejudice. After having exchanged ideas with colored students from every African colony and West Indian and South American country, and having visited most of the West Indies, I am ashamed to say that I choose to live in my prison.

Another student who travelled throughout the Southern States for three months before settling in New York drew this picture:

The whole situation down South filled me with bitterness and contempt. The utter ridiculousness of the sign in the cars " Whites to the front, colored to the rear ". The girl that pointed it out to me was so amused for I could not stop reading it and laughing. They told me of a white Y. W. C. A. leader who came to their meeting, but always stood by until they had eaten before she ate! I wished I could meet her. It did not seem possible to me that such conditions could exist in one of the centres of civilization. I liked the Southern Negroes very much; they seemed more hospitable and friendly than the Northerners. In spite of conditions, they have nice homes. Though I heard more of them had inferiority complexes than in the North, I enjoyed them. I met a very delightful but poor family where all the members were artistically gifted. The father and son sang the spirituals in a delightful manner. I never will stop loving the spirituals; I tell everyone I can that Negroes should be proud of it, for besides the American Indian's work, that is all the art America really possesses."

And an African woman speaks of a custom supposed to have originated on her native continent. The subsequent analysis reveals the great gulf to be bridged by Negro immigrant aliens:

Americans like show. I have been to speak at some meetings in Harlem and the love there for uniform, ceremony and organization is most wearisome; many are more concerned in having things just right than in listening to or being inspired by what speakers have to say.

The friendliness of perfect strangers in American social life startled and amused me. I have not yet become accustomed to it. Perfect strangers call me 'darling', 'dearie', 'honey', and they ask me to come and see them, but when you separate from that gathering they have forgotten you. I have come to the conclusion that I must not take American friendship too seriously. I did so once or twice only to be hurt by its shallowness.

Americans seem to me to be very sex-conscious. There seems nowhere a desire for platonic relations between man and woman. It is always sexual relations; always flirtations; women in the presence of men are always coquettish. Even the children in New York seem like hard-boiled grown-ups. They also have their girl friends and boy friends and imitate the examples of their elders. Sex education seems to be well given here. All speak of it unabashed, but something must be wrong somewhere for instead of it being healthy, it is unhealthy; all are conscious of it; every woman is waiting for a man; after she is married she has boy friends and he has his girl friends. This has been a very difficult thing for me to understand. The result is I feel I must avoid American boys.

Now I have been in the United States for over one year and I have learnt much. Maybe I would have learnt more had I spent the time in Harlem. All my friends remark now, 'How well and happy you look'. I feel well now for I am not fighting myself anymore; I know what to expect in mostly every situation now. Having been in many countries I have learnt versatility. I fit outwardly, though things may clash within. I have found a sense of humor necessary here and I have got it so it helps me many times, for, after all, Americans are funny. They can talk so much, they can advertise and are high pressure salesman. They want their things to be bigger and better. Whenever I wish to be cheered up I turn on the radio and listen to some of the advertisement!

I am not sorry I came to America though I long to go home. America has done much for me. It has given me a freedom of thought and broadening of mind never before known. I no longer idealize Americans, of course; I know more about political affairs, and I have more practical ideas on how to help my country; I know about economic and social problems, also about sex problems.

Here, needless to say, I have developed more bitterness towards the white man, but I am so certain he is afraid of the Negro that my bitterness does not lead to a hatred of all of them but to a determination to show them what my people can do. I laugh now when any American talks about the barbarities of other countries; these same barbarians could learn much that was new and tortuous in American civilization and, Christianity is mostly a mockery here; a polish over savagery.

It interested me to see the way the American Negroes rallied about the Ethiopian War; it certainly shows that new times are coming. They have all my sympathy and hopes for future successes, but I do not believe that the secret of their success is return to Africa, for they are now a part of Western civilization, and American whites cannot do without the Negroes.

America has broadened my thought and made it practical, but she has instilled no doctrines into me; true I have got into the ways of hurrying, being late at functions (for they start late anyway) and making some of my words sound like an American so I can be understood. I admire the gaiety of Americans at parties; it makes me wonder whether I am not taking life too seriously at times; I would like their gifts of being able to throw troubles aside, but that is a speciality of Western civilization. America, particularly New York, has some uncanny power about it that would in the end drive me to an asylum.

The color question seems to loom large in the heart of every American, as it naturally should; it seems to have given American Negroes an inferiority complex, which in some cases is subconscious. I will never forget my perplexity and resentment when a colored girl asked me whether I had joined 'the other side' because I had white friends. To me white and colored are no different in importance and I speak to all alike. Another colored girl asked me whether I did not feel at home with them more so than with the white. I said 'no' for American Negroes seem like Westerners to me. Many hold the whites as their copy, something they should look up to; they pursue the same activities as the whites when their race is shouting for dynamic leadership. I often ask myself can they not cooperate; can they not strike down this wicked color-barrier? Having done all they have under this suppression they could surely reach to greater heights.

When I leave this country it will be with the feeling that I have lived and with a thankfulness for the experience; here I saw life at its worst and glimpses of life at its best; I shall bid the Statue of Liberty ' farewell ' very sadly. I shall say: ' Farewell, land of liberty and home of slaves, you have given me much and robbed me of little except my hitherto blind faith in mankind; I go home still with the one purpose of being a great helper to my people and you have supplied me with much for that work. Be sure I will speak kindly of you for were you not once the land of my dreams, land of liberty? Always will I think of you and I wish the best for those of my race who are destined to spend their lives with you.'

Egocentrism and ethnocentrism are equally manifest in this estimate by a religious leader in one Negro community. Such statements are frequently the basis for conflicts and antipathies between the native-born and foreign-born:

Graduating from the Seminary in 1919 I was ordained to the sacred ministry of the Episcopal Church in the City of ———, in the month of August of that same year. I was sent to a large city where I did an outstanding piece of work for both my church and that community. I possessed youth, vision, tact and enthusiasm, and the white people and Negroes, foreign and native, gave me an almost 100 per cent cooperation. I built a church at a cost of $25,000 and freed it of mortgage debt. Later I built a rectory costing $2,000. I preached in the white Episcopal Church there at the 11 A. M. Sunday service. I was made president of the Interdenominational Alliance, Chairman of the colored branch of the local chapter of the American Red Cross, secretary of the Negro department of the State Fair, and chairman of the program committee of that department, in which capacity I had the honor of introducing to the public two now ex-governors of the state. I cooperated with the Juvenile court in handling Negro delinquents and organized a chorus of 300 voices for the Department of

Municipal Recreation. I was elected the first president of the Negro political club. In all these organizations the native-born Negro gave me full and hearty cooperation. Here was a city in which I was verily idolized by white and black. This fine spirit of cooperation led me to renounce my allegiance to His Majesty, King George V of England, and in due time I became an American citizen.

After ten years of ministry in this city I was promoted to the vicarage of the third largest Episcopal church for colored in all America. It has a nominal membership of almost 2,000 persons, and is the largest colored church in the city. From my last church I brought with me testimonials from the Mayor, the Welfare League, American Red Cross, Civil Service Board, Juvenile Court, Department of Recreation and others from colored organizations. I was now thoroughly American and almost anti-British. I arrived in my new charge in September, 1929, to serve a congregation with a foreign-born (or of foreign extraction) membership of fully 95 percent. My first task was to raise money to complete a church which had been under construction for seven years, and, for the finishing of which, hope had long been abandoned. Fourteen months after my arrival here we were worshipping in the new edifice. Everyone began to sing my praises. My Bishop told me I had worked a miracle. (This persecution complex is unusual among the professional people of foreign-birth.) Then both native and foreign-born Negro leaders set themselves against me and persecuted me for every cause. Baptist preachers preached against me from their pulpits warning their people against foreign-born leadership. Foreign-born preached against me proclaiming to their disciples that I had renounced His Majesty, the King. None of these things moved me and both native and foreign-born flocked to hear me. The first time I preached Naturalization to my people a near schism almost ensued. But I persisted; opened a class for training in American citizenship and, in two years, more Negroes have declared their intention to become American citizens than over any twenty-year period of that city's life.

Those who initiated the move to discredit my work were foreign-born Negroes. The man who told me that my expose of the poor housing conditions (practically all houses owned by white landlords) was 'putting yourself on the spot' was a foreign-born Negro whose native home was just ten miles from the place where I was born. Last year our National Church sent me to another city to lead two courses of study for the Clergy. Someone sent our National Chairman a letter (anonymous) in which he made some false and ugly charges against me. The coward that did that was, I suspect, a foreign-born Negro. Foreign-born Negroes are more prejudiced toward one another than are American Negroes toward the foreign-born. And, foreign-born Negroes prefer, and in some cases court, the friendship of the native-born. But if that same foreign-born Negro has the slightest suspicion that the friendship of the native is not true, he would never forgive him, and what is more, would influence all of his friends and fellow-countrymen to turn against him. In cities where there are many foreign-born Negroes the cleavage among them is greater than in their native lands. In the heyday of the Garvey Movement it is noticeable that Garveyism made its strongest bid where the percentage of British Negroes was largest and that, while the founder of that movement could not have gotten a respectable hearing at home, the same people flocked to his standard in the United States of America.

This man had never been gainfully employed when he arrived in the United States. He had just finished "prep" in England. He brought letters to the heads of many important commercial agencies, but the best they would offer him was a porter's job. His father was an outstanding business man in the West Indies.

I made friends readily at social affairs. At home I was a leader in youth movements and social life, and revelled in dancing. Then my favorite dances were the waltz, schottische, mazurka, and two-step. My admissions to many dances here were wasted until I compromised with what to me is a crazy indulgence, a potent weapon corrupting the morals of native-born Negro youth and adults—I refer to American jazz with all its sensuous, emotional appeal. While I admire the musical ability of Cab Calloway, Louis Armstrong and Tiny Bradshaw, I cannot enrich Jewish and Gentile promoters by paying them to insult me with their musical menus. My idea of truly representative native-born Negro musicians is found in Duke Ellington and Noble Sissle. I never miss an opportunity to patronize them. And I am still wondering why one must almost beg orchestra leaders to play the waltz, the most graceful and uplifting of all dance numbers.

There was fun in learning and using American slang. I fitted very well into the methods and policies of Negro journalism, making valuable friendships with editors, publishers, and members of the craft; working for and contributing to several newspapers.

After analyzing and initiating myself into the new life here, and duly appraising the assets and liabilities of the two schools of social and political thought, practices, and behaviorism—one native, the other foreign, I dropped many prejudices against the native-born and adopted new ways of living, devoting most of my leisure time to night school, Y. M. C. A. classes, forums and centres of racial life. I took special interest in politics, in fraternal, charitable and religious work, so much so that I automatically lost consciousness that I was a foreigner.

In seeking employment I had no scruples, realizing that, to make ends meet, a Negro, native or foreign-born must be adept at more than one occupation. I worked in a brickyard, washed dishes, carried hod, was the first Negro huckster in Camden, N. J., worked as a pick-and-shovel man and a dock-hand at Norfolk, Va., a salesman in Pennsylvania, a fraternal organizer, porter and messenger.

My entire social life was revolutionized during this adjustment, but it was a rocky road. Few of those interested in bridging the chasm between native-born and foreign-born Negroes realize the tense social situation aroused by the interest of native-born Negro women in foreign-born men and vice versa. I have been admired and won the infatuation of some of the finest and most representative types of American Negro womanhood, but, for each social triumph I earned the bitter hatred and enmity of native-born men who often charged me with spoiling their women folk with too much kindness, loyalty and devotion. The lack of confidence native-born men displayed in their women appalled me. They warned me against marrying or putting too much faith in a native-born wife or sweetheart. One of them told me some years ago,

'The white man has so infiltrated his blood into that of our race I am afraid it is almost impossible for most of our women to go straight'. However, I have found native-born Negro women as moral, ethical, and trustworthy as men permit them to be.

An intelligent young man now employed as an elevator operator gives these impressions:

I found religious life here too commercialized, vain, and farcical to give it the same enthusiasm and spiritual cleavage I gave the church at home. Religion, as I have seen it practiced by native-born Negroes, is a moral and spiritual liability rather than an enduring asset.

The fact that so great a percent of the followers of Negro religious opportunists like Father Divine, Elder Solomon Lightfoot, Michaux, Bishop Charles Emanuel Grace, Mother Horne, and 'Prophet' Costonie, were once active members of the Baptist, Methodist, Presbyterian, Episcopalian, and Holiness faiths; the fact that the intelligentsia of the Negro wing of the Christian Church brush Christian ethics lightly aside to lend comfort and encouragement to these parasites—for purely financial reasons, is weighty evidence that the intellectuals who guide the destiny of religion among native-born Negroes lack spiritual, moral, and social perspectives, and are still chained to religious mental attitudes borrowed from Reconstruction Days. If it be true that God does not dwell in any unclean places, then He is not often found in the churches of native-born Negroes.

I may summarize my experiences in the United States as a great adventure which ended in a great discovery and quickened mental, spiritual, and racial growth.

I no longer feel that Negroes born under the British flag are better than others. I find little to choose from between the white American, the Englishman, the Frenchman, the Russian, the Japanese, the German, the Italian. While their methods and attitudes in things racial might differ here and there they eventually lead to the same objective. They are all of one opinion on where the Negro's place should be in the scale of human values. Whether I am slave or free man, subject or citizen of one or the other, I shall have to fight intelligently, courageously, against their designs to annihilate, subjugate, and exploit the race.

The status of native and foreign-born Negroes under their respective governments binds me closer to the ideal of international comity between the two groups. The oppressor's first major objective in subduing people of color is to make them economically dependent and impoverished. We can best arrest this strategy by a counter-attack through the avenues of culture, commerce, trade, finance, science and languages.

To appreciably bridge the chasm between Africans, West Indians, American and Central American Negroes, all of us must meet on a common ground of racial understanding and found a defense mechanism capable of checking imperial plots to reduce all of us to the status of vassals.

America has made me what I am today and I am proud of my American citizenship. America has put a song on my lips and a star in my sky. I am reaching for my star.

ON RETURNING HOME

The ultimate test of adjustment, however, is found in the intentions of immigrants with respect to returning to their native lands. These two statements are representative opinions; one who plans to return, another who prefers remaining here. The first says:

I, myself, sometimes wonder what will be my reactions when I return home as I hope to do sometime in the future. I may be then likened to the man who, after drinking nothing but wine for fifteen years, found that he had lost his taste for milk. Certain it is that life in the West Indies will seem rather hum-drum after residence in the United States. In this country it seems as if I have run the gamut of my emotions from A. to Z. It will require, I fear, much self-control to live in an environment where life is so smooth and runs in so narrow a circle. But I feel that I can do a lot to help my own people to lead fuller, richer lives—at any rate I feel called upon to make an attempt to graft the new upon the old—the realistic upon the idealistic.

The second maintains:

My attitude towards my native land is similar to that of the man who divorced his wife, informing the press, ' We parted the best of friends '. British Honduras will ever remain dear and precious to me, but as long as she remains backward, unprogressive, an imperial pawn, I shall always be happier here and more useful to her as a son of the soil and a naturalized American citizen.

CHAPTER IX

CONCLUSION

GENERAL SUMMARY

THE Negro immigrant enters the United States in the dual role of Negro and immigrant. Moving into a few centers of Negro population in large numbers, threatening the existing order of Negro adjustments he brings the bases for intra-racial conflict. One factor only prevents the conflict from becoming intense, the visibility of the Negro immigrant is low. Except for those who are Spanish and Portuguese-speaking, and who usually move into their own language groups, the external characteristics of Negroes, native and foreign, are the same. Looking alike, they are not inherently estranged; differing in mores they are isolated.

The first contacts of the native and foreign-born Negro groups are not of the conflict type. They are accompanied by the usual fear, uncertainty and curiosity. There tends to be a symbiotic, categoric type of contact, which later becomes a social relation. The nature of the initial relationship determines the nature of future relationships. The first clashes between the native and foreign-born Negro involve questions of status. These are temporarily accomodated. As the immigrant is numerically weaker he is forced to subordinate his wishes and desires to those of the majority group. But this group that comes over for economic and utilitarian purposes soon seeks status, recognition, position and prestige within the existing political and moral order.[1] This struggle is at the root of such conflict as exists between the native and foreign-born Negro.

The culture of the Negro immigrant is not able to survive the intensity of the resultant subtle conflict, whether it be reflected in the term " monkey-chaser ", the aspersion cast upon the Garvey movement, or the effort to have foreign-born

1 Park, R. E., " Our Racial Frontiers in the Pacific ", *The Survey*, Vol. 56, 1926, p. 196.

Negroes deported. As a result the culture of the immigrant tends to disintegrate. The partial isolation set up by the conflict makes necessary a greater dependence upon the native Negro group. The immigrant must reevaluate his culture in terms of his needs and culture that can only be satisfied in terms of the native Negro's cultural adaptation. As, and if, these various immigrant cultures break, the Negro immigrant becomes a part of the native Negro community. This process is followed more readily by the English-speaking Negro group than by those of other languages. But most important in the whole process of adjustment is the fact that while the Negro immigrant may rise in the economic scale by coming to the United States, he frequently loses status as an individual, and seeks to acquire a new status, which, while more profitable in facilitating economic adjustment, is won, often at the cost of promoting personal disorganization and additional group conflict.

Early in the conflict between the two groups there tends to rise the intra-group counterpart of what Park calls the "marginal man." [2] This is the immigrant who first loses the traditional and externally obvious aspects of his culture and attempts to assimilate the standards of the larger and predominant group. The immigrant is not marginal if he is accepted by the native-born but he frequently is not so readily accepted. Under such conditions he is neither completely foreign-born or native in terms of the culture. As was frequently the case during the 1920's, failure to acquire status so easily leads to the immigrant-consciousness-rebelling upon treated as a pariah. He finds it difficult to become accustomed to the synonymous use of "Negro" and "colored", and in this respect adds fuel to that never-ending argument of what this group of people shall call themselves.[3] If he is a person who has enjoyed relatively high status previously, or who is capable of influencing the

2 Park, R. E., "Human Migration and the Marginal Man," *American Journal of Sociology*, Vol. 33, No. 6, 1928, pp. 881-893.

3 See: Miller, Kelly, "Negroes or Colored People," *Opportunity, Journal of Negro Life*, Vol. 15, No. 5, May, 1937, pp. 142-146.

masses, he articulates the group's grievances. As they experience the same treatment he becomes a leader, and foreign-born consciousness and movements, such as the Universal Negro Improvement Association, arise. Thus, Garvey aided and abetted the process of the inter-group conflict but he did not initiate it.

In defense, the native-born group develops and formulates stereotypes, myths and ideologies justifying its superiority over the immigrant, and designs methods to support its contention. Any myth that will give credence to its ideology is employed. Prejudices arise as the immigrant menaces the partially accommodated status of the native-born. Such reactions in course produce sentiments of nationality consciousness, which are reflected, in one instance by a double-reverse method of universal black unity—Back to Africa, for example—and in others by immigrant solidarity, pride, and national loyalties. All of these, of course, are directed toward securing status and rights. The problem becomes complicated because in the alignment of issues the status and rights of the immigrant have usually been higher and greater "back home" than in the United States. Nevertheless this conflict indicates the indefiniteness of the "place" to which the Negro immigrant is assigned, not by the white population, but by the native Negro group, which itself has no definite "place", except in the mind of the race-problem conscious white group.

The problem is further complicated by the tendency of the native group to lump all Negroes of foreign birth in one category. Virgin Islanders with American citizenship rate no higher in the group evaluation than the Jamaican, a British subject. Jamaicans and Barbadians become one and the same; and, Trinidadians are lumped with Haitians. The conflict between native and foreign-born, therefore, becomes not one of race—but one of social process, of absorption and assimilation in the common culture and the social patterns. In this study we have endeavored to identify some of the elements present in the problem of the Negro immigrant and his adjustment—elements that give it dimension. The statistical facts in themselves give no adequate interpretation of the problem. Equally as important are the attitudes and interests maintained by each group—what they think about themselves and what they think about the others.

The most significant differences between the native and foreign-born Negro groups are those of social backgrounds. These differences run the gamut of human experience and include the variations in the social settings of immigrant and native. Of particular moment in this connection is the immigrant's background of either a tripartite color system, or one where color was not a primary factor in group life.

The Negro immigrant is brought into a relatively isolated, partially assimilated Negro group in which he becomes part and parcel of a socially restricted population. Neither the immigrant nor the native is accepted as part of the dominant white society. The former having been more accustomed to fuller participation reacts more drastically than does the more accommodated native-born. In gaining greater economic security, with restricted occupational mobility he has sacrificed the rights of broad social participation. The immigrant moving from an area where he was the racial, if not the economic, dominant majority adjusts less easily to the net-like separation of the races in the United States. Diverse cultural heritages tend to accentuate the maladjustments. As the new group or personality seeks recognition intra-racial prejudices develop, the process being no different from that obtaining in other forms of social contact between groups of diverse cultural backgrounds.

The presence of these two groups in the same area presents intersecting parallels. The native-born Negro's church has been an agency of racial reform headed by his own leaders, and emphasizing racial respect and programs for social reform. It was a tremendous integrating force—evangelical, void of formalism, full of emotion. The formalism of the immigrant's church served as a compensation for the social disabilities he experienced. Pastored chiefly by non-Negroes, it rigidly adhered to the ritualistic service, avoided championing causes of immediate import, was dignified, aloof and " respectable ". But change is being experienced in the transplanted immigrant's church, for if it would survive it must meet the problems of its members.

Each group lacked social solidarity with the societal whole and developed mutual benefit societies. Among the immigrants, at home or abroad, the mutual benefit principle is still important; at home because of the absence of insurance and the persistence of economic-social relations within the primary groups; abroad, because of the change of habitat and the need for mutual protection. The development of the insurance principle in the United States made great inroads into the native Negro's benefit societies, and was offset only by an increasing population mobility after 1920. The survival rate of the native group's societies however is lower than that of the immigrant's. The " Sons and Daughters " of Virginia, Georgia and South Carolina wane as the local interests of New York, New Jersey and Pennsylvania increase. The immigrant societies that are based upon face to face relations and forms of mutual interest tend to survive with a greater vitality, being frequently rejuvenated by interest in any event or movement in the homeland. The Baltimore *Afro-American*,[4] for example reports that during the week of May 15, 1937, Harlem staged a little coronation of its own. More than 5,000 persons attended the coronation ceremonies mentioned above (See p. 126). *The British West Indies and Allied War Veterans Association* held another coronation ball in Harlem. One church conducted special coronation services, and another poured a coronation tea. One writer commented on the various affairs by saying that although the Harlem " West Indian population has checked out of the islands, it has retained the pawn tickets."

Each group, native and foreign, tends to find a vicarious comfort in the influence exerted on the affairs of the other.

4 Ottley, Roi, May 15, 1937.

The development of cultural interests by the immigrant group particularly is pursued in part because of the interest itself, and in part as a defense of its insecure position. There is a pride in the memory of Bert Williams as a West Indian almost equal to the appreciation of his great comedy art. The names of Denmark Vesey who led "the most elaborate insurrectionary project ever formed by American slaves, and who came the nearest to a terrible success;" John B. Russwurm, the first college graduate and the first Negro newspaper publisher; Marcus Garvey, leader of immigrant masses;[5] Peter Jackson, of boxing fame; Casper Holstein, the Virgin Island philanthropist; Matzeliger, the inventor; Samuel Ward, co-worker with Garrison and Lovejoy; Robert Brown Elliott, attorney general, speaker of the State assembly and twice elected representative from South Carolina in the United States Congress; Peter Ogden, organizer of the first Odd Fellows Lodge for Negroes in New York City; Arthur A. Schomburg, foremost bibliophile; Edward W. Blyden, former Liberian Minister to London; Claude McKay, the poet-novelist; Prince Hall, founder of Free Masonry among Negroes in the United States; Judge James S. Watson—and others, become important to the nationality-conscious immigrant as much because they represent foreign-born Negroes who "made good" in the United States, as because of their achievements. Pride in having representatives who have achieved higher status not only becomes an important constructive force in facilitating participation in the general culture, but also tends to perpetuate the group isolation. Their leaders, even as do the native Negro's and the white immigrant's, tend to wear the mantles of Moses and Messiah.

5 In the early days of his movement Garvey was proudly hailed as a "West Indian." Later, as social pressures diminished his importance he was referred to as a "Jamaican". This led the editors of *The Messenger* to write 'if you are talking of virtues in a West Indian, by all means say he is a West Indian; if discussing vices, for God's sake let the nationality slide." (Vol. III, March, 1923, p. 646). This is the perfect parallel of the interracial difficulty in the reporting of Negro news in the daily press.

The Negro immigrant is beyond a doubt more radical than the native. He was more radical in his various home islands; the mere emigration therefrom indicating a break with certain traditional values. His breaking away from the homeland was neither incidental nor accidental but, as Schrieke [6] has defined it, was intentional and symptomatic. Protests against social and economic conditions are more pronounced among groups not so adjusted to their peculiar functioning in the new country. Furthermore, the West Indian immigrant has long fostered a movement to provide better, more representative government for the islands. The fight for federation of the British possessions; the historic importance of Haiti's rebellion and consequent status as the first republic of the Antilles; the representation in Paris of the French islands; the Virgin Islanders' fight for political freedom, representation, better government, and now, home-rule; the chaotic uprisings in Puerto Rico—all these have engendered in the immigrants a sympathetic and aggressive attitude on matters of social adjustment, and have led them to wonder why twelve million Negroes cannot muster sufficient political strength to get a mere anti-lynching bill through Congress. The immigrants' fight has been one to enhance self-respect, and certainly to offer a means of escape. In the States the programs they originate are seldom those of universal radicalism, but of racial radicalism to stimulate group pride and group solidarity, a compensatory process to offset the partial adjustment he now accepts.[7]

The traditional background of the Negro immigrant varies from that of the native-born in other ways. The institutions of

6 Schrieke, B., *Alien Americans*, New York, The Viking Press, 1936, p. 73.

7 Charles S. Johnson in his recent study, *The Negro College Graduate* (Univ. of North Carolina Press, 1938) points out that foreign-born Negro College graduates formed 2.3 percent of the 5,512 persons studied, they formed 7.8 percent of the Negro "leaders" listed in *Who's Who in Colored America*. (See Sanford Winston, "The Migration and Distribution of Negro Leaders in the U. S.", *Social Forces*, Vol. X, December, 1931, pp. 243-255). The Who's Who compilation may be characterized as one of "successful and alert" Negroes.

the state, religion—even public opinion has exercised a much more rigid and uniform control over the immigrant. In the areas of greatest Negro concentration in the United States, the Negro's historical experience has been that the law and public opinion served to arrest rather than promote his complete adjustment. Here not only does the immigrant came more frequently into contact with the agencies of the law, but there is less respect for the institution. Thus personal problems involving standards for children become important in the parent-child relationship of the immigrant family. " Back home ", questions of morals would have been covered by the mores, here those mores are repudiated. Does not the child become non-foreign by so doing? Thus the child of foreign-born parents, or the immigrant child is subject to a double social maladjustment because of the self-consciousness of being Negro, and, West Indian.

Looking at the career of a youth born of Negro parents with foreign or mixed nationality seems to yield this sort of picture: Up to the age of six or seven he is greatly befuddled by the sombre stillness of his home which directly impresses itself on his mind when, with natural child-like curiosity he weighs the abandon with which native children can play and enjoy themselves. Up to this age has been stressed upon his mind the theories that it is not " nice " to be on the streets like a hoodlum at all hours of the day. He more or less envies those children he is able to see from his window. He wonders why he cannot do the things that such and such a child can do. In his subconscious mind there is a repressed thought that can be summed up by saying: " Oh yes? . . . Just wait until I get a chance." This is tantamount to saying " Until I begin going to school."

He approaches his apparently " great problem " in the school. He is quite accustomed to what he has imagined will be the routine in the school. He has been thoroughly drilled in his " A-B-C's " by his parents or more often grand-parents at home. He has in the pronunciation of many words a distinctly foreign accent. His language as he progresses in age and in his classes is a fascinating mixture of "Rather" and "Okie-doke" . . . of "Excellent" and "Not so hot". . . . In this very minor instance; we can perceive a psychological justification for his spiritual unrest and mental disorganization.

From his earliest days in school, he has been rather pampered by his teachers who, feeling, as has been often expressed, that the conduct of a child at school can be safely considered a reflection of his hometraining, have in many ways made him a sort of example to the class, in both his aptitude and deportment. This is a direct incitation to the growth of a superiority complex, fostered and encouraged by his recollection of adult conversation about "Those Americans".

This superiority, however, is over-shadowed by the attitude of his play-mates who sooner or later hurl at him an abrupt awakening of his consciousness when he is branded "West Indian." Among his play-mates, he sooner or later allies himself with some native chum. He has decided to "out-American" the American by the *fait accomplis* of so concealing his identity that it is nothing short of very grave astonishment if he is questioned about his foreign extraction.

This desire follows him persistently until such time as he begins to definitely form his likes and dislikes. He is fortunate, perhaps, in being able to see both the views of the West Indian domiciled in the United States and the native Negro. He is in reality near fusion of both, both by his attitude and approach. It becomes obvious that he is kept mentally unbalanced and spiritually unstable. It is to be seriously questioned whether or not his whole life is mantled by a gross insincerity. He never successfully adjusts himself, nor can he become reconciled to the Victorian ideas pervading the atmosphere in his home. His has been a life of daily routine of parents' harping on "conduct becoming a gentleman." His has been a life of daily admonitions based upon a comparison of life in the West Indies and in America. A stock phrase is hurled at him in no kindly tone—"If you were at home this could not happen." He hears it so frequently that he yearns for a freer expression.

This channel is found in his social life, and becomes a well-used one. Yet, in his quest and desire for spiritual liberation in his most exultant mood, he suffers emotional martyrdom. The sermon repeats itself. "A gentleman must know his limits." And his imbalance continues. We therefore, frequently, find him a thoroughly unadjusted individual so long as he is assured of some secrecy, out-nativing the native, forgetting his role as a "gentleman" and, resorting to chicancery with a finesse that beggars description; sometimes superficial, always stilted and at times stupidly superior among those to whom he feels he is merely extending patronage.

Similar situations confront the maladjusted adult as well. Each tends to become resentful—and not to "know his place" in interracial relations.

He is immediately impressed with the hugeness of the city. The high buildings, the helter-skelter of a new people utterly bewilder him. Psychologically, for a reason based more upon his reaction, he is forced into unconsciously being an impressionist. Being an impressionist, he carries the air of one who is superior. Yet, no one is more aware than he of that feeling of inferiority he constantly subdues.

His dominance and superiority in reality are only very evident in his association with his white employers and associates. In this instance, he is fortified by his adaptability. He is fortified by his confidence in himself to do a job well and thoroughly. He considers himself a self-appointed ambassador of a subjected peoples. He is willing and ready to sacrifice even his appointment for a principle. He views with a child-like enthusiasm the reactions of the white man when being honestly impressed by his views and perhaps his philosophy, he is rewarded with the stock-phrase. "You are so different, where are you from?"

Yet, in his dealings with the native-born Negro, he is both hesitant and careful. His foreign accent may provide the occasion for laughter and criticism to which he is most sensitive. His manner of dress is a subject for discussion. He is afraid to ask questions and extremely careful when he is impelled to. He, therefore, resolves that the need for adjustment is both desirable and pertinent. His earnings are immediately used in transforming his clothes. In this manner he is flattered when visibly he is able to " pass ". He makes an intensive study of the use of popular slang and intonation of lingo. He hopes to successfully state that he is from Georgia or Charleston, South Carolina. He glories in the fact that he is able to cloak his national identity. He bids good-bye to his " unnecessary " courtesies and tries desperately to assume the matter-of-fact manner of his native brother.

The resultant behavior is described by an immigrant as follows:

> In the process he becomes both unreliable and disgusting, vacillating and boastful. In time he eventually " knows " the people he so earnestly strove to emulate. He becomes the harbinger of erroneous information to the less venturesome and ambitious of his own group. In the cool shadow of fore-thought he becomes the apostle whose sermons begin with trifling fabrications and end with gross exaggerations.
>
> He now assumes the role of a reformer. He expostulates to his group the need for being wide-awake and alert. He in like manner tries to impress upon the minds of the native Negroes the various social amenities and graces he thinks, as the result of his observation and association with him they should observe. His unwanted advice and information meet with an indifferent reception. In this very feeling of being misunderstood, his vanity leads him to inscribe his name upon the tablets of the great.
>
> Fortunately, however, the personal lustre with which he migrated, is now tarnished. He is able to weather economic injustices, no longer gracefully, but philosophically. In his acute rejuvenation, he has developed a take-a-chance psychosis with which his native brother is gifted. This is counter-balanced and in some way restrained, by his native shrewdness and perspicacity from which subconsciously he has never been divorced. His mind is a mental turbine, generating power of intensive, vindictive, but utterly useless opinion. And if the young Negro West Indian

has not experienced these reactions then he becomes an "American" more easily than the rest of us.

But, while this failure to be or stay " put " may be a liability and cause loss of status in Negro-white relations, it makes for position and prestige within the racial minority, and with the radical groups.

Cleavages within the Negro group are accentuated by the presence of an immigrant population. While in the eyes of many persons, all Negroes as a horizontal group may rank lower than the whites, it must be remembered that within the Negro group there is a vertical stratification with numerous levels. The higher levels may be said to be composed of persons

1. who have achieved financial success.
2. who have high occupational ranking, particularly in fields where few Negroes are employed.
3. who receive public recognition.
4. who are race leaders.

Many Negro immigrants must go into a mental reverse to accept such stratification, for many of the positions and occupations regarded as important in the United States would be frowned upon in the homeland—as, being a policeman, for example. Furthermore, unrestricted mobility in the Negro group permits the sharecropper's son to become a leading luminary in the Negro world. This would not have been possible in a color-class strictured society. One West Indian commented as follows upon the naming of a prominent Negro of foreign birth to an important public post—" Why the very idea! I would not speak to the fellow at home."

Even as do the white immigrants, the Negro immigrants, particularly the British West Indians, bring a zest of learning that is not typical of the native-born population. High schools and colleges in New York City have an unusually high foreign-born Negro representation. Between 1867 and 1932 Howard University had more than one thousand West Indians in its student body. It seems a justifiable opinion that Negroes, foreign and native, and Jews have developed an almost exaggerated interest in higher education, as an avenue of escape equal to the accumulation of wealth.[8] About the West Indian Negro particularly there has arisen the highly exaggerated and mistaken notion that he is "smarter", and more intelligent than the native Negro. And though Smith[9] has pointed out that "the scholarship of the West Indian student in proporton to his numbers has been above average," this may mean nothing more than that the West Indian students are a more highly selected group than the native-born. The selective migration of the better educated West Indians has been a factor in the relatively high proportion of honors they have obtained in the schools of the United States.

The racial amalgam represented by American and West Indian Negroes is probably the most heterogeneous stock in the world. Yet the learned reactions of the particular geographical and cultural settings have such deep emotional content that actions which do not conform to the prevailing norms arouse immediate and violent emotional reactions from people who live in the culture in which they are prevalent. Thus the native-born Negro's reaction to the immigrant ways is immediate and violent. One simply does not do things that way, he says. It is not in accord with the unconscious scheme of behavior he has acquired. The Negro immigrant therefore must learn to adjust himself to the new cultural environment, if he would survive. And even if he only superficially accepts the current mores, and although his temporary isolation may bring about the creation of special cultural forms and practices with his own group, he realizes that he can only succeed as he adapts himself to the larger, the dominant culture. But one question, more or less academic, remains unanswered for the color-class conscious

8 Miller, Herbert Adolphus, "The Negro and the Immigrant" in *Social Attitudes* by Kimball Young, Holt & Company, New York, 1931, p. 338.

9 Smith, Alfred Edgar, "West Indians on the Campus," *Opportunity, Journal of Negro Life*, August, 1933, Vol. II, p. 239.

foreign-born Negro—why do native-born Negroes object to stratification on the basis of color-class when it is practiced in their everyday lives, within and without the group?[10] So far there has been only one overt reply, the rise of *black nationalism,* which has not only advocated the non-patronage of concerns not employing Negroes, but has openly and vigilantly, with fang and claw, opposed the affiliation of Negroes with the various associations of the Socialist and Communist groups whose appeals are based upon the uniting of white and black workers. And while this movement has been rather erroneously labeled *black nationalism* it may be more adequately interpreted as a racial patterning of nationalism—and better called *racialism.* Its social parallel is found in neo-Zionism.

This glorification of race purity, this extreme manifestation of race consciousness was a distinct product of West Indian immigration to the United States. In the English-speaking islands of the West Indies where " Negroes " have so outnumbered whites, race admixture has not developed to the extent that it has in the United States. West Indians of distinct African types, says Woodson, " are less inclined to undertake the impossible in trying to change their features with hair straightening and bleaching processes as do the native Negro victims of the slave psychology in the United States. The black West Indian is not ashamed of his color. He is very much like the African who boasts of being black and comely, black and beautiful, beautifully black."[11]

Meanwhile the movement for naturalization continues. The barring of aliens from employment on public works, proposals frequently advanced for excluding aliens from relief rolls, the fact that only citizens can qualify for old-age pensions and other benefits under social security laws, are all considerations which impel the Negro alien to seek naturalization. The plight

10 Herskovits, M. J., *op. cit.*, p. 54 ff.

11 Woodson, C. G., " West Indian Racial Purity Considered an Advantage ". Release of the Association for the Study of Negro Life and History. Washington, D. C., November 3, 1931.

of European Jews, and the anomalous conditions of English affairs in India and Africa have led many foreign-born Negroes to the conclusion that naturalization in the United States may be the better part.[12] And, though hearing little mention of returning to the islands, one notes the growing importance of nationality and culture groups within the immigrant population. In Harlem alone according to a West Indian journalist there are more than thirty benevolent organizations to look after the needs of a people coming from nine political areas.[13] Furthermore, specific culture traits are emphasized. Trinidadians are regarded as " sweet men ", Barbadians as " steady " and Jamaicans as " thrifty ". In the main, all West Indians are regarded as diligent and successful workers, with distinct aversions for manual labor. Attesting their increasing importance in Negro life is the presence of foreign news in Negro newspapers.

Reconciliation of the cultural heritages of the alien and native groups continues apace, following at least three paths of acculturation. By taking over a large portion of the American Negro's culture and folkways the Negro immigrant has in many instances assimilated not only the behavior patterns but also the inner values of the culture with which he has come into recent contact. In the second place there has resulted a smooth blending of the diverse heritages into a cultural whole that can be labeled neither native nor alien. Yet this adaptation frequently results in the retention of conflicting attitudes between the groups which, while reconciled in the main, may frequently flare up in some form of conflict as the occasion arises. Finally, contra-acculturative movements arise among the Negro alien population—sometimes mute and inglorious, sometimes enunciative and eminent—and maintain for that population a psychological prestige by either compensating for the imposed infer-

12 Schomburg, Arthur A., " Our Pioneers ", *The Amsterdam News*, New York, September 12, 1936.

13 Malliet, A. M. W., *The Amsterdam News* (New York City), March 2, 1937.

iority, or by perpetuating or returning to the older cultural conditions.

One is almost certain to ask " How do these problems compare with those of other immigrant groups? " Are there any differences in the methods and processes of adjustment? " In the first place, evidence of the partial assimilation of immigrant groups is rather widespread—the ghettoes of our large cities, though declining, are chief witnesses to the problem. Foreign born, generally, are committed to penal institutions only about a third as rapidly as are native born persons. Mexicans, Italians and Greeks, however, appear to have arrest rates as high as those of Negroes.[14]

Failure to assimilate is likewise noted in the studies of the " old " as well as the " new " immigrant stocks. English immigrants have always been accepted as our most assimilable stocks. The Irish immigrant was alleged to be protected from complete social demoralization in his new surroundings only because of his essentially religious spirit and his avidity for social contacts within his own race.[15]

The problems faced by the Germans in Pennsylvania and elsewhere closely parallel in pattern those faced by Negroes.[16] Italians, as have Negro immigrants, have built up a national consciousness, entered their young men in politics not alone as a matter of personal ambition but as a means of securing recognition of their social groups.[17]

Abel's study of a Polish community in New England, on the other hand, indicates how aspects of group differentiation, and geographical and social environments may singularly char-

14 Prisoners in State and Federal Prisons and Reformatories, 1933. U. S. Department of Commerce, Bureau of the Census, Washington, 1935.

15 O'Brien, Michael J., *A Hidden Phase of American History*, New York, Dodd, Mead and Company, 1929.

16 Davis-DuBois, Rachel and Schweppe, E., eds., *Germans in American Life*, New York, Thomas Y. Nelson and Sons, 1936.

17 Foerster, Robert Franz, *The Italian Immigration of Our Times*, Cambridge, Massachusetts, Harvard University Press, 1919.

acterize any immigrant group.[18] Each and all of these studies indicate that the problems of immigrant adjustment are on the one hand very real effects of human migration, and on the other *attitudinal,* subject to change with experience and the development of functional procedures directed toward adjustment. The difference between the adjustment of Negro immigrants within the Negro group, and of Poles, Germans, Italians, Mexicans and other races and nationalities within the white group, appears to be one of degree rather than kind.

Negro immigrants, beyond a doubt, have bettered their economic status, kept something of their group cohesion, lost or partly lost attachment to their families, and found greater economic opportunity in the United States. But the problems of cultural diversity in an urban society have their deepest roots not in race and nationality, but in the complex differentiation and stratification attending their economic functions, cultural interests and social status. The distinctions of folk adaptations that persist, and the distance in cultural diversity that develops, do but spell wide differences in social values, attitudes, and opportunity of life.

All in all, the presence of a foreign Negro population has broadened the social vision of the native Negro group. It has fostered and compelled unity and has certainly accelerated intra-racial progress. The complexities of social process have obtained within the Negro group in more intricate variety than are ever known in the predominant white group. And interestingly enough, the attitudes of that predominant white group exercise little influence upon these complexities and conditionings, except that the inter-racial prejudices and acts of suppression may increase the very qualities against which they are directed, and help to speed up the very forces of aggressiveness and self-assertion in the direction that prejudice would sup-

18 Abel, Theodore, "Sunderland—a Study of Changes in the Group Life of Poles in a New England Farming Community", in *Immigrant Farmers and their Children,* Edmund deS. Brunner, New York, Doubleday, Doran & Co., 1929, pp. 213-243.

press them. For the adjustment of Negro immigrants and Negro natives represents an activity in social process that is born of injustices faced by the Negro group and of its partial accommodation in the predominant culture. And while these injustices and this partial accommodation may present tragic consequences for the individual, and temporary maladjustments for the group, the devising of ways of meeting situations, represents a very real and vital asset of Negro life determining, in part, the future character of social relationships between the races.

The adjustment of the Negro immigrant is a process, evolutionary in character, constantly increasing in momentum, and ever-changing in direction and scope. The Negro immigrant is constantly seeking to procure more favorable and important places in all the phases of economic living, political preferment and social status that are possible to Negroes in the United States. If in the seeking he steps on the heels of the native Negro population it is only because both groups hear the same drummer and are aligning in a common cause.

APPENDIX A

REFERENCE TABLES

TABLE I

DISTRIBUTION OF THE NEGRO POPULATION OF THE UNITED STATES BY NATIVITY, 1900–1930

	1930	1920	1910	1900
TOTAL	11,891,143	10,463,131	9,827,763	8,833,994
NATIVE BORN:—Total ..	11,792,523	10,389,328	9,787,424	8,813,658
Native parentage ...	11,709,162	10,334,151	9,748,439	8,779,267
Born in outlying possessions	17,625	4,846	355	401
Mixed parentage ...	39,909	29,334	24,425	25,193
Foreign parentage ..	43,452	25,843	14,560	9,198
FOREIGN BORN:	98,620	73,803	40,339	20,336
TOTAL FOREIGN STOCK: .	177,981	128,980	79,324	54,727
PERCENTAGE DISTRIBUTION:				
Total	100.0	100.0	100.0	100.0
Native parentage ...	98.5	98.8	99.3	99.4
Mixed parentage ...	0.3	0.3	0.2	0.3
Foreign parentage ..	0.4	0.2	0.1	0.1
Foreign-born	0.8	0.7	0.4	0.2

Source: Fifteenth Census of the United States, Vol. II, Population, 1930, Table No. 6, p. 33. Adapted.

TABLE II

INCREASE IN THE WHITE AND NEGRO POPULATIONS OF THE UNITED STATES BY NATIVITY AND BY DECADES, 1900–1930

Color and Nativity	1920–1930	1900–1930	1910–1920	1900–1910
TOTAL:				
Number	17,064,426	46,780,471	13,738,354	15,977,691
Per cent	16.1	61.5	14.9	21.0
WHITE:				
Native-born				
Number	14,632,820	38,902,421	12,634,845	11,634,750
Per cent	18.1	68.4	18.5	20.6
Foreign-born				
Number	111,013	3,152,690	121,082	2,920,495
Per cent	0.8	30.8	0.9	28.6
NEGRO:				
Native-born				
Number	1,403,195	2,978,865	601,904	973,766
Per cent	14.4	33.8	6.1	11.4
Foreign-born				
Number	24,817	78,284	33,464	20,003
Per cent	33.6	384.9	82.9	98.3

Source: Negroes in the United States, 1920-32. Bureau of the Census, United States Department of Commerce, Government Printing Office, Washington, 1933. Adapted.

TABLE III

TOTAL AND NEGRO IMMIGRANT ALIENS ADMITTED AND EMIGRANT ALIENS DEPARTED: UNITED STATES, 1899–1937

Year	Total			African Black[1]			Percentage African Black[1] of total	
	Admitted	Departed	Excess	Admitted	Departed	Excess	Admitted	Departed
1937 ..	50,244	26,736	23,506	275	433	–158	.5	1.6
1936 ..	36,329	35,817	512	272	502	–230	.8	1.4
1935 ..	34,956	38,834	–3,878	246	597	–351	.7	1.5
1934 ..	29,470	39,771	–10,301	178	604	–426	.6	1.5
1933 ..	23,068	80,081	–57,013	84	1,058	–974	.4	1.3
1932 ..	35,576	103,295	–67,719	183	811	–628	.5	.7
1931 ..	97,139	61,882	35,257	884	737	147	.9	1.1
1930 ..	241,700	50,661	191,039	1,806	776	1,030	.7	1.3
1929 ..	279,678	69,203	210,475	1,254	425	829	.4	.6
1928 ..	307,255	77,457	229,798	956	789	167	.3	1.0
1927 ..	335,175	73,366	261,809	955	870	85	.3	1.1
1926 ..	304,488	76,992	227,496	894	865	29	.3	1.1
1925 ..	294,314	92,728	201,586	791	1,094	–303	.3	1.1
1924 ..	706,896	76,789	630,107	12,243	1,449	10,794	1.7	1.8
1923 ..	523,099	81,450	441,649	7,554	1,525	6,029	1.4	1.8
1922 ..	309,556	198,712	110,844	5,248	2,183	3,065	.1	1.0
1921 ..	804,828	247,718	557,110	9,873	1,807	8,066	1.2	.7
1920 ..	430,001	288,315	141,686	8,174	1,275	6,899	.1	.4
1919 ..	141,132	123,522	17,610	5,823	976	4,847	.4	.7
1918 ..	110,618	94,585	16,033	5,706	1,291	4,415	.5	1.3
1917 ..	365,403	66,277	299,126	7,971	1,497	6,474	.2	2.2
1916 ..	299,626	129,765	169,861	4,576	1,684	2,892	.1	1.2
1915 ..	326,700	204,074	122,626	5,660	1,644	4,016	.1	.8
1914 ..	1,218,480	303,338	915,142	8,447	1,805	6,642	.6	.6
1913 ..	1,197,892	308,190	889,702	6,634	1,671	4,963	.5	.5
1912 ..	838,172	333,262	504,910	6,759	1,288	5,471	.8	.4
1911 ..	878,587	295,666	582,921	6,721	913	5,808	.7	.3
1910 ..	1,041,570	202,436	839,134	4,966	926	4,040	.4	.4
1909 ..	951,876	225,802	726,074	4,307	1,104	3,203	.5	.5
1908 ..	782,870	395,073	387,797	4,626	889	3,737	.5	.2
1907 ..	1,285,349			5,235			.4	
1906 ..	1,100,735			3,786			.3	
1905 ..	1,026,499			3,598			.3	
1904 ..	812,870			2,386			.2	
1903 ..	857,046			2,174			.2	
1902 ..	648,743			832			.1	
1901 ..	487,910			594			.1	
1900 ..	448,522			714			.1	
1899 ..	311,715			412			.1	

Minus sign (–) denotes decrease.

[1] "African, Black" is the term employed by the Bureau of Immigration and Naturalization to include all immigrant and emigrant persons whose race has been specified as Negro.

Source: Reports of the Commissioner of Immigration and the Secretary of Labor, U. S. Department of Labor. 1899-1937. Adapted.

TABLE IV

YEAR OF ARRIVAL OF THE FOREIGN-BORN NEGRO POPULATION
BY SEX, FOR THE UNITED STATES: 1930

Year of immigration	Total		Male		Female	
	Number	Per cent	Number	Per cent	Number	Per cent
Total	106,202	100.0	57,887	100.0	48,135	100.0
1925-1930	7,582	7.1	3,806	6.6	3,776	7.8
1930 (to April 1) ..	302	0.3	142	0.2	160	.3
1929	1,357	1.3	632	1.1	725	1.5
1928	1,173	1.1	558	1.0	615	1.3
1927	1,261	1.2	652	1.1	609	1.2
1925 and 1926	3,489	3.3	1,822	3.1	1,667	3.4
1920-1924	27,372	25.7	13,391	23.1	13,981	29.0
1915-1919	18,181	17.1	9,699	16.8	8,482	17.6
1911-1914	10,951	10.3	6,008	10.4	4,943	10.2
1901-1910	15,356	14.5	9,178	15.8	6,178	12.8
1900 or earlier ...	7,601	7.2	4,551	7.9	3,050	6.3
Unknown	11,577	10.9	7,448	12.9	4,129	8.6

Source: Fifteenth Census of the United States. Population, Vol. II. Table No. 4, p. 498. Adapted.

TABLE V

COUNTRY OF BIRTH OF THE TOTAL AND NEGRO FOREIGN-BORN POPULATION OF THE UNITED STATES, 1930 AND 1920

Place of Birth	All Classes 1930	All Classes 1920	Negro 1930	Negro 1920
TOTAL FOREIGN-BORN	14,204,149	13,920,692	98,620	73,803
EUROPE	11,748,399	11,882,053	4,632	3,996
ASIA	275,665	237,950	44	27
China	46,129	43,560	1	6
India	5,850	4,901	29	—
Other Asia	152,693	107,987	14	21
AMERICA	2,102,209	1,727,017	87,094	63,684
Canada	1,286,389	1,124,925	5,817	5,651
Newfoundland	23,980	13,249	9	6
Cuba	18,493	14,872	2,362	1,934
Other West Indies	87,478	64,090	72,138	50,488
Mexico	641,462	486,418	915	3,123
Central America	10,514	4,912	2,662	816
South America	33,623	18,551	3,191	1,666
ALL OTHER	77,876	73,672	6,850	6,096
Africa	8,859	5,781	986	556
Australia	12,816	10,914	81	107
Azores	35,611	33,995	177	206
Other Atlantic Islands	9,461	10,345	5,411	5,143
Pacific Islands	4,527	3,712	96	40
Not specified, or born at sea	6,596	8,925	99	44

Source: Fifteenth Census of the United States, Population, Vol. II, Table 2, p. 231.

TABLE VI

POPULATION OF THE CARIBBEAN AREA BY NATIONAL AFFILIATION AND RACE, 1936

Political area	National affiliation	Population			
		Total	Colored	White	Other
TOTAL		12,397,204	8,084,770	3,861,058	451,376
Bahamas	Great Britain	62,679	48,679	13,000	1,000
Barbados	Great Britain	180,055	162,055	18,000	—
Bermuda	Great Britain	29,896	17,862	11,684	350
Cuba	Republic	4,011,088	1,300,000	2,443,000	268,088
Grenada	Great Britain	78,662	62,929	15,576	157
Guadeloupe	France	267,407	213,925	52,948	534
Haiti	Republic	2,650,000	2,646,000	3,500	500
Jamaica	Great Britain	1,090,269	1,040,269	20,000	30,000
Leeward Islands	Great Britain	132,973	106,378	26,330	265
Martinique	France	234,695	187,756	46,470	469
Puerto Rico	United States	1,623,814	473,664	1,150,000	150
St. Lucia	Great Britain	62,000	49,600	12,276	124
St. Vincent	Great Britain	47,961	44,549	2,173	1,239
Santo Domingo	Republic	1,478,121	1,444,621	30,000	3,500
Trinidad	Great Britain	425,572	265,572	15,000	145,000
Virgin Islands	United States	22,012	20,911	1,101	—

Source: Work, Monroe W., (Editor) *The Negro Year Book,* Tuskegee, Alabama, 1937, p. 327.

TABLE VII

NEGRO IMMIGRANT ALIENS ADMITTED TO THE UNITED STATES BY AREA OF LAST RESIDENCE
1899–1932

Year	Total number	West Indies		Central America		South America		British North America		Portugal		Other	
		No.	Per cent total	No.	Per cent total	No.	Per cent total	No.	Per cent total	No.	Per cent total	No.	Per cent total
1932	183	113	62.3	13	7.1	10	5.4	28	15.3	3	1.6	16	8.3
1931	884	674	76.2	77	8.7	61	6.8	30	3.4	9	1.0	33	3.9
1930	1,806	1,388	76.8	112	6.2	158	8.7	106	5.8	–	—	42	2.5
1929	1,254	803	64.0	169	13.5	89	7.1	123	9.8	8	.6	62	5.0
1928	956	586	61.3	136	14.2	57	6.0	134	14.0	9	.9	34	3.6
1927	955	581	60.1	125	13.1	53	5.9	153	16.0	2	.2	41	4.7
1926	894	480	53.8	197	22.0	50	5.6	114	12.7	7	.8	46	5.1
1925	791	308	38.9	174	22.0	47	5.7	224	28.3	13	1.6	25	3.5
1924	12,243	10,630	86.6	511	4.1	375	3.1	498	4.0	128	1.4	105	.8
1923	7,554	6,580	87.1	254	3.4	171	2.2	292	3.3	164	2.5	138	1.5
1922	5,248	4,424	84.3	188	3.6	154	2.9	172	3.3	201	3.8	109	2.1
1921	9,873	7,046	71.4	543	5.5	197	1.9	414	4.2	1,364	13.8	309	3.2
1920	8,174	6,059	74.1	417	5.0	193	2.3	415	5.1	845	10.3	245	3.2
1919	5,823	4,027	69.2	799	13.7	268	4.6	274	4.7	329	5.6	126	2.2
1918	5,706	3,993	69.9	906	16.0	158	2.7	142	2.5	407	7.1	100	1.8
1917	7,971	5,769	72.3	622	7.9	135	1.7	409	5.1	940	11.8	96	1.2
1916	4,576	3,257	70.9	160	3.5	100	2.2	364	7.9	653	14.3	82	1.2

TABLE VII (*Continued*)

Year	Total number	West Indies		Central America		South America		British North America		Portugal		Other	
		No.	Per cent total	No.	Per cent total	No.	Per cent total	No.	Per cent total	No.	Per cent total	No.	Per cent total
1915	5,660	4,104	73.9	252	4.5	38	.7	286	5.1	838	13.1	144	2.7
1914	8,447	5,724	67.7	348	4.1	111	1.3	342	4.1	1,711	20.2	211	3.6
1913	6,634	4,891	73.8	277	4.2	91	1.4	338	5.1	972	14.6	65	.9
1912	6,759	4,885	72.2	245	3.6	94	1.4	329	4.8	1,103	16.3	103	1.7
1911	6,721	4,973	73.9	154	2.3	111	1.6	304	4.6	1,101	16.1	76	1.5
1910	4,966	3,769	75.9	120	2.4	38	.8	212	4.3	778	15.7	49	.9
1909	4,307	3,340	77.5	107	2.5	30	.7	172	4.0	615	14.3	43	1.0
1908	4,626	3,563	77.0	116	2.5	77	1.7	102	2.2	705	15.2	63	1.4
1907	5,233	4,561	87.3	99	1.7	48	.9	105	2.0	349	6.7	71	1.4
1906	3,786	3,018	79.7	91	2.4	43	1.1	57	1.5	301	8.0	276	7.3
1905	3,598	3,034	84.3	37	1.0	66	1.8	9	.2	347	9.6	105	3.1
1904	2,386	1,762	73.9	3	.1	25	1.0	5	.2	439	18.4	152	6.4
1903	2,174	1,134	52.1	1	(1)	2	(1)	—	—	934	42.9	103	4.9
1902	832	805	96.7	—	—	—	—	—	—	—	—	27	3.3
1901	594	520	87.5	—	—	—	—	—	—	—	—	74	12.5
1900	714	703	98.4	—	—	—	—	—	—	—	—	11	1.6
1899	412	388	94.1	—	—	—	—	—	—	—	—	23	5.9

(1) Less than one tenth of one per cent.

Source: Reports of the Commissioner of Immigration, United States Department of Labor, 1899-1932.

TABLE VIII

AGE DISTRIBUTION OF TOTAL AND NEGRO IMMIGRANT ALIENS ADMITTED IN 1930. (By Sex)

	Total				Negro			
	Number		Per cent		Number		Per cent	
Age groups	Males	Fe-males	Males	Fe-males	Males	Fe-males	Males	Fe-males
TOTAL	117,026	124,674	48.4	51.6	785	1,021	43.5	56.5
Under 16	20,906	19,871	8.6	8.2	184	165	10.2	9.1
16-21	28,627	29,109	11.8	12.0	220	228	12.2	12.6
22-29	36,878	34,692	15.3	14.4	196	285	10.9	15.8
30-37	14,495	17,548	6.0	7.3	102	162	5.6	9.0
38-44	6,666	9,044	2.8	3.7	49	88	2.7	4.9
45 and over	9,454	14,410	3.9	6.0	34	93	1.9	5.1

Source: Report of Commissioner General of Immigration, 1930, p. 154.

TABLE IX

Age Distribution of Total and Negro Populations of Known Ages By Sex, 1930

	Total Population					
	Number			Per cent		
Age groups	Total	Male	Female	Total	Male	Female
All ages	122,681,024	62,085,264	60,595,760	100.0	100.0	100.0
Under 16 ...	38,352,575	19,410,707	18,941,868	31.2	31.3	31.1
16-21	13,689,878	6,782,069	6,907,809	11.1	10.9	11.4
22-29	16,270,524	8,018,103	8,252,421	13.3	12.9	13.6
30-37	15,680,963	7,384,107	7,296,856	12.2	11.9	12.1
38-44	11,638,298	5,993,998	5,644,300	9.4	9.7	9.4
45 and over .	28,048,786	14,496,280	13,552,506	22.8	23.3	22.4

	Negro Population					
	Number			Per cent		
Age groups	Total	Male	Female	Total	Male	Female
All ages	11,877,412	5,848,605	6,028,807	100.0	100.0	100.0
Under 16 ...	4,090,566	2,031,269	2,059,297	34.4	34.7	34.2
16-21	1,496,942	702,733	794,209	12.6	12.0	13.2
22-29	1,788,127	829,993	958,134	15.0	14.2	15.9
30-37	1,399,125	677,093	722,032	11.8	11.6	11.9
38-44	1,043,712	509,577	534,135	8.9	8.7	8.9
45 and over	2,058,940	1,097,940	961,000	17.3	18.8	15.9

Source: Fifteenth Census of the United States, 1930 Population, Vol. II, Table 20, pp. 593-594.

TABLE X

Marital Status of Negro Immigrant Aliens United States, By Sex
1923-1932

Year	Total					Male					Female				
	Total	Single	Married	Widowed	Divorced	Total	Single	Married	Widowed	Divorced	Total	Single	Married	Widowed	Divorced
1932 ..	183	134	41	8		66	54	11	1		117	80	30	7	
	100.0	73.2	22.4	4.4		100.0	81.8	16.6	1.6		100.0	68.3	25.7	6.0	
1931 ..	884	688	160	36		352	294	57	1		532	394	103	35	
	100.0	77.8	18.1	4.1		100.0	83.5	16.2	0.3		100.0	74.0	19.4	6.6	
1930 ..	1,806	1,363	396	46	1	785	636	146	3		1,021	727	250	43	1
	100.0	75.5	21.9	2.5	0.1	100.0	81.0	18.6	0.4		100.0	71.2	24.5	4.2	0.1
1929 ..	1,254	935	279	39	1	563	454	101	7	1	691	481	178	32	
	100.0	74.6	22.2	3.1	0.1	100.0	80.6	17.9	1.3	0.2	100.0	69.6	25.7	4.7	
1928 ..	956	662	247	45	2	463	325	134	4		493	337	113	41	2
	100.0	69.2	25.8	4.7	0.3	100.0	70.1	29.0	0.9		100.0	68.3	22.9	8.3	0.5
1927 ..	955	667	242	43	3	415	309	96	8	2	540	358	146	35	1
	100.0	69.9	25.3	4.5	0.3	100.0	74.5	23.1	1.9	0.5	100.0	66.3	27.0	6.5	0.2
1926 ..	894	605	245	43	1	388	293	86	9		506	312	159	34	1
	100.0	67.6	27.4	4.8	0.2	100.0	75.5	22.1	2.4		100.0	61.6	31.4	6.8	0.2
1925 ..	791	521	220	48	2	357	254	99	4		434	267	121	44	2
	100.0	65.8	27.0	6.1	0.3	100.0	71.1	27.7	1.2		100.0	61.5	27.9	1.0	0.5
1924 ..	12,243	8,865	2,954	420	4	5,558	4,062	1,444	51	1	6,685	4,803	1,510	369	3
	100.0	72.4	24.1	3.4		100.0	73.1	26.0	0.9		100.0	71.8	22.6	5.5	0.1
1923 ..	7,443	5,524	1,659	258	2	3,325	2,586	707	30	2	4,118	2,938	952	228	
	100.0	74.2	22.3	3.5		100.0	77.8	21.3	0.9	0.1	100.0	71.3	23.1	5.6	

Source: Annual Reports Commissioner General of Immigration 1923-1932.

TABLE XI

DISTRIBUTION OF NEGRO IMMIGRANT ALIENS ADMITTED BY OCCUPATIONAL GROUPING AS SPECIFIED UPON ARRIVAL

1901–1935

Year	Total Negro admissions	Total reporting specific occupations	Miscellaneous	Per cent reporting occupations	Occupational classification: All occupations	Agriculture		Industry		Commerce and finance		Laborers and servants		Professions	
					Per cent	No.	Per cent	No.	Per cent	No.	Per cent	No.	Per cent	No.	Per cent
Total	141,125	103,232	37,893	73.1	100.0	14,971	14.5	32,424	31.4	10,345	10.1	41,737	40.4	3,755	3.6
1931-35	1,575	746	829	48.6	100.0	14	1.9	301	40.4	132	17.6	209	28.1	90	12.0
1926-30	5,865	3,208	2,657	54.7	100.0	96	3.0	1,364	42.5	415	12.9	1,064	33.2	269	8.4
1921-25	35,709	24,713	10,996	69.2	100.0	2,872	11.6	8,374	34.0	2,792	11.3	9,634	34.0	1,041	4.2
1916-20	32,250	23,888	8,362	74.1	100.0	2,727	11.4	8,176	34.2	2,721	11.4	9,373	39.2	891	3.8
1911-15	34,222	26,076	8,146	79.1	100.0	5,426	20.8	6,997	26.8	1,618	6.2	11,292	43.4	743	2.8
1906-10	22,920	17,469	5,451	76.2	100.0	3,152	18.0	5,007	28.7	1,512	8.6	7,257	41.6	541	3.1
1901-05	8,584	7,132	1,452	83.1	100.0	684	9.6	2,205	30.9	1,155	16.2	2,908	40.8	180	2.5

TABLE XII

Negro Immigrant Aliens Admitted By States of Intended Future Permanent Residence 1923–1932

State of intended residence	Year Ending June 30th										Total
	1932	1931	1930	1929	1928	1927	1926	1925	1924	1923	
Total	183	884	1,806	1,254	956	955	894	791	12,243	7,554	27,520
New York	89	663	1,341	850	601	543	461	435	8,214	4,986	18,183
Florida	—	4	144	55	64	62	140	35	1,992	1,086	3,582
Massachusetts	16	43	80	92	70	90	58	87	691	521	1,748
New Jersey	3	36	34	22	19	30	40	30	351	262	827
Michigan	10	16	40	42	51	52	41	40	181	99	572
Pennsylvania	8	12	16	32	25	22	26	19	207	136	503
California	7	13	27	14	18	18	32	19	61	58	267
Connecticut	1	6	9	8	9	12	3	5	98	68	219
Illinois	2	7	18	18	10	20	6	—	73	45	199
District of Columbia ...	2	17	11	14	9	16	14	—	41	54	178
Others	45	67	86	107	80	90	73	121	334	239	1,242

Source: Reports of the Commissioner of Immigration, 1923-1932.

TABLE XIII

DISTRIBUTION OF THE FOREIGN-BORN NEGRO POPULATION OF THE UNITED STATES, BY NUMBER AND PER CENT OF TOTAL NEGRO FOREIGN-BORN BY DIVISIONS: 1900-1930

Divisions	1930 No.	1930 Per cent	1920 No.	1920 Per cent	1910 No.	1910 Per cent	1900 No.	1900 Per cent
United States	98,620	100.0	73,803	100.0	40,339	100.0	20,336	100.0
Middle Atlantic ..	64,565	65.5	37,625	51.0	16,322	40.0	4,875	24.0
New England ..	11,786	12.0	12,256	16.6	7,710	19.1	4,368	21.5
South Atlantic ..	12,584	12.8	12,962	17.6	8,075	20.0	5,495	27.0
E. North Central ...	5,157	5.2	4,262	5.8	3,384	8.3	2,316	11.4
W. North Central ...	528	0.5	1,049	1.4	807	2.0	412	2.1
E. South Central ...	532	0.5	636	0.9	625	1.5	512	2.5
W. South Central ...	1,412	1.4	2,991	4.0	1,869	4.6	1,556	7.7
Mountain.	187	0.2	581	0.9	373	0.9	217	1.1
Pacific ...	1,869	1.9	1,441	1.8	1,174	2.9	585	2.8

Source: Fifteenth Census of the United States, 1930, Population, Vol. II, Table XVII, pp. 41-45. Adapted.

TABLE XIV

Distribution of the Negro Population by Nativity and Urban, Rural-Farm and Rural-Non-Farm Areas, by Number and Per Cent of Total, United States, 1930

	New England	Middle Atlantic	East North Central	West North Central	South Atlantic	East South Central	West South Central	Mountain	Pacific
Total Urban									
Number	81,443	939,064	848,627	259,195	1,462,904	759,166	744,255	21,032	78,227
Per cent	100.0	100.0	100.0	100.0	100.0	100.0	100.0	100.0	100.0
Native-Born									
Number	71,588	875,798	843,804	258,751	1,452,649	758,799	743,117	20,904	76,626
Per cent	87.9	93.3	99.4	99.8	99.3	99.9	99.8	99.4	98.0
Foreign-Born									
Number	9,855	63,266	4,823	444	10,255	367	1,138	128	1,601
Per cent	12.1	6.7	0.6	0.2	0.7	0.1	0.2	0.6	2.0
Total Rural-Farm									
Number	1,133	11,016	18,195	35,257	1,940,501	1,451,742	1,186,543	2,363	3,773
Per cent	100.0	100.0	100.0	100.0	100.0	100.0	100.0	100.0	100.0
Native-Born									
Number	965	10,957	18,152	35,215	1,939,838	1,481,692	1,186,423	2,350	3,689
Per cent	85.2	99.5	99.8	99.9	99.9	99.9	99.9	99.4	97.8
Foreign-Born									
Number	168	59	43	41	663	50	120	13	84
Per cent	14.8	0.5	0.2	0.1	0.1	0.1	0.1	0.6	2.2
Total Rural-Non-Farm									
Number	11,510	102,819	63,628	37,332	1,017,983	418,330	351,153	6,830	8,122
Per cent	100.0	100.0	100.0	100.0	100.0	100.0	100.0	100.0	100.0
Native-Born									
Number	9,747	101,579	63,337	37,289	1,016,117	418,215	350,999	6,784	7,938
Per cent	84.7	98.8	99.5	99.9	99.8	99.9	99.9	99.3	97.7
Foreign-Born									
Number	1,763	1,240	291	43	1,866	115	154	46	184
Per cent	15.3	1.2	0.5	0.1	0.2	0.1	0.1	0.7	2.3

Source: Fifteenth Census of the United States, 1930. Population, Vol. II, Table 22, pp. 65-66.

TABLE XV

DISTRIBUTION OF NEGRO POPULATION BY NATIVITY FOR CITIES HAVING MORE THAN 500 FOREIGN-BORN NEGROES IN THE POPULATION: 1930

	Total	Native-Born	Foreign-Born	Per cent Foreign-Born
TOTAL	1,409,902	1,335,546	74,356	5.2
MASSACHUSETTS:				
Boston	20,574	17,287	3,287	16.0
Cambridge	5,419	4,264	1,155	21.3
New Bedford	3,631	2,500	1,131	31.1
RHODE ISLAND:				
Providence	5,473	4,821	652	11.9
NEW YORK:				
New York City	327,706	272,952	54,754	16.7
Bronx Borough	12,930	11,186	1,744	13.5
Brooklyn Borough	68,921	57,655	11,266	16.3
Manhattan Borough	224,670	184,837	39,833	17.7
Queens Borough	18,609	16,909	1,700	9.1
Richmond Borough	2,576	2,365	211	8.2
NEW JERSEY:				
Atlantic City	15,611	15,092	519	3.3
PENNSYLVANIA:				
Philadelphia	219,599	217,582	2,017	0.9
ILLINOIS:				
Chicago	233,903	232,656	1,338	0.6
MICHIGAN:				
Detroit	120,066	118,621	1,445	1.2
MARYLAND:				
Baltimore	142,106	141,382	724	0.5
FLORIDA:				
Miami	25,116	19,604	5,512	21.9
Tampa	21,172	20,541	631	3.0
LOUISIANA:				
New Orleans	129,632	128,966	666	0.5
CALIFORNIA:				
Los Angeles	38,894	39,369	525	1.3

Source: Fifteenth Census of the United States, 1930. Population, Vol. II, Table 23, pp. 67-73. Adapted.

TABLE XVI

CITIZENSHIP OF THE FOREIGN-BORN NEGRO POPULATION BY STATES: 1930
(For states having 500 or more foreign-born Negroes)

State	Total	Naturalized					
		Total		Males		Females	
		No.	Per cent	No.	Per cent	No.	Per cent
UNITED STATES ...	98,620	24,815	25.2	14,379	28.3	9,052	22.3
Massachusetts ...	8,934	2,133	23.9	1,151	23.9	877	23.9
Rhode Island	1,063	221	20.8	137	19.3	78	24.8
Connecticut	1,378	274	19.8	176	19.6	85	20.8
New York	57,895	13,582	23.5	7,783	28.0	4,879	10.0
New Jersey	3,719	1,258	33.8	701	36.1	482	30.8
Pennsylvania	2,951	1,243	42.1	811	42.5	389	43.7
Ohio	1,077	500	46.4	271	42.3	218	55.6
Illinois	1,566	747	47.7	406	45.5	302	52.6
Michigan	2,262	959	42.4	441	38.6	461	49.7
Maryland	872	271	31.1	218	30.7	50	35.5
Florida	10,347	1,271	12.3	668	13.6	554	12.9
Louisiana	809	244	30.2	180	31.0	56	30.1
California	1,652	453	27.4	302	29.3	141	27.1
All other states ..	4,095	1,659	40.5	1,134	39.6	480	45.5

Source: Fifteenth Census of the United States, 1930. Population, Vol. II, Table No. 18, p. 446. Adapted.

APPENDIX B

LEGAL DEFINITIONS OF IMMIGRANTS, NON-QUOTA IMMIGRANTS, AND QUOTA IMMIGRANTS[1]

Section 3. When used in this act the term " immigrant " means any alien departing from any place outside the United States destined for the United States, except (1) a government official, his family, attendants, servants, and employees (2) an alien visiting the United States temporarily as a tourist or temporarily for business or pleasure (3) an alien in continuous transit through the United States (4) an alien lawfully admitted to the United States who later goes in transit from one part of the United States to another through foreign contiguous territory (5) a bonafide alien seaman serving as such on a vessel arriving at a port of the United States and seeking to enter temporarily the United States solely in the pursuit of his calling as a seaman, and (6) an alien entitled to enter the United States solely to carry on trade under and in pursuance of the provisions of a present existing treaty of commerce and navigation (Sec. 203).

NON-QUOTA IMMIGRANTS

Section 4. (As amended by sections 1 and 2 or joint resolution approved May 29, 1928, 45 Stat. 1009.) When used in this act the term " non-quota immigrant " means—

(a) An immigrant who is the unmarried child under twenty-one years of age, or the wife of a citizen of the United States, or the husband of a citizen of the United States by a marriage occurring prior to June 1, 1928;

(b) An immigrant previously lawfully admitted to the United States who is returning from a temporary visit abroad;

(c) An immigrant who was born in the Dominion of Canada, Newfoundland, the Republic of Mexico, the Republic of Cuba, the Republic of Haiti, the Dominican Republic, the Canal Zone,

1 U. S. Dept. of Labor, Immigration and Naturalization Service, Immigration Laws and Rules of January 1, 1930, Washington, D. C., United States Government Printing Office, 1935, pp. 2-4.

or an independent country of Central or South America, and his wife, and his unmarried children under eighteen years of age, if accompanying or following to join him;

(d) An immigrant who continuously for at least two years immediately preceding the time of his application for admission to the United States has been, and who seeks to enter the United States solely for the purpose of, carrying on the vocation of minister of any religious denomination or professor of a college, academy, seminary, or university; and his wife, and his unmarried children under eighteen years of age, if accompanying or following to join him;

(e) An immigrant who is a bona fide student at least fifteen years of age and who seeks to enter the United States solely for the purpose of study at an accredited school, college, academy, seminary, or university, particularly designated by him and approved by the Secretary of Labor, which shall have agreed to report to the Secretary of Labor the termination of attendance of each immigrant student, and if such institution of learning fails to make such reports promptly the approval shall be withdrawn; or

(f) A woman who was a citizen of the United States and who prior to September 22, 1922, lost her citizenship by reason of her marriage to an alien, but at the time of her application for an immigration visa is unmarried (Section 204).

QUOTA IMMIGRANTS

Section 5. When used in this act the term "quota immigrant" means any immigrant who is not a non-quota immigrant. An alien who is not particularly specified in this act as a non-quota immigrant or a non-immigrant shall not be admitted as a non-quota immigrant or a non-immigrant by reason or relationship to any individual who is so specified or by reason of being excepted from the operation of any other law regulating or forbidding immigration (Section 205).

BIBLIOGRAPHY

Abbott, Edith, *Immigration: Selected Documents and Case Records,* Chicago, University of Chicago Press, 1921.

Barzun, Jacques, *Race: A Study In Modern Superstition,* New York, Harcourt, Brace and Co., 1937.

Beals, Carleton, *America South,* Philadelphia, J. P. Lippincott Co., 1937.

Bogardus, E. S., *Immigration and Race Attitudes,* Boston, D. C. Heath and Co., 1928.

Bowen, Lawrence Guy, *Immigration: Cultural Conflicts and Social Adjustments,* New York, Longmans, Green and Co., 1933.

Brown, Francis J., and Joseph Slabey Rouchek—(Editors) *Our Racial and National Minorities,* New York, Prentice-Hall, Inc., 1937.

Brunner, Edmund de S., *Immigrant Farmers and Their Children,* New York, Garden City Publishing Company, 1929.

Bunche, Ralph, *A World View Of Race,* Bronze Booklet Number 4, The Associates in Negro Folk Education, Washington, D. C., 1936.

Carlson, Fred A., *Geography of Latin America,* New York, Prentice-Hall, Inc., 1936.

Carpenter, Niles, *Immigrants and Their Children,* U. S. Bureau of the Census, 1920, Census Monograph VII, 1927.

Carr-Saunders, A. M., *World Population—Its Past Growth and Present Trends,* New York and London, Oxford University Press, 1936.

Chenault, Lawrence R., *The Puerto Rican Migrant in New York City,* New York, Columbia University Press, 1938.

Clark, Victor S., (Director) *Porto Rico and Its Problems:* A Survey by the Brookings Institution, Washington, D. C., 1930.

Commons, John R., *Races and Immigrants in America,* New York, The Macmillan Co., 1920.

Davie, Maurice R., *World Immigration: With Special Reference to The United States,* New York, The Macmillan Co., 1936.

Duncan, Hannibal G., *Immigration and Assimilation,* Boston, D. C., Heath and Co., 1933.

Fairchild, Henry Pratt, *Immigration, A World Movement and Its American Significance,* New York, The MacMillan Co., Revised Ed., 1925.

Frazier, E. Franklin, *The Negro Family in Chicago,* Chicago, University of Chicago Press, 1932.

Garis, Roy L., *Immigration Restriction,* New York, The Macmillan Co., 1927.

Garvey, Amy Jacques, *Philosophies and Opinions of Marcus Garvey,* New York, Universal Publishing House, 1930.

Gamio, Manuel, *The Mexican Immigrant, His Life Story,* Chicago, University of Chicago Press, 1931.

——, *Mexican Immigration to the United States,* Chicago, University of Chicago Press, 1930.

Greaves, Ida C., *The Negro in Canada*, McGill University Economic Studies, No. 16, 1929.

Herskovits, M. J., *The American Negro*, New York, Knopf, 1928.

Jenks, J. W. and Lauck, W. J., *The Immigration Problem*, New York, Funk and Wagnalls Co., 6th Edition 1926, Revised and Englarged by Rufus D. Smith.

Johnson, James Weldon, *Black Manhattan*, New York, Knopf, 1930.

Johnston, Sir Harry H., *The Negro in the New World*, New York, The Macmillan Co., 1910.

Jones, Chester Lloyd, Henry Kittredge Norton and Parker Thomas Moon, *The United States and the Caribbean*, Chicago, University of Chicago Press, 1929.

Kepner, Jr., Charles D., *Social Aspects of the Banana Industry*, New York, Columbia University Press, 1936.

Kiser, Clyde V., *Sea Island to City*, New York, Columbia University Press, 1932.

Mathieson, William Law, *British Slavery and Its Abolition, 1823-1838*, London, Longmans, Green and Co., 1926.

——, *British Slave Emancipation, 1838-1849*, London, Longmans, Green and Co., 1932.

——, *The Sugar Colonies Under Governor Eyre, 1849-1866*, London, Longmans, Green and Co., 1936.

Mayo-Smith, Richmond, *Emigration and Immigration*, New York, Charles Scribners Sons, 1890.

MacIver, Robert M., *Society, Its Structure and Changes*, New York, Long and Smith Company, 1931.

——, *Society, A Text Book of Sociology*, New York, Farrar and Rinehart, 1937.

MacLean, A. M., *Modern Immigration*, Philadelphia, J. B. Lippincott and Company, 1925.

McKay, Claude, *Harlem Shadows*, New York, Harcourt, Brace Co., 1922.

——, *Home to Harlem*, New York, Harper and Brothers, 1928.

——, *Banjo*, New York, Harper and Brothers, 1929.

——, *Ginger Town*, New York, Harper and Brothers, 1933.

——, *A Long Way From Home*, New York, Furman, 1937.

Miller, Herbert A., *Races, Nations and Classes*, Philadelphia, J. P. Lippincott and Co., 1924.

National Commission on Law Observance and Enforcement, Report on Crime and the Foreign Born, Vol. III, Washington, Government Printing Office, 1931.

National Commission on Law Observance and Enforcement, The Causes of Crime, Vol. VI, Part III, "Notes on the Negro's Relation to Work and Law Observance," Ira De A. Reid, pp. 219-255.

National Resources Committee, The Problems of a Changing Population, Report of the Committee on Population Problems, Washington, Government Printing Office, May, 1938.

Naturalization and Immigration Service, Reports of the Commissioner of Immigration and Naturalization, Immigration and Naturalization Statistics of the United States, Lecture No. 3, January 7, 1935, Department of Labor, Annual Reports of the Secretary of Labor, 1899-1936.

Olivier, Lord, *White Capital and Coloured Labor*, London, Hogarth Press, 1929.

Panunzio, Constantine, *Immigration Crossroads*, New York, The Macmillan Company, 1927.

Reuter, E. B., (Editor) *Race and Culture Contacts*, New York, McGraw-Hill, 1934. See especially (1) Charles S. Johnson's article "Negro Personality in a Southern Community," Chapter XIII, pp. 208-227; (2) E. Franklin Frazier's "Traditions and Patterns of Negro Family Life in the United States," Chapter XII, pp. 191-207.

Reynolds, Lloyd G., *The British Immigrant, His Social and Economic Adjustment in Canada*, Toronto, Oxford University Press, 1935.

Robertson, James A., *Louisiana Under Spain, France and the United States, 1785-1807*, Cleveland, Arthur H. Clark and Co., 1911, 2 vols.

Schrieke, B., *Alien Americans*, New York, Viking Press, 1936.

Seeber, Edward D., *Anti-Slavery Opinion in France During the Eighteenth Century*, The Johns Hopkins Studies in Romance, Literatures and Languages, Extra Volume X, Baltimore, The Johns Hopkins Press, 1937.

Siegfried, Andre, *America Comes Of Age*, New York, Harcourt, Brace and Company, 1927.

Stephenson, George M., *A History of American Immigration, 1820-1924*, Boston, Ginn and Company, 1926.

Stoddard, Lothrop, *Clashing Tides of Colour*, New York, Charles Scribner's Sons, 1935.

Stonequist, Everett V., *The Marginal Man:* A study in Personality and Culture Conflict, New York, Charles Scribner's Sons, 1937.

Taft, Donald Reed, *Human Migration: A Study of International Movements*, New York, Ronald Press, 1936.

——, *Two Portuguese Communities in New England*, New York, Columbia University Studies in History, Economics and Public Law, Vol. CVII, New York, Columbia University Press, 1923.

Tannenbaum, Frank, *Whither Latin America: An Introduction to its Economic and Social Problems*, New York, Crowell, 1934.

Thompson, Warren S. and Whelpton, P. K., *Population Trends in the United States*, Recent Social Trends Monograph, New York, McGraw Hill Book Company, 1933.

Thomas, W. I. and Znaniecki, Florian, *The Polish Peasant in Europe and America*, Chicago, University of Chicago Press, 1918-1920, 5 vols.

United States: Bureau of the Census, *Negroes in the United States, 1920-1932*, Washington, Government Printing Office.

——, *Reports of the Immigration Commission* Appointed under the Congressional Act of February 20, 1907. Senate Documents 61st Congress, 1911, 42 vols., Abstracts of the Reports, 2 vols., Government Printing Office, Washington, 1911.

Walrond, Eric D., *Tropic Death*, New York, Boni and Liveright, 1926.

Willcox, Walter F., Editor, *International Migrations*, New York National Bureau of Economic Research, 1929-1931, 2 Vols.

Williams, Joseph H., *Voodos and Obeahs*, New York, Dial Press, 1933.

Wirth, Louis, *The Ghetto*, Chicago, University of Chicago Press, 1928.

Woodson, Carter G., *The Negro Professional Man and His Community*, Washington, D. C., Associated Publishers, 1934.

Woofter, T. J., *Races and Ethnic Groups in American Life*, New York, McGraw Hill Book Company, 1933.

Young, Donald, *American Minority Peoples: A Study in Racial and Culture Conflicts in the United States*, New York, Harper Brothers, 1932.

——, *Research Memorandum On Minority Peoples in the Depression.* Prepared under the direction of the Committee on Studies in Social Aspects of the Depression, New York, Social Science Research Council, 1937.

Articles and Unpublished Manuscripts

Beals, Carleton, "The Black Belt of the Caribbean", *The Fortnightly Review*, Vol. 130, pp. 356-368, No. 777, September, 1931.

Beckwith, Martha Warren, "Jamaica Anansi Stories", In Memoirs of the *American Folklore Society*, pp. xi-xii, 1924.

Bagnall, Robert W., "The Madness of Marcus Garvey," *The Messenger*, Vol. V, No. 27, February 21, 1925.

DuBois, W. E. B., "Inter-Racial Implications of the Ethiopian Crisis," *Foreign Affairs*, Vol. 14, pp. 82-92, No. 1, October, 1935.

——, "Marcus Garvey", *The Crisis*, Vol. 21, pp. 58-59, No. 2, December, 1920 and Vol. 21, pp. 112-115, No. 3, January, 1921.

Dunbar, Barrington S., "Factors in the Cultural Background of the American Southern Negro and the British West Indian Negro that condition their Adjustment in Harlem," M.A. Thesis, Political Science, Columbia University, 1935.

Frazier, E. Franklin, "The American Negro's New Leaders," *Current History*, New York, Vol. 28, pp. 56-59, April, 1928.

——, "Garvey, A Mass Leader," *Nation*, New York, Vol. 123, pp. 147-148, August 18, 1926.

——, "The Garvey Movement," *Opportunity, Journal of Negro Life*, Vol. 4, pp. 346-348, November, 1926.

Hart, Rollin Lynde, "The Negro Moses," *The Independent*, pp. 205-208, February 26, 1921.

Herrick, Robert, "The Race Problem in the Caribbean, II, The French Way," Vol. 118, pp. 669-670, June 18, 1924.

Hill, Edwin C., "Primitive Superstitions in the United States," *Human Side of the News*, May 18, 1930, Washington, D. C.

Hubert, James H., "Are We Forging Ahead? And How?", *The West Indian Committee Journal*, Vol. I, pp. 17-19, No. 5, 1928.

Hurlbutt, Mary E., "The Invisible Environment of the Immigrant," *The Family*, Vol. IV, pp. 160-164, No. 6, October, 1923.

Johnson, James Weldon, "The Making of Harlem," *Survey Graphic*, Vol. 53, March, 1925, Vol. 6, pp. 635-639.

Malliet, A. M. Wendell, "On West Indian Colonization in British Guiana," *Education, A Journal of Reputation*, Vol. I, No. 4, p. 3, July-August, 1935.

Matthews, Ralph, "Wedding Bells Ring Loudest in Harlem," *The Baltimore Afro-American*, May 2, 1936.

Mecklin, John M., "The Philosophy of the Color Line," *American Journal of Sociology*, Vol. XIX, p. 345, Nov., 1913.

Miller, Kelly, "Negroes or Colored People?" *Opportunity, Journal of Negro Life*, Vol. XV, pp. 142-146, No. 5, May, 1937.

Miller, Herbert Adolphus, "The Negro and the Immigrant," in Kimball Young's *Social Attitudes*, New York, Holt and Company, pp. 328-346, 1931.

Moore, Garrie Ward, "A Study of A Group of West Indian Negroes in New York City," M.A. Thesis, Faculty of Political Science, Columbia University, 1913 (Typewritten).

Park, Robert E., "Our Racial Frontiers in the Pacific," *The Survey*, Vol. 56, p. 196, 1926.

——, "Human Migrations and the Marginal Man," *American Journal of Sociology*, Vol. 33, pp. 881-893, 1928.

Parsons, Elsie Clews, "Folk-Lore From the Cape Verde Islands," *In Memoirs of the American Folk-lore Society*, Vol. 15, Part I, pp. 40-45, 1922.

Patterson, Harvey T., "American Democracy In the Canal Zone," *The Crisis*, New York, Vol. 20, pp. 83-84, No. 2, June, 1920.

Petioni, Charles A., "The Intra-racial Problem," *Education, a Journal of Reputation*, Vol. II, No. 2, May-June, 1936, p. 2.

Reid, Ira De A., "Negro Immigration to the United States," *Social Forces*, Vol. 16, No. 3, pp. 411-417, March, 1938.

Roller, Arnold, "Black Ivory and White Gold in Cuba," *The Nation*, Vol. 128, pp. 55-56, January 9, 1929.

Schomburg, Arthur A., "Our Pioneers," *The Amsterdam News*, New York, September 12, 1936.

Smith, Alfred Edgar, "West Indians On the Campus," *Opportunity, Journal of Negro Life*, Vol. 7, p. 239, No. 7, August, 1933.

Sutherland, Louis G., "Panama Gold," *Opportunity, Journal of Negro Life*, Vol. 12, pp. 336-339, No. 11, November, 1934.

Talley, Truman Hughes, "Garvey's Empire of Ethiopia," *World's Work*, Vol. 41, pp. 265-270, No. 3, January, 1921.

Walrond, Eric, "Imperator Africanus," *The Independent*, January 3, 1923.

Warner, W. Lloyd, "American Caste and Class," *American Journal of Sociology*, Vol. 42, No. 2, September, 1936, pp. 234-237.

Weatherly, U. G., "The West Indies as a Sociological Laboratory," *American Journal of Sociology*, Vol. 49, No. 3, November 1923, pp. 290-304.

Wesley, Charles H., "The Emancipation of the Free Colored Population of the British Empire," *The Journal of Negro History,* Vol. XIX, pp. 137-170, No. 2, April, 1934.

PAMPHLETS

American Negro Churches of Manhattan, A Study by the Greater New York Federation of Churches, New York, N. Y., 1930.

Best, Ethel L., *Economic Problems of the Women of the Virgin Islands of the United States,* The U. S. Dept. of Labor, Women's Bureau, No. 142, 1936.

Forester, Robert F., "The Racial Problems Involved in Immigration from Latin America and the West Indies to the United States," *Hearings Before the Committee on Immigration and Naturalization,* House of Representatives, 68th Congress, 2nd Session, March, 1925. Washington Government Printing Office, 1925.

Garvey, Marcus, *Aims and Objectives of a Movement for Solution of the Negro Problem Outlined,* New York, 1924.

Morgan, Dwight C., *Foreign Born in the United States,* The American Committee for Protection of Foreign Born, 1930.

James, C. L. R., *The Case for West Indian Self Government,* Day to Day Pamphlets, No. 16, The Hogarth Press, London, 1935.

INDEX